design

pocket essentials

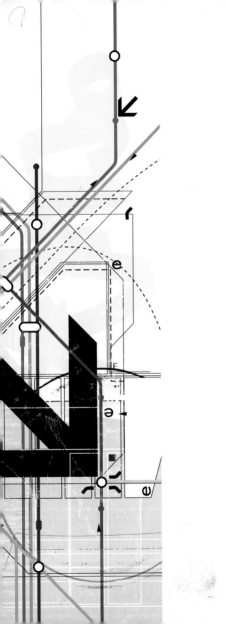

graphic
design pocket
essentials

ILEX

GRAPHIC DESIGN POCKET ESSENTIALS

First published in the United Kingdom in 2010 by
I L E X
210 High Street
Lewes
East Sussex BN7 2NS
www.ilex-press.com

Publisher: Alastair Campbell
Creative Director: Peter Bridgewater
Managing Editor: Nick Jones
Editor: Ellie Wilson
Art Director: Julie Weir
Designer: Graham Davis

British Library Cataloguing-in-Publication Data
A catalogue record for this book is available from
the British Library

ISBN: 978-1-907579-03-5

10 9 8 7 6 5 4 3 2 1

Printed in China

Colour Origination by Ivy Press Reprographics.

◼ Introduction

◼ Design basics

◼ Surface design

Screen design

Color/image

Reference

INTRODUCTION

"DIGITAL," "GRAPHIC," AND "DESIGN" have become three very potent words in our vocabulary. There can be few people in the developed world whose life has not been influenced by information and design technology. Personal computers and the ubiquitous silicon chip have found their way into the homes and workplaces of millions of people.

Introduction

Most common as an all-encompassing descriptor is "digital"—computers depend on streams of electronically generated "digits" to function. So we have digital telephone lines, digital printing, digital radio, and digital television, among the many areas connected with information, communication, and design. Virtually all data, whether in the form of words, numbers, images, sound, or movement, can be digitized and transmitted using a range of technologies.

Digitization has created a common method of recording and transmitting data, allowing a high level of interactivity across media. This interactivity allows sound, image, text, and other creative elements to work together in a single context, and has radically changed designers' working methods by providing access to the vast storehouse of knowledge on the Internet and corporate intranets and by enabling them to send and receive a range of media electronically via email from their own computers.

Digital data transmission speeds are limited by the size of files, the medium through which data flows, and the speed at which computer processors can handle the information. But every day sees an improvement in all of these areas—files can be compressed more efficiently, broadband Internet connections and high-speed wireless networking are being used more and

more, and processor speeds are getting faster and faster. There is also a growing convergence of media, bringing about a merging of personal computing, television, radio, telephone, publishing, games, web, email, and e-commerce. Computer and TV monitors are getting larger, with clear flat-screen technologies replacing CRT, while mobile phones and other portables gain full-color displays. This takes us into an era where the quality of visual content will play an increasingly important role in the way we communicate to a wider range of audiences. The quality of visually received information is the responsibility of the digital graphic designer.

Design finds its way into every aspect of daily life. From clothes, buildings, and consumer goods to reading matter, entertainment, interior and exterior environments—almost every form of modern communication and production—graphic design plays a key part. It is almost impossible to avoid being bombarded by visual messages.

Much of what is published in print or on screen can be visually discordant or jumbled, partly due to the speed at which it can now be generated and delivered. In this information- and message-orientated world, it is increasingly important for the graphic designer to strive for order and clarity. Understanding how audiences react to visual material, their levels of concentration and comprehension, and how they can be influenced by trends is key to the problem-solving process. Equally important is understanding how eye and brain work together in scanning and processing words, pictures, and the subtler visual cues of form, color, and composition.

Since prehistory, humans have used signs and shapes to communicate about the real world as well as their imagination. While the earliest scribes could be described as the first "graphic designers"—arranging text in a logical and efficient way—it was the invention of printing, along with mass production, that formed the bedrock for graphic design as a recognizable trade.

The development of movable type in the mid-15th century, widely attributed to Johann Gutenberg, radically changed the design of letter shapes. Whereas the handwriting of the scribe evolved slowly over centuries, with equal emphasis on composition and embellishment as on letter forms, type design became a relatively fast-moving commercial process. Letter shapes were standardized, and it was necessary to devise different varieties to help convey meaning.

Graphic design continued to evolve as a hybrid activity, owing as much to mathematics, engineering, and psychology as to the fine arts. Changes in art, fashion, and taste, dramatic advances in reprographic technologies, and the changing demands of commerce and lifestyle exerted massive influence, along with the creative contributions of innumerable artists, typographers, designers, and stylists. Yet the overwhelming impression given by the more influential graphic designers of recent times is of a reluctance to draw on history. Following World War I, members of the Bauhaus School saw history as dead convention, and preferred to redefine or reject the parameters within which their predecessors had worked. All avant-garde thinking—a major component of graphic design—is driven by the need to escape from the past and explore the possibilities of the future.

The emphasis of this book is on digital graphic design, a field created by the development not of the computer itself but of the "graphical user interface" (GUI)—the means by which users can interact with graphic symbols on screen. In place of text-based operation, it allowed the innovation of a graphical screen display to be exploited for the creation of graphical content, and thus digital graphic design was born.

Since the launch of the Mac in 1984, the digital revolution has overtaken traditional graphic design practices with extraordinary speed. Many specialist trades and crafts have become almost redundant. Much of the responsibility for technical aspects of production has shifted to the desktop, and designers themselves are required to master an ever-expanding new skillset, ranging from the operation of different software packages to the digital representation of color and the processes involved in reproducing digital content in print and on screen.

There are, however, areas of graphic design that remain relatively unaffected. These include generating and developing ideas and concepts, design and typographic principles, and creative problem-solving—all attributes that distinguish graphic design from other professions. Happily, digital technologies have provided new tools for exploring, extending, and realizing ideas in faster, more flexible, and more cost-effective ways.

Graphic design is in a state of permanent revolution. Web design, for instance, has already changed beyond recognition as new softwares have been developed and new standards adopted. Who knows what media we may be designing for, and with what tools, in another decade? As the saying goes: "If we can see into the future, then we're not looking far enough ahead."

PROFESSIONAL GRAPHIC DESIGN will continue to thrive because ideas and innovation, good composition, and a creative eye cannot be "packaged." Paradoxically, in an era that has seen many industries and professions having to specialize in order to survive, the digital graphic designer has been required to diversify.

The graphic designer's role

The biggest growth is in the Internet and multimedia industry. Many graphic designers are engaged in web page design involving typography, imagery, animation, movies, and sound. The computerization of graphic design, with the rise of many disparate, yet often overlapping, software programs has enlarged the range of work of "graphic" designers. In addition to the rich creative elements of many programs, there are built-in productivity and labor-saving features. Many once specialist areas of graphic design now share similar programs.

The digital power available to the designer is immense. A project can be created and finished to a high professional level on a single Apple Macintosh or PC. Not only has the origination process been made easier, but the ways in which the finished result can be previewed has transformed the way people work. Affordable color proofers show how printed materials will look; technologies such as PDF files allow instant transmission and distribution; walk-through software previews three-dimensional creations; packaging software makes up packs from flat designs; and slide shows and movies bring presentations to life.

Many of the chores linked with repetitive design or editing tasks have been lessened by automated features built into most applications: search and replace, spellchecking, "style sheets,"

and "content management" systems, to name a few. If you can't find a suitable automated feature, you can likely create it yourself by recording a "macro," "script," or "action."

As graphic designers can work across so many fields, they need to be familiar with a wide range of production and manufacturing processes and related professions and skills. This may include photographers, illustrators, musicians, writers, and film-makers, as well as technical specialists in web design and programming. Digitization of sound, image, animation, movies, and production processes has enabled professionals to collaborate and work across a wider spectrum.

Graphic design is exciting and vibrant and, as such, is a rewarding profession. It combines creativity and innovation with analytical and methodical ways of working. Designers need a knowledge of budgets, manufacturing, and reproduction processes. Successful graphic designers aim to devise inventive solutions to visual communication problems in response to clients' needs, and in order to do so often work closely with clients in formulating a brief and strategy prior to starting any job. A good understanding of human nature and the cultural environment, as well as the ability to lead or be a team player, together with a keen eye for detail, distinguish the truly excellent designer from the average.

How to use this book

The aim of this book is to both inspire and inform by exploring a wide range of visual communication and graphic design contexts, while introducing essential design methodology and concepts on which to build. It explores the diversity of graphic design and showcases the work of inventive and talented designers in digital media.

The *Graphic Design Pocket Essentials* seeks to demystify some of the technical jargon often associated with computing and the design world.

Throughout the book are examples of work from a wide range of visual communication contexts, setting the scene for further in-depth exploration within individual sections.

Part One, *Design Basics*, explores the fundamental principles that underpin good and efficient graphic design. This section is, in essence, "away from the screen" as it involves creative processes related to idea generation and informed design decision-making. It includes an appreciation of the "building blocks" of good graphic design: shape and form, spatial awareness, what type is and how to work with it, as well as the emotive use of color and how it can work as a powerful tool rather than just decoration.

Part Two consists of sub-sections that explore defined areas of surface graphic design. These include: *Design for Print*, *Advertising*, *Packaging*, *Signage*, and *Exhibition*.

Part Three looks at web design for the Internet, intranets, and multimedia. This part is particularly useful for those who may feel somewhat swamped by the terminology in this area. It shows clearly how designers have to respond and adapt to a fluidity of display by different web browsers and computer platforms, and explains the significance of new standards of good practice for accessibility to disabled users.

Part Four takes a focused look at the technical intricacies of color and image-making.

The use of color is also discussed in the *Design Basics* section, but it is essential for the practicing graphic designer to understand how color is created and why. As mixing, controlling, and adjusting color plays such an important role in graphic design, the attributes and terminology of color and how it works are looked at closely.

Computer programs have made retouching, montaging, and technical and fine art image-making readily accessible to the designer and artist. The essential way in which bitmap programs work compared to vector-based programs is made clear. The creation of special effects, the use of painting programs or drawing programs and how they interact with each other is discussed and explained.

DESIGN BASICS

PRIMARY SHAPES The familiar shapes—square, circle, and triangle—together with their three-dimensional derivatives—cube, sphere, and pyramid—underpin all the structures seen around us. There is very little that will not break down into, or visually relate to, some form of primary shape.

Basic design principles are the building blocks of graphic communication. To appreciate their value and relevance it is best to begin by looking at their particular characteristics away from an applied context.

Graphic designers find themselves working at both large and small scales across increasingly varied areas at local, national, and international levels. The flexible, innovative perspective they need must be underpinned by basic principles if they are to make informed design decisions and aesthetic judgments. These principles are common to other design disciplines and provide a valuable constant in the midst of the continually developing opportunities with which the graphic designer is presented.

The square, like the cube, is a wholly static form with no directional pull. It can be used to frame, exclude, include, attract, or define area, or for modular division, and it will sit comfortably in almost any arrangement of multiples. Even when rotated and in a more dynamic, diamond form, it retains its inherent, fixed quality. Minor modification to a linear square will, however, begin to direct the eye and also create associations. For example, if the corners are opened, or if a side is removed or tilted, the eye will move into the shape and associations of exit or entrance will be made. An extended square, or rectangle, directs the eye along, up or down its length and beyond, making the eye look for common alignments.

The circle has two main attributes—it provides a powerful focus for the eye and at the same time invites it to take a circular journey round either itself or a circular layout of any kind of element. By contrast, a series of circles suggests self-contained units and so makes the eye "jump" from one unit to the other, quickly tiring it. Although circles do not easily fit together, the eye can be made to spin across the surface by

Right: The primary shapes and bright colors that underlie the concept of this 3D, giant-sized children's hospital sign are familiar things with which a child can comfortably identify. Variations on the playful and cheerful signage theme are used through the system.
DESIGN BY EMERY VINCENT DESIGN, AUSTRALIA

physically linking a series of circles. The pace of the spin is controlled by the size of circle.

The triangle is a balanced and completely stable form in both two- and three-dimensional form, but also suggests a dynamic energy, even when equilateral. Unlike the circle or square, the proportions of a triangle can be radically altered to give it directional force without affecting its basic shape. The eye finds this directional force difficult to ignore.

It is important to understand the significant influence that these key forms have on the viewer's perception. Such an understanding will enable the designer to organize confidently the form and content of a design in order to communicate a visual message.

POINT, LINE, AND AREA are the basic elements used in all graphic design and, as with primary shapes, the way in which they are used will affect the overall perception of any communication. Most basic visual design decisions involve some representative combination of these shapes and elements. These may be used explicitly or implicitly, and with varying levels of complexity.

Using space

The point indicates position and acts as a visual stopping point. A single point placed on a blank page instantly attracts and focuses the eye (diagram 1). The eye senses a relationship between it and the edges of the paper. Adding a second point suggests relative positioning and sets up an automatic relationship with the first point, deflecting attention away from the sur-rounding area (diagram 2). As the eye moves between the points it "sees" an imaginary straight line. When a third point is added, it will relate these points of reference and "create" a triangle (diagram 3). As more points are added, grouping and subgrouping patterns occur. The positioning of these groupings determines the viewing sequence and levels of importance (see diagrams 4, 5).

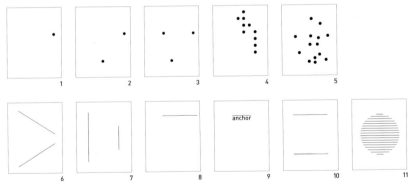

Diagrams:

1. A point of focus.

2. Points suggesting a line.

3. Points suggesting a shape.

4. Organized grouping of points leading the eye from start to finish in an ordered way.

5. Random grouping of points. This causes the eye to scan the area constantly looking for starting and finishing points.

6 & 7. Lines creating an illusion of depth.

8. Placing a line closer to one edge of an area will direct the eye along it.

9. Centering a line on a page closer to either the top or bottom will visually anchor it.

10. Lines may be used to direct the eye to a given area.

11. Rules of different lengths build an image. Lines of type can produce the same effect.

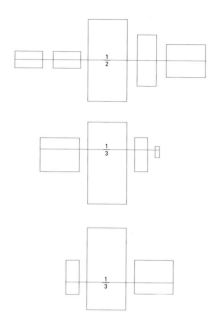

Left: Creating an axis through proportional division of space can be an effective way of visually coordinating radically different-sized elements within a single design concept, such as an exhibition or display.

within a design at any scale. It is easy to be distracted by disparate elements on the surface without realizing that area is also a powerful element in its own right—"empty" areas can create energy within a design—and can be used to direct the eye from one place to another. This energy is known as dynamic white space.

Choice of format (rectangular or otherwise) may be dictated by either job content or production practicalities or both. There are some time-tested formats that have proved to be particularly suited to a wide range of uses. Print, for example, makes frequent use of the international standard series of A and B paper sizes, which are based on a rectangle having sides in the ratio of 1:1.414, the latter remarkable number being the square root of 2. Repeated folding parallel to the short side allows paper in this proportion to be halved into further rectangles—all in the same 1:1.414 proportion—giving the designer a flexible range of proportionally related sizes with which to work.

Although screen-design formats generally follow the maximum allowable vertical and horizontal dimensions, there is no reason why this must be rigidly adhered to.

Equal division of an area conveys a static feel, whereas contrasting division communicates greater dynamism. The golden section has been used for centuries as a formula for creating harmony. In this formula, the relationship of the smaller area to the larger area is equal to the relationship of the larger area to the whole— approximately 8:13.

Line essentially indicates direction and so leads the eye. It will also encourage the eye to continue beyond its length. It may be either implied through the juxtaposition of two elements, as with points, or actual, as in a drawn line, a line of text, a typographic rule or set of images or other elements. The strategic placement of several lines can create an illusion of depth (linear perspective) (diagrams 6, 7). Lines may also be used to suggest form, delineate, enclose or divide, emphasize, and act as a visual marker (diagrams 8, 9, 10, 11).

Area is a defined surface or plane, and it acts as a visual container, drawing attention to its content or edges. Graphic designers are concerned with area as a means of defining format and proportion and as a way of pacing the viewing

DYNAMICS, EMPHASIS, AND CONTRAST Visual emphasis is a means of specifically directing the viewer, ordering complex information by creating a visual hierarchy and highlighting elements. Four basic ways of creating visual emphasis are through the use of size, weight, color, and disposition (placement).

Visual emphasis

The skilled use of emphasis is essential to communicating with clarity and pace, and works to focus and progressively direct the viewer through or around a design. Emphasis, like all other design basics, should always be considered in relation to the design as a whole. Many examples of size, weight, color, and disposition used as emphasis can be seen in newspapers and magazines where the visual pace is broken down into small parcels of information. These are identified (or emphasized) in many different ways, for example, by a heading (size), bold introductory text (weight), a colored rule or tonal change in text setting (color), placement or discrete arrangement of elements (disposition).

Size creates emphasis through contrast in proportions of format, type, image, relationship of elements, dimension (length and height), and volume (area and depth). Reducing an element to a small size on a large format can be just as powerful as enlarging it to fill the area, if not more so.

Weight suggests visual substance and mass, which can range from heavy or bold to light. It is often used in conjunction with size but works successfully when used across uniformly sized elements. Contrast in weight alone between individual words or lines can be effective in large amounts of text. Changes of weight between elements or blocks of continuous or display text

will set up different spatial planes and can influence the viewing and reading order. Degrees of density and openness in text and the tonal value of images can be used to increase or decrease levels of emphasis.

The use of color not only highlights, but also adds depth to every aspect of emphasis through association, mood, temperature, and emotion. Appropriate color choice can be based on any one or a combination of these areas. Random choice or personal preference in the use of color can wrongly emphasize or detract from the content or message. Interaction and/or contrast between individual colors together with the level of saturation (intensity) and brightness (tone) will significantly modify the degree and volume of emphasis (see *Color*, pages 44–47). Typographic "color" created by weight change from one body of text to another can also be used as a means of subtle emphasis or contrast.

Disposition, like color, interfaces with every aspect of emphasis. It is so integral to visual communication that its potential is often undervalued. Disposition is inextricably linked to area and refers to the strategic placement of elements. It can subtly or dynamically draw attention to elements within an overall design. For example, the small folio on its own at the bottom or top of a page does not shout but is instantly found by the reader through its unique positioning. Similarly an indent (the disposition of the first word in sequences of paragraphs) quietly creates pace. It is surprising how successfully judicious use of disposition can work without recourse to other methods of emphasis. However, poorly considered placement of elements on a page can be confusing for the reader.

Contrast is used to create visual interest in the same way that tone and intonation add interest to speech. Without contrast, graphic communication would become dull and flat, with little to attract attention or sustain interest. Contrast draws on visual opposites or dissimilarity to emphasize,

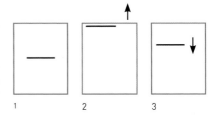

Above: Diagram 1: The exact central placement of an element within an area will produce a fixed appearance. Diagram 2: Placing an element close to the top edge of an area will encourage the eye to travel upwards beyond it. Diagram 3: Placement to the left and a third of the way down will draw the eye downwards.

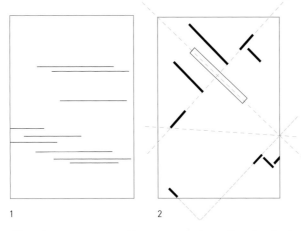

Left: 1. Asymmetrical placement works best if the elements are informally grouped, with the space inbetween and around used to lead the eye though them. 2. Diagonal arrangements need careful consideration in structuring in order to avoid causing the eye to dart from element to element. Setting up basic directional lines can help avoid this.

differentiate, set up competition, attract, and change the reading pace. It can be both quantitative and qualitative, obvious or subtle. Its use should be considered in relation to the concept and the design as a whole. As there is little limit to how contrast may be used, it can be helpful to look initially for potential within the main emphasis groups—size, color, weight, and disposition.

Everyday visual opposites (loud and quiet, warm and cool, balance and motion) can also be a source of inspiration for graphic contrast. To be effective, contrast needs to be appropriate to the concept and be linked to emphasis. Overuse may result in a lack of focus in the design, with elements fighting for the viewer's attention and the eye being pulled in different directions.

THE MECHANICS OF TYPE The designer needs to understand how type is constructed and assembled as well as having an aesthetic appreciation of it. Letters of the alphabet are made up of complex combinations of straight lines and curves that give them their individual character.

Type basics

All letters have common, notional points of reference in their physical make-up, regardless of the typeface design, style, or size. These notional points are the baseline (the line on which all letters sit), the x-height (the height of the lowercase letters), the ascender line (the extent of the vertical upstrokes of lowercase letters), and the descender line (the extent of the downstrokes of lowercase letters).

The terms used to identify the different parts and structures of letterforms within this notional framework help to ensure accurate recognition and reference (see diagram below). Some characters have detailing unique both to themselves and to the typeface, for example the ear of

Below: What distinguishes one font from another are the different graphical characteristics of its set of glyphs—the slope of its "counters," the relative size of its "x-height," the shape of its "descenders" and height of its "ascenders," for example—all of which will have been carefully designed to make a specific impression.

Further variation comes from the different styles and weights that may be produced for each font "family": plain (often called "Roman" or "normal"), italic, semibold, bold, extra bold, condensed, thin, light, and so on. The differences among fonts, and among styles and weights, can be marked, or they may be very subtle.

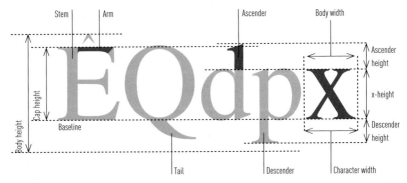

Stem   Arm   Ascender   Body width

Cap height   Body height   Baseline   Ascender height   x-height   Descender height

Tail   Descender   Character width

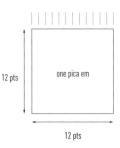

12 pts

one pica em

12 pts

lowercase g or the tail of uppercase Q. However, although letterforms are recognized by these specific characteristics, the overall shape of the characters and the counter-shapes (enclosed areas) also contribute to the character of a typeface. Although there is considerable individuality within the different characters of a typeface, each is designed to form a cohesive whole and give a global color and texture when typeset. Appreciating the physical make-up of type helps the designer identify points to look for and so facilitates typeface choice for different purposes.

Although the size of type is described by a common system (usually in points), different typefaces at, say, 10 pt, may look quite different in size. This happens because of the relative proportions of the characters. Helvetica, for instance, has a large x-height and comparatively short ascenders and descenders, whereas some Garamonds have a relatively small x-height and longer ascenders and descenders. These differences in proportion result in different typographic color when text is set—the bigger the x-height, the more open the texture and color, making it vital to look at different samples. For the same reason, the number of characters that will fit on a given line length varies between typefaces at the same size. Even if this makes little difference to small amounts of copy, it can make a big difference to many pages of text.

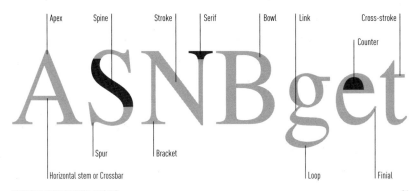

Apex Spine Stroke Serif Bowl Link Cross-stroke

Counter

ASNBget

Spur Bracket

Horizontal stem or Crossbar

Loop Finial

Type basics

THE POINT SYSTEM

Digital processing allows designers to work on screen in a range of interchangeable measurement systems, to their own choice. However, when dealing with type, most people find it more practical to work with a common system that allows everyone to grasp and quickly appreciate the values being talked about. The point system used for measuring type—unique to the printing industry—has, surprisingly, remained the same since the days of metal type. In the days of phototypesetting, an attempt was made to use millimetres as a basic unit for type measurement, but it was never taken up.

Type size, as shown in the diagram, is determined by the size of the type body (which, in the past, was a piece of movable metal) rather than by the actual letter. Nowadays, the body can be considered as the distance between the top of the highest part of the letterform (usually an ascender) to the bottom of the lowest (a descender), plus a notional amount of clearance, which varies from typeface to typeface.

The typographer's point is approximately 0.3 mm or 1/72 inch. Such a very small unit is necessary when describing very small sizes of type. However, attempting to express large

Adobe Garamond

measurements in points is cumbersome, so a larger unit of 12 pt, the pica em, is used. In many programs, it is possible to select pica ems or picas as a unit of measurement, for example, as the horizontal measurement for setting column widths. In practice, digital graphic designers will probably find themselves working in several measurement systems—points for type, millimetres for area or page size, and inches for scanning resolutions (dpi).

The em (without the pica) is a measurement notionally based on the width of a capital M. Therefore, the value of the em is the same as the point size being used. Units of digital letter spacing and character construction are based on dividing the em of the given type size (be it 8 pt or 24 pt) into hundredths or thousandths—infinitely more subtle than in earlier times.

Every word in this line

Verdana   Helvetica   Futura

Below and bottom: Although these words are all set in exactly the same size type, the differences in their appearance are pronounced. Note particularly the relative sizes of the x-heights: Verdana's large x-height is the main reason why that font looks bigger than the others.

Type Type

Helvetica

Gill Sans

* Before you start designing a publication, read the text and think about the readership.

* Begin any job with just two fonts. Use more only if you are sure you need them.

* Invest in a specimen book showing the characteristics of different fonts or compile one yourself. Use a font utility program to print out custom specimen sheets for the fonts already owned.

* Use tried and tested combinations—for example, a serif font such as Bembo for body text, with a sans serif such as Franklin Gothic Heavy or Gill Sans Extra Bold for headings. Some font families, such as Adobe Stone, contain a combination of well-matched serif and sans serif versions.

* Keep body text between 9 point (for books) and 12 point (for newsletters and marketing materials).

* Use leading (the spacing between lines of text) to aid legibility. One rule of thumb is that body text should have leading around 2 points greater than the size of the type. For example if the text is set in 9 point, then the leading should be at least 11 point. Most design software automatically applies leading 120 percent of the type size, giving 12 point leading with 10 point type.

* Do not use ALL CAPS or underlining to highlight text. Bold or italics (but not both together) are better for emphasis. However, avoid using any of these devices for long blocks of text—it makes the text harder to read.

* Ensure your chosen fonts have all the cuts, styles, and weights necessary to set the text. For example, an animal encyclopedia will probably require an italic cut in which to set Latin species names.

is Set in 32 POINT Type

AGaramond

Bodoni small caps

Times

TYPEFACE DESIGN EVOLVED slowly as printing technology developed, but, given the flexibility of digital technology, recent typeface design has had few constraints. Radically different letterforms, often challenging typographic convention, have emerged alongside the digitization of many classic typefaces originally designed for older typesetting methods.

Designing with type

Rather than being limited to a few fonts in a fixed number of sizes, the digital designer will typically have access to hundreds of typefaces that can be instantly scaled to any size required. Each font, moreover, is increasingly likely to contain extra characters beyond the basic alphanumeric set, including symbols, ligatures (letter combinations), fractions, accents, and even foreign alphabets.

Many typefaces fall into one of the following broad groups: serif, sans serif, glyphic, decorative and display, script, blackletter, and contemporary. More recent, innovative digital typeface designs, however, follow their own rules and do not fit easily into these groups. The terms used are derived from basic characteristics such as whether or not the letters have serifs, the shape of any serif, the contrast between thick and thin strokes, and the angle of stress or axis of the letters. These characteristics combine to give a typeface its unique character, typographic color, and rhythm. They should be carefully considered when you choose a typeface. Trying out different text settings is always useful in assessing the typographic color and rhythm in a particular context (see page 20).

Although letterforms are necessarily restricted in shape and almost always monochromatic, it would be blinkered to consider type as a limited graphic medium, because it can equally well be used in its own right as an "image." In a context where pictorial images are inappropriate or do not exist, a heading, single word, or letterform can be inventively used as a graphic focal point to create interest, evoke mood, or set the scene for the rest of the design scheme. Visual onomatopoeia, in which type is made to suggest the meaning of the word visually and "talk" to the viewer, is also an engaging way of getting the message across.

Zapf Chancery
ABCDEFGHIJKLMNOPQRSTUVWXYZ
abcdefghijklmnopqrstuvwxyz

Vag Rounded
ABCDEFGHIJKLMNOPQRSTUVWXYZ
abcdefghijklmnopqrstuvwxyz

Gridnik
ABCDEFGHIJKLMNOPQRSTUVWXYZ
abcdefghijklmnopqrstuvwxyz

Serpentine
ABCDEFGHIJKLMNOPQRSTUVWXYZ
abcdefghijklmnopqrstuvwxyz

Reactor
ABCDEFGHIJKLMNAOPQRSTUVWXYZ
ABCDEFGHIJKLMNOPQRSTUVWXYZ

Above: Recent innovative typeface designs (commonly produced digitally) follow their own rules and do not fit easily into the standard typographical family groups.

Abqoe

1

Abqoe

2

Abqoe

3

Abqoe

4

Abqoe

5

Abqoe

6

1. Old Face: marked axis inclined to the left, subtle change from thick to thin in the letterstrokes, bracketed serifs that are angled on the ascenders and an ¨e¨ with a horizontal bar. Capital letters are sometimes shorter than ascenders.

2. Transitional: axis that is slightly inclined to the left (can also be vertical), bracketed serifs that are angled on the ascenders.

3. Modern Face: vertical axis, abrupt contrast between thick and thin letterstrokes, unbracketed (or minimally bracketed) hairline serifs.

4. Geometric Sans Serif: normally monoline letterstrokes, based on simple geometric shapes. Often with a single-storey lowercase ¨a.¨

5. Humanist Sans Serif: some contrast in the letterstrokes, based on inscriptional letterforms, with two-storey lowercase ¨a¨ and ¨g.¨

6. Slab Serif: monoline or with minimal contrast in the letter strokes. Unbracketed, heavy serifs.

DECIDING ON A TYPEFACE

Typefaces are the voices of words and determine the visual tone of the text. The success of typographic communication depends as much on the choice of typeface as on the use of space and layout. Deciding on one typeface over another is a matter of visual judgement, fitness for purpose, and style. A close look at the basic characteristics of different typefaces within the broad groups will help to make the choice more manageable. A typeface can be specifically chosen to reflect, or contrast with, the content and mood of the text in relation to feel of the overall design, but care should be taken to ensure that this does not conflict with the message or overpower the look of the text. Identifying the purpose and context of the text—advertising, signage, packaging, print, web, or multimedia, the audience and the location in which it will be read—will inform the choice of size, weight, and style of type.

Type is used for informing, entertaining, providing reference, instructing, directing, or otherwise involving the reader in some way. Each of these contexts will require a different level of concentration and reading pace, and both of these factors are relevant to the choice of typeface. For example, road signage has to be instantly recognizable: using a decorative face

Designing with type

for a directional road sign might dangerously distract the driver's attention from the road. Reading may be sustained (as for a book), intermittent (as for a magazine, on a website, package, or exhibition panel), or focused (as for a set of instructions or reference source). Text may need to be read under compulsion (as for a warning), or as an option (as for a disclaimer). The choice of size, weight, and style of the typeface, as well as the typeface itself, should be linked to the reading pace. For example, it would be inappropriate to set instructional text in small, closely spaced, bold type: the difficulty in reading and understanding would be reflected in the reader's attitude to the task.

It is generally felt that serif, rather than sans serif, typefaces are easier on the eye and less tiring to read over lengthy continuous text. Magazines commonly break the rule, but complete novels are not often set in sans serif. Discussion of the relative merits of serif and sans serif text faces will inevitably continue. Display faces are suitable for setting a few words at a large size, rather than continuous text. Quirky or gimmicky typefaces are usually best reserved for display work. Text faces can be scaled to display sizes, but care should be taken to consider whether the letterforms still look well proportioned, and the overall character spacing (tracking or range kerning) may need to be reduced.

Most typefaces are designed with a basic roman (upright) and true italic style (or oblique, for sans serif faces) and perhaps one or two other weights (light, bold, etc). Those intended for professional text setting, however, may have extensive families of weights ranging from extra-light to ultra-black, and of styles ranging from condensed to expanded. This can be useful when complex information needs different levels of emphasis; it will ensure that changes of type will work well together stylistically. The aim should be to choose a small set of ideal weights for a given purpose, however, not to mix dozens of variants.

TYPE FOR SCREEN DISPLAY

Text for monitor display must be set larger than for print, since small letterforms cannot be formed legibly by the restricted number of pixels on screen. Similarly, typefaces with fine serifs are unsuited to screen display: fine detail is lost in the rendering. Many type manufacturers now offer faces optimized for screen display, such as AgfaMonotype's ESQ (Enhanced Screen Quality) series. The color of background and type needs consideration; dark backgrounds can ease glare.

SPACING TYPE

Type is spaced both horizontally and vertically. Vertical spacing, or "leading" (to rhyme with "bedding"), is measured in points from the baseline of one line of type to the baseline of the next. The amount should balance continuity and legibility.

Horizontally, each character is spaced proportionally to its width, using units as small as one-thousandth of an em. Digital typeface designers program special adjustments to the

Modernism, as we have known it, has served as the aesthetic, spiritual and moral conscience of our time. It embodies the essentially democratic idea of the creative artist as the inventor of a personal style, a unique vision of the

Modernism, as we have known it, has served as the aesthetic, spiritual and moral conscience of our time. It embodies the essentially democratic idea of the creative artist as the inventor of a personal style, a unique vision of the world. Modernism fosters

Above: "Range kerning" or "tracking" can be used to adjust text to fit to a given space. However, designers must be careful not to distort the text by over exaggerating the spacing.

Right: The vertical spacing of type is measured in points from the baseline of one line of text to the next.

The space between lines of type is known as leading

Right: Characters are horizontally spaced proportionally to their width. Sometimes it may be necessary to make one-off adjustments to the spacing between certain pairs of characters.

Word

Kerned

Word

Unkerned

Interstate Light Compressed
Interstate Compressed
Interstate Bold Compressed
Interstate Black Compressed
Interstate Light Condensed
Interstate Light Condensed Italic
Interstate Condensed
Interstate Condensed Italic
Interstate Bold Condensed
Interstate Bold Condensed Italic
Interstate Black Condensed
Interstate Light
Interstate Light Italic
Interstate Regular
Interstate Italic
Interstate Bold
Interstate Bold Italic
Interstate Black
Interstate Black Italic

spacing or "kerning" of difficult pairs of charac-ters—such as AV and Te—into their fonts, and software will apply these automatically. However, sometimes one-off adjustments to kerning are needed, particularly in headlines.

Increasing or decreasing the spacing across several words or lines is known as tracking or range kerning, and can be used to alter the visual color of the typeface or, on rare occasions, as a cheat to help fit the text to the space available.

When text is justified across a column, rules must be set up to deterine how spacing is to be adjusted to the required line length. Word spacing can be controlled independently to balance char-acter spacing against unsightly gaps.

Above: A selection of typefaces from the extensive Interstate family. Using related typefaces within a document will help to ensure a professional-looking result.

PLANNING DESIGN Design is normally carried out in response to a need, and inevitably involves planning. The parameters may not always be clear at first, as clients can have difficulty in pinpointing their exact requirements. Graphic designers are employed to bring their creative ability and practical understanding to solving a particular problem.

The design process

Acquiring an insight into the clients' businesses is an important part of informing the creative process. This can often be done simply by listening to and learning from clients, who usually know their own businesses intimately. Sometimes a client may be convinced that a particular medium or context is the best way to promote a product or service but, after careful analysis of the brief by the designer, an entirely different medium or approach may emerge as more suited to the actual, rather than the perceived, needs of the client.

The designer needs to make a reasonably accurate assessment of the size and complexity of the job and level of budget allocation. It is, for instance, unwise to embark on a corporate identity design without first agreeing which specific elements are going to need design consideration—is it a logo or letterhead, or will there also be a requirement to look at packaging, vehicle livery, and uniforms, a signage system, website, and design standards manual? Even a small-scale design can involve unexpected work, such as having to include, or rework a highly complicated diagram. Preliminary inquiries have to be made as to the feasibility and timescale of any reprographic and production processes from the completion of digital artwork before a realistic timetable can be worked out and agreed with the

client. These initial planning stages are all essential to the design process. The only real drawback to digital design is that it allows designers to explore endless variations of ideas and colorways in a process where time is usually at a premium and decisions have to be made quickly.

When it comes to the creative element of the design process, there is little doubt that paper, pencil, and digital software can work well in partnership. Paper and pencil are valuable basic tools for the digital graphic designer—much creative inspiration can come from doodling and note-making both on- and off-screen. Whichever starting point you use, your creative approach should always be informed by the brief. Basic guidelines for possible approaches can be set up by identifying from within the brief the answers to four simple questions. This exercise will also help you to clarify your intentions for the design (see page 30). Working out and evaluating the answers to these questions should give you a

A company logo is very often only the first step in creating a corporate identity. This range of elements from a corporate identity design for Skywash— a car-wash company based in Atlanta—illustrates how a whole range of graphics can be developed by cleverly picking up on key elements of the logo.
DESIGN BY WINK DESIGN, USA

Logo

Air Freshner

Icons

Business and Compliments Slip

Letterhead

Service Menu

Thank You Card

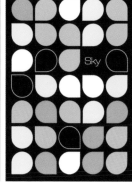

Posters

The design process

The questions are:

What

is the message to be communicated?
is the reason for the brief?
is the problem to be solved?

Why

does the client want to communicate
the message?

Where

is the message going to communicate
and under what conditions?

Who

is the intended audience or market?

springboard for idea generation that will help you maintain a reasoned link between the brief and even the most lateral approaches. One or more key words, images, or points should emerge from the analysis. These can be used as the basis of short but intensive visual brainstorming sessions on paper or screen to help start ideas and associations flowing.

Drawing need not be restricted to paper for these sessions, as many designers find working with a digital tablet creates a natural progression from hand to screen. But, whichever method you use, the value of drawing as a tool for visual thinking and exploration is important to recognize. Thinking through drawing focuses the mind and, as it rarely throws up "finished" or resolved ideas,

its flexible immediacy can suggest alternative routes for exploration, allowing for "happy discoveries" along the way. For this reason, put down every response that comes to mind, whether or not the relevance is immediately clear—often, it is not! Wit and humor can also play an important part in graphic communication, and they often make for entertaining, informative, and memorable designs.

When working in a three-dimensional field, any initial two-dimensional creative thinking can be developed through the making process with small-scale maquettes and mock-ups or by using a three-dimensional modeling program.

Drawn or doodled ideas, whether on paper or screen, should be stored, and those with potential should be researched and developed further without imposing too many constraints. Although ideas are generated by the creative intellect, they normally need some form of reference to underpin them, as the imagination cannot always be relied on for accuracy. Access to the Internet is extremely useful for this purpose—the web offers a vast storehouse of knowledge and visual references that can both inform and stimulate the design-making process. Digital-image libraries offer royalty-free images to download. Ideas should always be thoroughly explored until they are fully resolved, and all research should be kept as it can sometimes throw up different ideas worth following.

When an idea seems right, the designer should assess how it can be realistically applied to all the components of the job. Decisions as to choice and use of type, images, and color then need to be made. If you do not have the typeface you feel is suitable, font manufacturers have many browsable websites where it may be possible to find a face that fits your particular requirements. To assess colors and make choices, alternative colorways can be set up and viewed in most graphic art software packages. Images and graphics may either be supplied by the client or may need to be commissioned by the designer. They in turn may also help to generate ideas and influence the final design (see *Image Creation*).

Pulling the creative and informative strands of your design together and fine-tuning it can be done using drawing, image-manipulation, page-layout, or three-dimensional modeling programs, as the job demands. These programs can produce superficially seductive results, so you should always make sure that your design concept has "substance."

Most clients will have computing set-ups that allow you to communicate by email and to send visuals in a digitally viewable form. The graphic designer should be in a position to make PDF files, which can be viewed on any computer, and should also have a commonly used compression program. Once initial ideas have been approved or modifications agreed, the detailed design for each and every component of the job can be finalized before work can be prepared for production.

Every production process demands varying amounts of execution from the designer, but it will inevitably involve a digital file being prepared in a graphic arts program. The designer's file may be used directly to drive a printing device or a process with little or no intervention from the printer or anyone else. This raises two very important points. First, the content of your digital files must be correct in every aspect, with type and image information appropriately supplied. Second, it is extremely valuable to develop a good working relationship with your supplier, and ensure that there is a clear indication and understanding of responsibilities. Never assume that everything created digitally is going to be perfect—it is absolutely essential to have proofs for all print work, regardless of how small or big the job may be. Never rely on output from your studio printer being identical to that of the printer's or bureau's device.

CONTINUOUS TEXT needs special attention, as it contains large amounts of detailed information that needs to be easily understood. Readability is concerned with the speed and ease with which the reader can assimilate and retain information printed on the page or screen.

Legibility versus readability

Although individual components (letters) may be legible, this does not automatically mean that reading is easy. Readers perceive words not simply as sequences of letters, but as groups of letters and words. These letter and word groupings facilitate speedy recognition as the eye scans the text. Anything that contributes to the breaking up or the slowing down of this scanning process makes for harder and more tiring reading. For example, exaggerated tracking (character and word spacing) will disrupt the normal shape of words (recognizable letter groupings) causing strain to the eye and brain.

Character and word recognition are more easily achieved with upper- and lowercase letters, since they create a greater range of word-icon shapes and individuality than uppercase alone. Capital letters all appear to occupy equal spaces when set in a line of text, so the words they form are more difficult to discern at a normal reading speed. The relative weight of type can also affect legibility. Medium weights are easiest to read because of the visual balance between the counter-shapes and letterstrokes. Extreme weights of both light and bold type are more difficult and tiring to read as the contrast

Modernism, as we have known it, has served as the aesthetic, spiritual and moral conscience of our time. It embodies the essentially democratic idea of the creative artist as the inventor of a personal style, a unique vision of the world.

Modernism, as we have known it, has served as the aesthetic, spiritual and moral conscience of our time. It embodies the essentially democratic idea of the creative artist as the

Above and right: A comparison of over-long and readable line lengths.

Left: Setting justified type to an overly narrow measure throws up exaggerated letter spacing to fill the measure and makes for difficult and tiring reading.

Modernism, as we have known it, has served as the aesthetic, spiritual and moral conscience of our time. It embodies the essentially democratic idea of the creative artist as the inventor of a personal style, a unique vision of the world.

Below: Tight tracking makes an interesting but illegible typographic pattern. Loose tracking weakens the horizontal character of lines of type and so slows and hinders reading.

Modernism, as we have known it, has served as the aesthetic, spiritual and moral conscience of our time. It embodies the essentially democratic idea of the creative artist as the inventor of a personal style, a unique vision of the world.

V
E
R
T
HORIZONTAL
C
A
L

Below: Although display type set vertically is economical in one way, it puts added reading strain on the eye as it is forced to jump unnaturally downwards, from letter to letter.

straight left-hand edge. However, small group-ings of text can normally be read in most of the setting styles. Justified setting (text that is aligned at both sides) is not suitable for very small blocks of text, where ugly word spacing will occur. Justification can also sometimes create difficulties with hyphenation and word spacing in longer, continuous text unless this is carefully controlled. Hyphenation at line ends can sometimes create an unnecessarily "spotty" look and should be avoided where possible.

Line length also affects how text is read. If lines of text are too long, the eye has difficulty in returning to the start of the next line. Conversely, if lines of text are too narrowly set, the eye is made to progress too quickly from line to line and may skip lines, interrupting the flow of comprehension. Although these disturbances will have little effect over a few lines, they will tire the eye over large amounts of text. As a rough guide to line length, an average line of text in the English language reads comfortably with

between the letterstrokes and counter-shapes is distracting.

The style of text setting—justified, flush left or right, centered or asymmetric—together with line length, also has an effect on the readability of text. In reading any length of text, the eye is generally more comfortable in returning to a

Left: Lowercase letters have individual key characteristics which tend to be in the top half of the letterform. These characteristics are more important to letter and word recognition than those in the bottom half. This is particularly noticeable in serif typefaces where the tops of letters are more easily identifiable. In sans serif designs, there can be greater similarity between the top half of letters
DESIGN BY BRIAN COE, UK

approximately sixty-three to sixty-five characters (counting word spaces as characters).

Digital technology enables both display and text type to be very flexibly set into shapes. Running text round images is also easily done. However, in working with either, care has to be taken to maintain coherent, readable text by controlling each individual line break.

Display type is normally restricted to a few words and presents fewer problems due to its size, weight, and dominant position in the design area. The designer should, however, look carefully at the spaces between characters and words in larger type sizes. Pairs of letters may need kerning to aid readability. Where several words are involved, one or more word spaces may need to be optically balanced—to counteract the effects produced by the shapes of the last and first letters of the words at either side, which may be exaggerated at display sizes.

EXTENDED OR EXPERT SETS

Many digital typefaces have extensive ranges of characters well in excess of the basic set of letters, numerals, punctuation marks, and symbols included as standard in most fonts. Where these are included within a single font file, the font is said to have an extended character set. The Unicode character encoding system, now the industry standard, encompasses a huge range of characters in many languages, although this is no guarantee that a particular font will include them. OpenType fonts can also store multiple glyphs (letterforms) for each character. For example, there may be "optical" variants designed for use at a different range of sizes

Garamond Alternate ligatures   Garamond Alternate italic

Garamond Alternate regular

Adobe Caslon Alternate ligatures   Garamond Regular/Garamond Alternate terminal letters

Bembo roman accents

Left: Some of the alternative glyphs available in expert font sets. Most expert sets include "old style" or non-aligning numerals, which rise above and below the x-height and baseline. This style of numeral works well within text, as it is less disruptive to visual continuity. It can also be softer to read in tabular form, although lining numerals are often preferred for technical and financial material.

DESIGN BASICS

(such as text and display); or a ligature glyph may represent multiple characters, such as "ffi."

Many fonts on the market predate these technologies, and any extra characters are supplied as a separate font, known as an expert set. In either case, the typographer is provided with a range of extra letterforms that share the inherent form and structure of the basic typeface.

Another example of an alternative glyph is a swash character: a decorative version of a letter with an exaggerated sweeping entrance or exit stroke that may overlap the preceding or following character. Swash characters can add a flourish to the start or the end of a word. Capitals ("swash caps") are common, but some designs include swash initial, terminal, and even medial lower-case letters (see below opposite).

Non-lining or old-style numerals, which ascend and descend like lower-case letters rather than lining numerals, are a useful option, and can help soften large quantities of numerical information. Specially designed small capitals are essential for setting text in small caps, as ordinary caps reduced in size will not match the weight and proportion of other characters.

Below: This page, from a brochure for Entec, creates a precise yet complex typographic "sound image" which reflects the nature of the product: high-fidelity speakers. The three-dimensional, broad-ranging nature of sound is suggested through strong contrast in size, weight, color, and type style, and semi-abstraction of parts of the letterforms.
DESIGN BY MAUK DESIGN, USA

THE DESIGN AREA or page format and margins are the basic components of layout, which—like everything else in the design process—should always be informed by the content of the job and the creative approach. How and where the end-product is to be used or viewed must be taken into account in deciding the size and format.

Layout

Size and format can range from pocket to wall-size, in both two and three dimensions. When designing for the web or multimedia, where the maximum area is predetermined, page proportions should still be given thought.

In almost every design context, the graphic designer will need to set up an appropriate page or design area structure (see below). This is normally done in a page-layout program, and it initially involves making a series of interrelated design decisions: width of the top, foot, and side margins (essentially there for handling purposes and for leading the eye), the number of columns for text and image organization and, where appropriate, the number of pages or surfaces that may be involved. Once these decisions have been made,

the page structure can be set up as single or facing pages in templates (or master pages in desktop publishing programs) to allow automatic repetition of the original structure across numerous pages.

Multipage surface design benefits from adding a further underpinning structure or grid to the basic page. This is done by subdividing the basic page structure into sets and subsets of equal vertical column widths. The greater the number of divisions or columns, the greater the flexibility. The modularity that is created can be used invisibly to structure the relationship of quite disparate elements, with some running across several or all of the columns. If the complexity of the job requires additional underpinning, a horizontal grid can be constructed in a similar way. A grid system can be

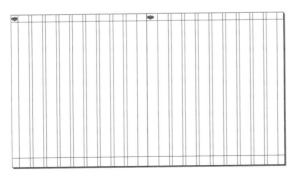

Left: Structuring the design area across a series of pages or surfaces so as to give maximum flexibility without losing continuity is important to holding the viewer's attention.

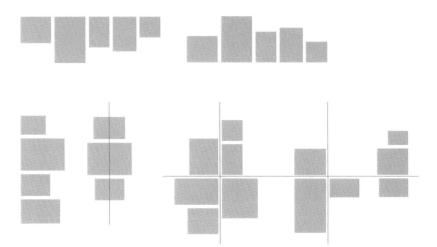

particularly useful in helping to keep a sense of continuity across a range of different pages, sizes, scales, or formats. Corporate identities, exhibitions, advertising campaigns, and multi-media can all benefit from the controlling influence of a grid system.

Diagonal layouts can be very powerful but need to be kept simple as they may hinder the reader if too many elements are involved.

Above: Different sized and proportioned elements are coordinated within a given area. This diagram shows "hanging," "sitting," vertical, and centered alignments, and combined horizontal and vertical axes around which different clusters of elements can be grouped.

Below: Margin proportions will vary depending on the design context as in the diagram above, but as a guideline, the foot margin is normally double the head margin and the fore-edge margin half the width of the back margin.

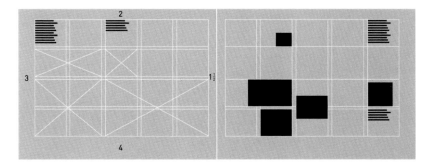

DOCUMENT SIGNPOSTING Most graphic design includes working with some element of text or copy. Most copy needs ordered presentation, so before any design work starts the designer should work through it to establish some basic organization or hierarchy.

Organization and hierarchy

Breaking the copy down into digestible passages, if only by white space, will automatically pace the reader. Controlling the space between elements will determine the reading sequence. Hierarchical conventions will direct and signpost the reader through, for example, a book, via the title page, the contents page, the page numbers (folios), chapter headings, subheadings, paragraphs, and footnotes.

Designing a website will often involve developing an ordered, functional, and user-friendly navigation process to take the viewer through the various pages. In advertising, the hierarchy of information may be as simple as a main heading and strapline, whereas an instruction manual may contain many layers of information. Developing a visual hierarchy will order information and make it easily accessible. The exercise will normally include typeface and style together with varying levels of emphasis for other elements through the use of size, weight, color, and disposition. Even the structuring of the basic paragraph needs many decisions about detailing.

Bullet points (circular, square, or triangular) and selected dingbats (for example, Wingdings) can be used to highlight and draw attention to listings, instructions, or blocks of text, but the level of emphasis should be compatible

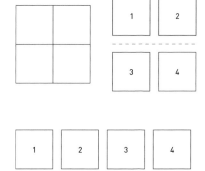

with the rest of the text and overall context. The size, weight, or color of bullets and dingbats should complement, rather than compete with, the other elements in the design, and should direct the reader to and through the points in a relevant sequence.

Frames and rules are devices that can help to isolate, contain, formalize, contrast, and draw attention to text, image, or area. The weight, style, and color of the line used for a frame will control the level and intensity of focus, but the design and proportion should be integrated with the main context. Framed text or other elements often appear within a main body of text, but they

DESIGN BASICS

should still be capable of being read independently. To achieve this, the framed text needs to be set to a narrower width than the main text to allow for the thickness of the frame and a reasonable space between it and the text. Surrounding white space can suggest a frame (as with margins on a page) through the placing of single element within a large area. Decorative frames should be used sparingly as they can easily distract attention from the content.

Desktop publishing programs make a distinction between rules that can be placed before or after paragraphs and underlining, which is a feature of the type style (character underlining or word underlining).

Typographic rules have considerable potential in their own right as design elements and need not be restricted to being used in conjunction with paragraphs. They can direct and arrest the eye, physically divide areas or separate elements, pace

Left and below: Where it is essential that the viewer reads the design in a particular sequence, subtle grouping—through the use of white space one-and-a-half to two times the spacing between the individual elements in a group—will naturally guide the eye through the grouping sequentially. When elements are butted up to each other, the eye will read the surface as an entity in itself.

Headings	Captioning	Numbering	Indexing	Examples of conventions that are used to make sense of copy and so guide the reader through documents.
Chapters	Illustrations	Pages	Index	
Sections	Photographs	Paragraphs	Table of contents	
Major topic headings	Charts	Footnotes	Glossaries	
Subheads	Diagrams	Cross-referencing	Appendices	
Sub subheads	Tables		Bibliographies	
	Quotations		**Punctuation**	
	Speech		Pace	
	Extracts		Sense	

Organization and hierarchy

the viewer, and be a facilitating device in leading the eye along the horizontal, vertical, or diagonal direction. When placed above, below, or to the side of an element, a rule has an anchoring effect on it. The level of focus and emphasis created in this way can be accentuated or diminished by modifying the relative size, color, texture, or weight of either the rule or the element. If different weights of rule are used in the same design area, they should be distinctly contrasting—if they are too similar in weight, they may look like a mistake or be indistinguishable from each other. Whichever type of frame or weight of rule is used, it is generally better to keep the scheme simple.

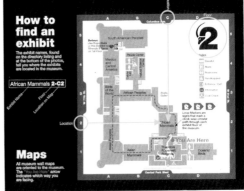

Left top: A contrasting rule will anchor text. A further rule below text or images will contain them. Middle: With marginal headings or two different column widths, fine and bold vertical rules can help set the reading hierarchy. Bottom: Rules can both separate and coordinate elements.

Above: Size, type style, icon, disposition, and typographic devices are combined to pinpoint key locations in the wayfinding system for the American Museum of Natural History in New York. Clarity is essential to prevent visitors from getting lost. DESIGN BY LANCE WYMAN, USA

Above: The impenetrable nature of the Berlin Wall is graphically conveyed in this exhibition display through the use of heavy typographic rules carrying tightly contained, reversed-out type.

Left: The structure of even basic paragraphs needs to be carefully considered to determine a visual hierarchy of information and make it easily accessible.

Column width	
Typeface	La puerta con dos casas es lo permanente, inacesible. Esta casa de alforja se encuentra en el territorio de los acontecimientos simultáneos. Dos espacios que se aman, que se besan, pour una puerta que no se sabe si separa o une.
Indents	Aquí todo tiene la suficente claridad y la deliciosa oscuridad de la armoniá. No nos sabemos dentro hasta que unos pasos más allá de la primera puerta, nos encontramos fuera del edificio; nunca sabemos qué es demasiado.
Alignments	
Type size	Todo recuerdo de este viaje será el instante en que abandonamos esa sensación de recogimiento, memoria irrecuperable de un espacio inmenso, inmensamente.
Type style	*La puerta con dos casas es lo permanente, inacesible. Esta*
Leading	*casa de alforja se encuentra en el territorio de los acontecimientos simultáneos. Dos espacios que se aman,*
Inter paragraph spacing	
Case	AQUÍ TODO TIENE la suficente claridad y la deliciosa oscuridad de la armoniá. No nos sabemos dentro hasta que
Tracking	unos pasos más allá de la primera puerta, fuera del edificio; nunca sabemos qué

IMAGE SELECTION The client may provide a set of images that are integral to a job, which leaves the designer with no say in the content or design of the image and little say in the selection. However, the designer can control how the images are used and, when selecting from a range, should ensure that the selection "tells the story" appropriately.

Images

Initial impact may be of prime importance, but drawing the viewer in through secondary and tertiary levels of interest should also be considered. There are, however, some occasions when it is better to invest in a completely new set of images. The designer can then advise on them or be involved in selecting them or commissioning them from a photographer or illustrator. As coordinator of all the elements in a design and manager of the process, the designer has a responsibility to prepare a focused brief outlining the aims, purpose, format and context of the image-making. This should be agreed with the client and photographer or illustrator, and supplemented with detailed instructions concerning appropriate file formats and resolution values (see *Image Creation*).

Every aspect of an image should contribute in some degree to the overall message and mood of the design. Images may clarify, contrast, enhance, and partner text or other elements, but they should never be used simply as gratuitous

Left: Even if the budget for images is zero, it is possible to make use of clip art or the Custom Shapes supplied with Photoshop to create effective images. Composition and color are as always the key, enabling even the humblest of source material to look good.
DESIGN BY GRAHAM DAVIS, UK

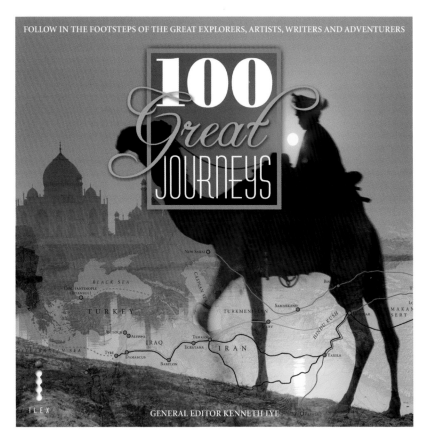

100
Great
JOURNEYS

GENERAL EDITOR KENNETH LYE

ILEX

"add-ons." Scaling and cropping images and deciding on a presentation method (color, black-and-white, duotone, cutout, squared-up) needs considerable care and attention, and should bear a direct relevance to the overall design. Judicious cropping can substantially affect the visual impact and balance of the image itself, as well as influencing the message and other design elements.

Above: Merging pictures can result in an image that is more than just the sum of the parts, particularly if creatively combined with text, as in this book cover.
DESIGN BY GRAHAM DAVIS, UK

DESIGNING WITH COLOR Color is the element that brings an added, almost magical dimension to visual communication. It reflects the everyday world and human experience, giving the designer a strong common language with which to express mood, emotion, and significance.

Color

The digital graphic designer has an almost limitless color palette with which to work and evoke specific responses in the viewer. Color can be used as appeal, inspiration, entertainment, a focus, or an identifying marker.

Color is always relative and never works in isolation. The viewer responds to color within a context and in association with other colors and graphic elements. Environmental and lighting conditions affect the way color is perceived, which is a particular consideration when choosing colors for packaging, signage, and exhibitions.

Color can be used as a means of identification and coding, as in pie and bar charts, where a range of different elements of equal importance need to be identified. In such contexts, care should be taken to mix colors (hues) of similar tones (brightness) and intensity (saturation) to avoid giving undue emphasis to any one element. In a situation where it is necessary to create levels of relative importance, a change in color intensity or brightness, or both, can be used as a hierarchical device.

Combining complementary colors (true opposites on the color wheel) will set up a natural vibrancy if a sense of excitement and energy is needed. To use color emotively, it is essential to have an understanding of the design subject matter and the audience to which it is directed, so that color choice can be appropriately related.

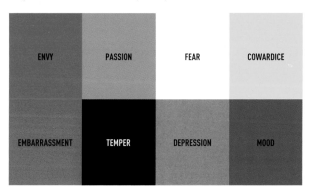

| ENVY | PASSION | FEAR | COWARDICE |
| EMBARRASSMENT | TEMPER | DEPRESSION | MOOD |

Left: Color and meaning varies widely according to different cultures. For example, in much of Asia white is associated with death whereas in the West it is associated with purity. These associations and differences can be useful in making unusual connections or changing perceptions depending on the design context.
DESIGN BY ALAN FLETCHER, UK/USA

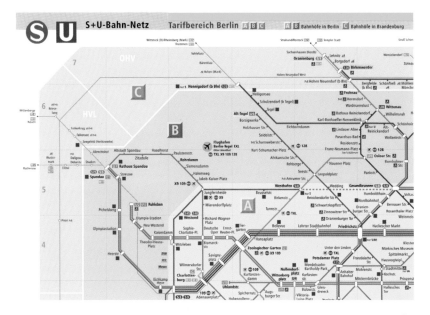

Colors can be considered as warm or cool, soft or hard, light or dark, passive or active—all of which characteristics can be used individually or in association with each other. Mood is greatly affected by color temperature.

Color association forms an important part of color language in all areas of graphic design. This can be seen in the way that greens are used for freshness, blues and whites for hygiene, red for danger, and purple for richness. There are many examples of color combinations that are associated with politics, nationality, sport, religion, or cultural and social conventions. The designer has to be aware of all of them, in order to avoid creating confused messages. For example, red and green are recognized across the world as symbolizing "stop" and "go."

Above: Color coding in diagrammatic maps ensures a clarity of communication and quick recognition that can be flexibly applied to related graphics and signage.
DESIGN BY METADESIGN, GERMANY

Right: This inventive annual report for the Linear Technology Corporation is made up of two books packaged in this bright sleeve. The Digital book is monochrome and only contains indecipherable streaming ascii code. The Linear book dramatically makes the point that "Digital means nothing without Linear" through pages of brilliant digital color and succinct, accessible black text on pure white.
DESIGN BY CAHAN & ASSOCIATES, USA

Color

It is impossible to provide a set of rules for particular harmonious color combinations since these change according to different environments, fashions, and culture. The designer may consider setting up disharmonies as a way of creating shock or provocation, which may be a perfectly legitimate way of communicating the intended message.

Graphic art software provides tools for selecting and mixing colors in a variety of models. These give the designer unprecedented control over color creation and usage (see *Color Matters*). The hue, saturation, and brightness (HSB) model is particularly useful as it enables the creation either of different hues of the same brightness and intensity or of varying intensities or brightnesses of the same hue.

Designers should be aware that their color perception can be affected if they set strong background colors for their monitors. Large areas of color and poor lighting in the working environment will have a similar effect on perception. It is advisable, therefore, to set the monitor to a neutral gray when working intensively with color, and to paint design studios in neutral colors.

TYPE AND COLOR

All the uses of color to express mood, emotion, or significance can be equally well applied to type. Color may be used to modify the way in which type works: bold type can be softened, hierarchies can be developed without recourse to change of size or weight, text can be enlivened, and typographic emphasis can be subtly enhanced.

When designing with colored type on a colored background, the designer must consider the choice of color combination carefully in order to ensure legibility. In general, type and background need to be significantly contrasting. Dark type on a pale background, rather than on a white background, will result in less glare (particularly with screen-based designs, for example on web pages). Type and backgrounds of equal brightness (tone) will reduce legibility considerably. Color can be used with type to create a sense of progression and recession, to enhance spatial quality and suggest depth and perspective. The reading pace and sequence of text and display type can be further controlled through the use of color.

Setting type in dark colors may be unsuccessful if the letters have a small surface area with which to carry color; the result may appear to be a poor version of black. Type, particularly text type, has little surface area compared to the background surface on which it appears, so dark-colored type generally appears darker and light-colored type generally appears lighter. A heavier weight of type can be used to compensate for this phenomenon.

Interestingly, the millions of easily accessible digital colors have also brought a revived energy to the use of black and white that should not be underestimated.

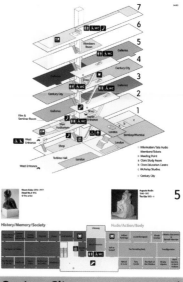

Century City:
Art and Culture in the Modern Metropolis

4

Above: Black was an unusual but distinctive choice for a coordinating element in the new, Suma supermarket identity in Barcelona. Together with special lighting, it is used as a means of focusing the eye on the different colors of their merchandise. These aprons show color used as coding for fish, meat, and vegetables.
DESIGN BY SUMA, SPAIN

Right: Subject areas are grouped together into discrete gallery displays in the Tate Modern, London. Each is identified in the plan (or on the website) by a unique color used in both the titles and floor plan, facilitating visit planning and wayfinding through the vast building.
DESIGN BY HALMES WOOD, UK

Left: Colored text can be effective but it can result in legibility problems so take particular care when it is displayed on a colored background. Smaller text sizes in particular can be difficult to read so when in doubt use colored text on a white background.
DESIGN BY GRAHAM DAVIS, UK

THE VALUE OF DESIGN BASICS

SURFACE DESIGN

2

TYPE is one of the graphic designer's core tools. With attention to detail, the designer can use type to communicate appropriately, to suggest mood and character, and to contribute to page or surface layout dynamics. However, type does need to be handled with care and understanding.

TYPE MATTERS

Designers should not only have an appreciation of the aesthetic values of type (see *Design Basics*), but also know how type is stored, controlled, and output digitally. All these issues have a direct bearing on how type is printed and displayed on screen.

A typeface is an alphabet (along with numerals and punctuation) considered as a designed or aesthetic visual entity. A font is a collection of letterforms in that typeface, and is stored in one file on the computer. One font may contain the alphabet in upper and lower case, with related numerals and punctuation, plus any number of alternative or additional characters and symbols (see page 34). Several fonts will be required to use a typeface effectively for text setting, typically including at least italic, bold, and bold-italic variants. Many typefaces are available as "families" of several dozen fonts.

Font-related issues are among the most common causes of problems when collaborating on documents with other users, sending desktop publishing files to press, and even keeping the designer's own system running smoothly. The following brief overview should help to clear up any confusion and avoid the potential pitfalls.

Opposite: An example of some of the glyphs available for the font Times New Roman Regular. Below: On the Mac, many special characters can be accessed by key combinations. The Keyboard Viewer shows which combinations generate which characters in a given font. To activate it, open System Preferences, click International and, under Input Menu, tick Keyboard Palette. You will then find Keyboard Viewer in the menu accessed from the national flag symbol in the main menu bar at the top of the screen. Hold down the modifier keys (Control, Alt, and Command) to see the characters they will give.

Recently Used:

Show: Entire Font ▼

	!	"	#	$	%	&	'	(	)	*	+	,	-	.	/	0	1	2	3
4	5	6	7	8	9	:	;	<	=	>	?	@	A	B	C	D	E	F	G
H	I	J	K	L	M	N	O	P	Q	R	S	T	U	V	W	X	Y	Z	[
\	]	^	_	`	a	b	c	d	e	f	g	h	i	j	k	l	m	n	o
p	q	r	s	t	u	v	w	x	y	z	{	|	}	~	¡	¢	£	¤	¥
¦	§	¨	©	ª	«	¬	®	¯	°	±	²	³	´	µ	¶	·	¸	¹	º
»	¼	½	¾	¿	À	Á	Â	Ã	Ä	Å	Æ	Ç	È	É	Ê	Ë	Ì	Í	Î
Ï	Ð	Ñ	Ò	Ó	Ô	Õ	Ö	×	Ø	Ù	Ú	Û	Ü	Ý	Þ	ß	à	á	â
ã	ä	å	æ	ç	è	é	ê	ë	ì	í	î	ï	ð	ñ	ò	ó	ô	õ	ö
÷	ø	ù	ú	û	ü	ý	þ	ÿ	Ā	ā	Ă	ă	Ą	ą	Ć	ć	Ĉ	ĉ	Ċ
ċ	Č	č	Ď	ď	Đ	đ	Ē	ē	Ĕ	ĕ	Ė	ė	Ę	ę	Ě	ě	Ĝ	ĝ	Ğ
ğ	Ġ	ġ	Ģ	ģ	Ĥ	ĥ	Ħ	ħ	Ĩ	ĩ	Ī	ī	Ĭ	ĭ	Į	į	İ	ı	IJ
ij	Ĵ	ĵ	Ķ	ķ	ĸ	Ĺ	ĺ	Ļ	ļ	Ľ	ľ	Ŀ	ŀ	Ł	ł	Ń	ń	Ņ	ņ
Ň	ň	ŉ	Ŋ	ŋ	Ō	ō	Ŏ	ŏ	Ő	ő	Œ	œ	Ŕ	ŕ	Ŗ	ŗ	Ř	ř	Ś
ś	Ŝ	ŝ	Ş	ş	Š	š	Ţ	ţ	Ť	ť	Ŧ	ŧ	Ũ	ũ	Ū	ū	Ŭ	ŭ	Ů
ů	Ű	ű	Ų	ų	Ŵ	ŵ	Ŷ	ŷ	Ÿ	Ź	ź	Ż	ż	Ž	ž	ſ	ƀ	Ɓ	Ƃ
ƃ	Ƅ	ƅ	Ɔ	Ƈ	ƈ	Ɖ	Ɗ	ƌ	ƍ	Ǫ	Ǝ	Ə	Ɛ	Ƒ	ƒ	Ɠ	Ɣ	ƕ	ɩ
Ɨ	Ƙ	ƙ	ł	ƛ	Ɯ	Ɲ	ƞ	Ɵ	Ơ	ơ	Ƣ	ƣ	Ƥ	ƥ	Ʀ	Ƨ	ƨ	Σ	ƪ
ƫ	Ƭ	ƭ	Ʈ	Ư	ư	Ʊ	Ʋ	Ƴ	ƴ	Ƶ	ƶ	Ʒ	Ƹ	ƹ	ƺ	ƻ	Ƽ	ƽ	ƾ
ƿ	ǀ	ǁ	ǂ	ǃ	DŽ	Dž	dž	LJ	Lj	lj	NJ	Nj	nj	Ǎ	ǎ	Ǐ	ǐ	Ǒ	ǒ
Ǔ	ǔ	Ǖ	ǖ	Ǘ	ǘ	Ǚ	ǚ	Ǜ	ǜ	ǝ	Ǟ	ǟ	Ǡ	ǡ	Ǣ	ǣ	Ǥ	ǥ	Ǧ
ǧ	Ǩ	ǩ	Ǫ	ǫ	Ǭ	ǭ	Ǯ	ǯ	ǰ	DZ	Dz	dz	Ǵ	ǵ	Ƕ	ƿ	Ǹ	ǹ	Ǻ

Times New Roman ▼ Regular ▼

LETTERFORM INFORMATION can be stored digitally in bitmap or vector form. Bitmap data—effectively a black-and-white image—is fine for screen display at a fixed size, but gives a "pixelated" appearance when scaled up.

Bitmaps and vectors

Vector or "outline" descriptions of each character provide scalable forms which can be displayed and printed at any size, provided that the computer or printer has the means to "rasterize" the outlines to a bitmap (all screen or printer output is ultimately bitmapped). The outlines are filled with black or whatever color you choose for the text.

In the early days of scalable type on desktop computers—dating from the launch of PostScript in 1985—the processing power was not available to rasterize outline fonts "on the fly" for screen display. Instead, characters were represented on screen by bitmapped fonts in a fixed range of

sizes, and outline fonts substituted on printing. This meant that what you saw on screen often bore little resemblance to what appeared on paper. Later, outline fonts could be rendered on screen using Adobe Type Manager (ATM).

Today, font display is handled by the computer's operating system, whether OS X or Windows. (Users with obsolete versions of these will still need ATM.) You can be sure that, with very few accidental exceptions, the shapes and positions of the characters you see on screen in your page layouts will be precisely reproduced when you print.

Left: Some pairs of characters do not sit comfortably together. Type designers set up "kerning pairs"—sometimes hundreds per font—to adjust the trickier combinations, but you will always need to fix a few instances yourself using manual kerning.

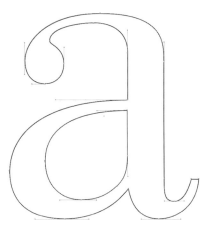

Above: Every character in a font is described by a set of vectors, its "outline" description.

Below: The common accents used in most Latin alphabets can be obtained on the Mac by pressing Option plus another key before typing the character that you want to accent. For example, to place a circumflex over an e (ê), hold down Option and press i, let go of Option, and type e. The keys for accents have a white outline in Keyboard Viewer (see page 50).

áéèüöçôåñ ˘

Meta.t1		Font Suitcase
MetaBol		PostScript Type 1 outline font
MetaIta		PostScript Type 1 outline font
MetaNor		PostScript Type 1 outline font
MonacoCY.dfont		Datafork TrueType font
Nadeem.ttf		Windows TrueType font
NewsGothicStd-Bold.otf		OpemType font
NewsGothicStd-BoldOblique.otf		OpenType font
NewsGothicStd.otf		OpenType font

Left: Font files on the Mac are identified in Finder windows by their icon and "Kind" attribute. PostScript fonts traditionally comprise an outline file for each instance along with a "suitcase" of bitmaps for the set, although Mac OS X can recognize the outline files, and render them on screen and in print without the bitmaps. Double-clicking a font shows a visual preview, and an option to install it will appear.

DESIGNERS producing materials for the screen, such as web graphics, have different concerns. At small sizes, the area into which a letterform is to be rasterized may contain only a few pixels. Using anti-aliasing (see page 57), a fair impression can be given of the shape, but the character will be fuzzy, and text set this way is hard to read.

Font formats

Bitmapped fonts, designed for on-screen use at a fixed size, are a better choice when text is set as a graphic at small sizes (this is also why operating systems have an option to anti-alias the fonts used for labels and buttons only above a certain size). For headings and other large text, an outline font rendered with anti-aliasing is ideal.

POSTSCRIPT TYPE 1 FONTS

PostScript, Adobe's page description language, can be used to store any kind of vector graphic from a simple shape to the structure of a complete page layout. Fonts for professional use, particularly with Macs, traditionally contain outlines in this language, and more specifically in a format known as Type 1. PostScript Type 1 fonts consist of two parts: a bitmap file for screen display, for the reasons explained earlier, and an outline file. (They may also have extra files with the extension ".afm" and/or ".inf"—these are rarely used by software.) Several bitmap files—contained in a "suitcase" on the Mac—are usually supplied in different sizes. Older operating systems can use these to show characters on screen, and they will also be used if the outline file is missing. The outline font file is traditionally downloaded to the printer (which must have a PostScript engine) to enable it to rasterize characters, but many applications now pre-rasterize their output in

software, using the operating system's PostScript interpreter rather than the printer's. One advantage of this is that layouts can be output on non-PostScript printers; cheaper lasers, and almost all inkjets, fall into this category.

Although they contain the same information, Mac and PC PostScript font files are not interchangeable—you need the right ones for your computer platform.

TRUETYPE

TrueType is a rival format to PostScript which was adopted as a standard by both Microsoft and Apple, although it only really caught on with Windows users. A TrueType rasterizer is built into both Macintosh and Windows operating systems. TrueType fonts are held in a single file which can contain variants such as regular, italic, bold, and bold italic. From Mac OS 8.5 onwards, Macs can use the same TrueType file format as PCs, with the extension ".ttf" or ".ttc." However, Macs also have their own TrueType format, ".dfont," which is not compatible with Windows.

OPENTYPE

OpenType, a relatively new font format from Adobe and Microsoft, can contain TrueType and PostScript data, and works on both Macs and PCs. OpenType fonts have the extension ".otf."

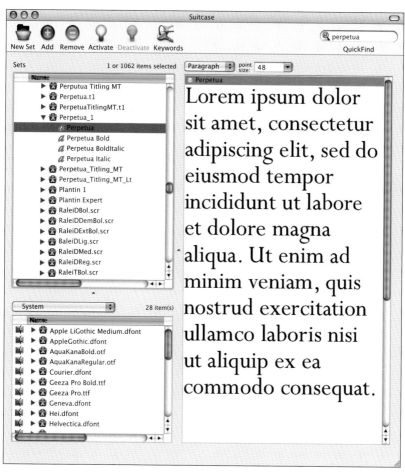

Above: Font management software such as Extensis Suitcase can help rationalize the large number of fonts likely to be found on a designer's system. User-defined "sets" arrange fonts by type, usage, client, or job. Sets or individual fonts can be activated and de-activated as required, rather than having a huge number constantly installed, which can slow down the system and cause conflicts between copies of the same font. Some of this functionality, however, is now built into Mac OS X and, to a lesser extent, Windows.

Font formats

2

Despite the undoubted benefits, such as the inclusion of extended character sets and alternative glyphs (see page 34) in a single font file, so many pre-OpenType fonts exist that adoption of the new standard can only proceed fairly slowly. Significantly, though, Apple is supporting it and supplies OpenType fonts with the Mac OS.

MULTIPLE MASTER FONTS

Multiple Master fonts, developed by Adobe, contain several sets of outlines that represent either end of up to four "design axes": weight, width, style, and optical size. Using a software utility, designers can create custom fonts by choosing points between these extremes. The result is not a distortion of the original letterforms but a newly generated font. Sadly, only a few Multiple Master fonts have appeared, and they are not directly supported in either Windows or the Mac OS.

WHERE ARE MY FONTS?

TrueType and Type 1 fonts can be installed and used on the same system and even within the same page. To avoid confusion, it is safest not to install the same font in more than one format. When using PostScript Type 1 fonts, always make sure you have the outline font as well as the bitmap. In general, you should stick to Type 1 fonts in documents that are to be sent for commercial printing, but TrueType and OpenType fonts are increasingly accepted by prepress equipment.

In Windows, installed fonts are normally stored in the Fonts folder inside the Windows folder on the main hard disk, although they can be kept elsewhere. In Mac OS X, fonts are normally only available for use if they are stored in one of four Library folders, depending on whether they are essential system fonts; to be used by everyone with access to the Mac; only for one named user; or stored on a network server. A built-in utility called Font Book makes this clearer than it sounds, and also allows installed fonts to be turned on and off. Fonts used in OS X's Classic mode, which provides access to OS 9 for older programs, are stored in the Fonts folder inside the OS 9 System Folder.

FONT PROBLEMS

Font problems are less common than they used to be, but graphic designers are particularly prone to them, simply because they tend to have more fonts and do more with them than other users.

"Jagged" type on screen is caused by missing PostScript outline files; try using Find (Mac OS) or Search (Windows) to see if they have simply ended up in the wrong folder. With older systems, it could be that ATM is switched off.

When you click the Italic or Bold button in software, the selected text should be reset in the corresponding italic or bold font. However, if no such font is present, or if (in the case of Type 1 fonts) the software does not know which file it is, then the ordinary letterforms are either just slanted to simulate italic or offset for bold. Not only are these effects unsightly, but they may not print. To be safe, choose the italic or bold version of the font from the font menu, unless it is a TrueType font which has them in a single file.

Some fonts may not be listed alphabetically where you expect, usually because their makers have added a variant prefix, as in "I Bodoni Italic," or a foundry name, as in "ITC Garamond."

If you open a previously laid-out document and find text looks wrong or has moved, there are two possible causes. Either you do not have the correct font installed, and the software has substituted another; or you have more than one version of the font, and the wrong one is active. Sort this out before editing the document.

When you send a job to a bureau or printer, always include the fonts, either by embedding them, if using PDF, or by sending the necessary font files with the document and image files. The latter route is technically an infringement of copyright unless the contractor already owns the exact same font, but it is common practice and the font companies have never come up with a workable alternative.

Sometimes the bureau or printer may report that a font is missing, even though you have no recollection of using it. A blank line or single character in a font—even a space—will create an error if that font is missing. Many programs let you check the fonts in a document and switch any mis-styled characters to the correct font.

FONT COPYRIGHT

Remember that fonts are protected by copyright law. When you "buy" a font, you only acquire a licence to use it, usually on one to five computers. You should not pass fonts to friends, colleagues, or contractors. It is very common practice to do so for one-off jobs where it would be uneconomical for everyone in the production chain to buy their own copy, but you should be aware that there is no legal protection for this. Embedding fonts in PDFs largely obviates the problem.

IMPROVING TYPE ON SCREEN

Good digital typeface designers tweak the "hinting" in their fonts to help computers rasterize characters accurately at low resolutions. The quality of hinting varies between fonts, but some are specifically optimized for use at the relatively low resolution of the monitor. Ideally the weight, width, spacing, and stroke variation should all be considered in this light, as well as the hinting.

When you rasterize type in a program such as Photoshop, you can choose between different anti-aliasing methods—for example, Smooth or Crisp. This option should not be overlooked when setting type as graphics for websites.

The future of type in on-screen media could lie in a system such as Bitstream's TrueDoc. This allows fonts to be embedded in multimedia content, and rasterizes them using "subpixel" technology, improving sharpness and accuracy. At present, there is little sign of this becoming the norm.

jaggies
jaggies

Above: "Jaggies" is the name given to the crude pixelated rendering of type on screen which occurs when bitmapped fonts are enlarged. Smooth results are obtained when working from the outline information in OpenType, PostScript, or TrueType fonts.

THE ROOTS OF GRAPHIC DESIGN lie in our desire to communicate information —more especially by the arrangement of type and pictures on a printed page. Although the development of digital technology has made the possibilities virtually limitless, graphic design and print remain inextricably linked.

DESIGN FOR PRINT

Graphic design for the medium of print embraces an extensive and varied range of products. These include promotional applications such as brochures, leaflets, flyers, direct mail, catalogs, and posters. Business communication tools include stationery, newsletters, training manuals, reports, or menus. The publishing industry, producing magazines, books, and newspapers, is still one of the largest sectors employing graphic designers.

With ever-increasing market and client pressure to create eye-catching, innovative ways of presenting printed information, there are jobs that call for more specialized print processes. The use of materials other than paper—plastic, metal, or even fabric—is also becoming more prevalent.

The processes that take the concept to the printed product affect many design decisions made at concept stage. The choice of paper or other media, or the size of the print run, will dictate not only the type of print technology used but also the way the production files are created—including the appropriate choice of type and the size of the halftone dot.

The computer has shaped not only conceptual design, by encouraging freedom of layout and the breaking of typographic conventions, but also the linear process of transferring the design from screen to printed page. The traditional boundaries of the design-for-print process have been blurred. The designer equipped with a PC, or more commonly an Apple Macintosh, linked to a desktop scanner, a color output device, and a high-speed Internet connection can take conceptual ideas through to press, and today even the printing press itself may be a digital device.

With the adoption of Adobe's PDF (portable document format) as a medium for delivering press-ready documents, there need be virtually no human intervention between the designer and the printed product.

Right: Design for print, especially in multi-page documents, relies upon first establishing adequate foundations and this means a grid. Usually set up on master pages, it is the skeleton on which each layout is fleshed out. A successful grid will balance flexibility and variety in layouts, while imposing consistency overall.
DESIGN BY GRAHAM DAVIS, UK

Facil exerit dolesequisi bla con henisse niamcon sequamet in henim nim del ut lortion ullutat nosto ectem autetum ip enit ad miniatem iniam, consed ming

Et consed dunt iureet ercing et velismo dignisi in veros dunt acip ent vullupt ationsecte facidunt

Facil exerit dolesequisi bla con henisse niamcon sequamet in henim nim del ut lortion ullutat nosto ectem autetum ip enit ad miniatem iniam, consed ming

---

Facil exerit dolesequisi bla con henisse niamcon sequamet in henim nim del ut lortion ullutat nosto ectem autetum ip enit ad miniatem iniam, consed ming

lorem ipsum dolor pretu ectem autetum

Et consed dunt iureet ercing et velismo dignisi in veros dunt acip ent vullupt ationsecte facidunt

Facil exerit dolesequisi bla con henisse niamcon sequamet in henim nim del ut lortion ullutat nosto ectem autetum ip enit ad miniatem iniam, consed ming

THE SOFTWARE Over the past few years, there have been significant developments in software dedicated to both design and production, providing more streamlined digitally driven systems that take design directly to print.

Print designer's toolkit

Creating designs for print demands page precision and the flexibility of working with multiple creative sources. A page-layout package therefore needs to combine vector artwork, bitmap images, fonts, and color in one place using a what-you-see-is-what-you-get interface. But modern page-design software goes way beyond these basics, also supporting long documents with indexing, tabular layouts, automated type styling, and special graphics effects that can be output at high resolution to film, plate, and press.

QUARKXPRESS

Although QuarkXPress was not the first page-layout software to hit the market, it was the first to offer professional-strength design features back in the late 1980s. It has defined and dominated the print design industry ever since. Familiarity with QuarkXPress is mandatory in virtually every studio and publishing house, and for every freelance designer.

QuarkXPress is often seen as the one steady rock in a sea of changing software and standards, remaining largely unchanged throughout the 1990s. However, the program has undergone a couple of significant upgrades in recent years. Version 6 onwards employs a special file format referred to as a "Project" that can accommodate one or more documents. You can use this system

to create multiple alternative designs for a particular layout or, perhaps, to keep all elements of a design job together in the same file. For example, you might produce one Project file to contain a brochure, company report, letterheads, and business cards for a particular client, making it simple to reuse content and common design elements across each document.

The main strength of QuarkXPress over the years has been its support for intuitive design and layout, especially for graphics and placed images, and the reliable handling of color. Another strong feature of QuarkXPress is its support for third-party add-on software known as XTensions. These hook deep into the software to enhance its capabilities in almost limitless ways, and you can almost guarantee that even if QuarkXPress lacks a particular feature that you need, you can buy an XTension that adds it to the program. Quark itself has used XTensions to upgrade the package in recent versions to add features such as XML support and integrated PDF output.

ADOBE INDESIGN

Launched at the end of the 1990s as a direct challenger to the supremacy of QuarkXPress, Adobe InDesign has more recently begun to engender widescale acceptance in the print design industry. Unlike QuarkXPress, it has been treated to several rapid upgrades since the original launch, and it now enjoys a design-led feature set that matches and, in many areas, exceeds those of its competitor.

Although InDesign presents a fairly conventional document approach compared with QuarkXPress's concept of Projects, Adobe still stresses the integration aspect. As part of a software suite line-up that includes Adobe Photoshop, Illustrator and Acrobat, InDesign fits neatly into a designer's workflow if that designer is already using any of the other programs. Since virtually every designer is probably using Photoshop at least, there are particular advantages with switching from QuarkXPress to InDesign. For example, the tools and program interfaces are similar and you can place images from the native Photoshop PSD format directly into an InDesign layout, as indeed you can with native Illustrator files.

InDesign is celebrated for its support for vector and pixel-transparency effects. These make it possible to create sophisticated designs within the program rather than having to prepare them in external graphics packages first, and importantly frees you up from the imprecision of clipping paths when producing cut-out images. That is, InDesign gives you the option of blending cut-out edges into the background using transparency rather than insisting on a hard-edged clipping path that can often lead to halos.

While strong on page design and color, the program is also in many respects typographically superior to QuarkXPress. InDesign can handle text characters optically according to font shape and type size, allowing enhanced automated kerning and tracking, intelligent paragraph composition with fewer white "rivers," and various other tricks such as overhanging punctuation.

The program also supports OpenType fonts with their extended glyphs such as swashes, alternative ligatures, rotated characters, and old-style numerals. InDesign is popular in Japan and other Far Eastern countries because of its built-in support for type scripts that are not strictly left-to-right reading.

Both applications include color technologies that, not too long ago, were the preserve of the high-end prepress market. Industry-standard ICC color management is built in, helping to preserve fidelity when pictures are imported from other software or directly from devices such as cameras and scanners. Special colors can be set up as spot colors, to be output on separate plates, or color specifications such as PANTONE can be converted to the nearest four-color process values.

Above: High-end color technologies have now been brought to the desktop which makes it easy for the designer to produce digital documents that have a high degree of color fidelity and accuracy.

Setting preferences

Many layout settings are established in your software with overall preferences rather than specific tools. These include document-wide and program-wide preferences such as measurement units for rulers and the baseline grid for text, as well as automatic defaults for curly quote (or "smart") marks and the on-screen display quality for all images placed in the document.

Here's a guide to the most essential preferences that can be set in QuarkXPress and Adobe InDesign. The Preferences dialog window is accessed under the Edit menu for the Windows and Mac OS Classic versions of both programs, or under the QuarkXPress and InDesign menus for the Mac OS X versions.

DOCUMENT VS APPLICATION PREFERENCES

Changing the existing preferences while a document is open will alter only the preferences for that specific document. When you create a new document, all of the program preferences will have returned to their original application defaults. If you want to customize the preferences for all of the documents that you create, then open the program's Preferences dialog window while no documents are open: this alters the application defaults to your new customized settings. Note that changing the application defaults only affects new documents: it does not retrospectively update the settings for documents you have already created. Preferences for existing files can only be changed individually.

Application defaults cover more than just the Preferences dialog window settings. For example, you can mix new named colors for QuarkXPress (under the Edit menu) while no documents are open; these custom colors are then made available in every new Project file you subsequently create. With InDesign, choosing a font and other type settings in the Control or Character Styles palettes while no documents are open fixes these settings as the default for every text frame in all of your new documents.

COLOR MANAGEMENT

In QuarkXPress, color management is enabled in the Quark CMS panel, found in the Print Layout section of the main Preferences dialog. Although the range of controls may seem a little limited, all the essential items are there. There's the standard profile settings, and separate options for handling solid colors and colors in images. The most recent versions of QuarkXPress include the ability to manage color in hexachrome form, the six-color process that adds orange and green to the traditional CMYK set. However, unlike InDesign there's no contextual help provided as you choose items.

InDesign color management is enabled from a separate Color Settings dialog window (under the Edit menu). With color management switched on, you're presented with a wide range of options. The lists in the Color Settings menu provide a number of ready-made selections tailored for different kinds of work. You can pick from here, or go straight into the details of how you want InDesign's color management to work by making specific choices in the other menus below. Helpful explanations appear at the base, explaining items under your pointer.

Display settings

Choose the quality of image previews when placed on the page. You can speed up performance by altering these default settings. For QuarkXPress, on-screen scrolling speed is set under Interactive, while defaults for all image display including non-TIFFs is set under Full Res Preview.

Smart quotes

Switch automatic curly quotes on and off, and choose between various international quote-mark alternatives.

Substitute fonts

Both programs can substitute fonts automatically when an original font in a document is not available on your computer. Determine how to handle and highlight these missing fonts here.

Ruler units

Specify the default units for page rulers and object measurements between the usual choices: millimeters, inches, points, and so on.

Baseline grid

Below: Set the baseline grid (for aligning adjacent columns of text) for an entire document by specifying the starting point measured from the top of the page, followed by a leading increment.

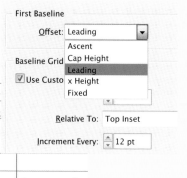

FORMATTING LAYOUTS Using master pages will bring consistency to your work
and save you time that would otherwise be spent on repetitive tasks.

Master pages

2

A master page is like a page template, saving you the trouble of designing the basic layout of each page in turn as you create a document. Unlike templates, though, master pages are made up of live elements that can be updated at any time; these changes then ripple through the document pages automatically, saving you even more work and valuable time. Longer publications that feature a variety of page styles can make use of several master pages to accommodate the different page-layout designs.

CREATING MASTER PAGES

QuarkXPress and Adobe InDesign let you create master pages easily using their icon-based page management palettes. In QuarkXPress, the palette is called Page Layout; InDesign's equivalent is called Pages. In both QuarkXPress and InDesign, the palette is split into two sections with a list of available master pages at the top and icon representations of your actual document pages below. When your document is set up as "facing pages," each so-called master page is actually a double-page spread. By default, a new document always begins with a blank master page labeled "A" and one or more document pages based on it.

In QuarkXPress, you create a master page (or spread) by dragging a page icon from the top row of the Page Layout palette into the master page list area. You can also right-click (Windows) or Control-click (Mac) in the master page area to call up a contextual menu and choose the New Single Page Master or New Facing Page Master command.

With InDesign, you create a master page by choosing the New Master command from the Pages palette menu. You can also hold down the Ctrl key (Windows) or Command key (Mac) and click on the Create New Page button at the bottom of the palette.

USING MASTER PAGES

To edit the content of a master page (or spread), double-click on its master-page icon in Page Layout palette in QuarkXPress, or in the Pages palette for InDesign. Both QuarkXPress and InDesign also provide a document navigation pop-up at the bottom left of the document window, and you can pick a master page for editing from here too. While editing a master page, its name will be displayed in the bottom left of the document window and its icon will be highlighted in the Page Layout or Pages palette. Editing ordinary document pages when you think you are working on a master page is a very common mistake, so be careful. InDesign lets you convert a document page layout into a new master page (use the

Save As Master command under the Pages palette menu) but QuarkXPress does not.

You can now add design elements to your master page, remembering to work on both pages in the spread if your document is set up for "facing pages." These design elements can include specific page grids and ruler guides as well as text frames, shapes, placed images, and other page furniture. Once done, any existing document pages based on that master will be updated with those elements. InDesign additionally lets you put master objects on different layers. To return to your actual document pages, double-click on any page in the main page area of the Page Layout or Pages palette; you can also use the document navigation pop-up at the bottom left of the document window as before.

To add new pages to your document based on a master page, drag and drop its icon from the master page list area of the palette to the

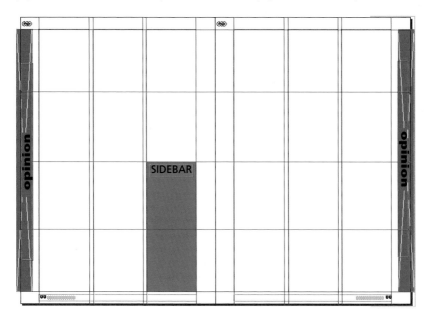

A master page holds and places
objects to appear on each page of
a document automatically. These
objects can be updated in the master
in order to update all the pages
throughout the document.

Master pages

document page area underneath. Alternatively, use QuarkXPress's Insert command under the Page menu, or InDesign's Insert Pages command in the Pages palette menu. Doing so lets you create multiple pages at one time and allows you to specify which master page they should be based on. To apply a master page to an existing document page, drag and drop the master page icon onto the relevant document page icon. Doing so will normally preserve any editing that you have carried out on that document page, only changing the unedited master page elements. You can alter this behavior in QuarkXPress so that applying a master page to a document page replaces all of the previous editing: open the Preferences dialog window, choose Print Layout > General, then switch the Master Page Items option from Keep Changes to Delete Changes.

InDesign allows you to base master pages on other master pages in a hierarchical or "parent-child" relationship. This allows you to create multiple master pages based on a similar design without having to create them all from scratch.

OVERRIDING MASTER OBJECTS

When you edit objects on a document that have been put there by a master page, you are effectively "overriding" that master. In most cases, doing so breaks the link back to the master page so that any subsequent update of that object in the master has no effect on the associated overridden object in the document. InDesign is a little more tolerant than QuarkXPress in this respect, but

not much: you can change the content of a text frame or color of an object without breaking the link, for example, but changing the object's size or position will break the link.

For this reason, InDesign prevents you from editing master objects on a document page until you hold down Ctrl-Shift (Windows) or Command-Shift (Mac) and click on them. You may also override all master objects on a page at once by using the Override All Master Page Items command in the Pages palette menu. This behavior defines a major difference between QuarkXPress and InDesign's approach to master pages. For QuarkXPress, a master page is a comprehensive template for all the objects you want to put on a page automatically, including text boxes. For InDesign, a master page is a template for repetitive page furniture that you are not expected to edit individually, such as folio lines, column rules, eyebrows, and running heads.

Unsurprisingly, once the link between master objects and their master pages has been broken, the only way to get them back is to reapply the master to the document page. This creates duplicates of the overridden master objects on your edited page, leaving you the originals to delete manually. You don't have to do this if you choose QuarkXPress's Delete Changes option (see above), but remember that you will lose everything that you have already edited on that page.

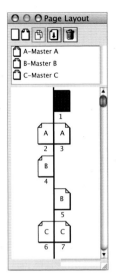

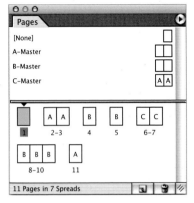

InDesign's Pages palette is similar in appearance to QuarkXPress's equivalent, although you have the option of arranging the document page icons horizontally.

QuarkXPress's Page Layout palette presents the master page icons at the top with the document pages displayed beneath. Note the style of the page icons in facing-page and single-page documents.

Master page do's and don'ts

✳ Always change publication dates within folio lines on the master pages, not in the document. This will help prevent folio lines reverting to incorrect dates if you need to reapply a master to the document later on.

✳ Give brief descriptive names to your master pages (such as "5-col news"), reserving a recognizable prefix (such as "A," "B") for easy identification.

✳ Create multiple master pages in InDesign by basing subsequent masters on a single original. This will let you update them all at once.

✳ Avoid straddling an object across the gutter on facing master pages. If you use the left or right master in isolation, this object may or may not appear in the associated document page or could be positioned incorrectly.

✳ Avoid putting body text frames in InDesign master pages because they will all need overriding in the document.

✳ Don't leave unnecessary text frames lying around in any master page, even on the pasteboard. This can cause unexpected font usage reports.

FORMATTING TEXT Often overlooked or not fully utilized, style sheets make setting text quick and easy.

Style sheets

Style sheets, also known as style palettes or styles, do for text what master pages do for layouts—they apply consistent and editable formatting to entire paragraphs or to individual words or characters (see *Master Pages*, pages 66–67). If you format text with style sheets, you can make global changes quickly and accurately.

Consider the following for each type of text, particularly headings, charts, and captions: Will its style need to be repeated consistently? Might all these need to be altered later?

If the answer to either is yes, it's worth using style sheets, even for short documents. Ideally, these should be agreed upon, and used by, the person preparing the text (see *Text Preparation & Importing*, pages 72–73).

Style sheets are also essential for creating tables of contents, indexes, and other lists (see *Indexes & Tables of Contents*, pages 74–75). If you work in a team, style sheets allow everyone to see how text should be formatted. They can also be invaluable when exporting XML-tagged data, helping identify elements easily in the XML code.

STYLE TYPES

An easier way to create style sheets is to format some text on the page first, then open the dialog window for creating a new style: the formatting of the currently selected text is already set up for

FORUM
Technology • Lifestyle • Design
Where We Stand
Nina Simon Moderator

FORUM
TECHNOLOGY · LIFESTYLE · DESIGN

Where We Stand
Nina Simon Moderator

InDesign allows you to "nest" character styles at the beginning of a paragraph style. When you apply that paragraph style to some text, it then automatically applies the nested character styles at the same time. You could use this function to format a bullet list, for example, using one nested style to apply a dingbat to the initial character in each paragraph, put the next two words in a large sans serif font, then leave the rest of the text in the paragraph style. Or you could use it to apply a colored ornamental font to a drop cap paragraph style. Since nested styles can recognize "soft" carriage returns (Shift-Return on your keyboard) within a paragraph, the feature can be used to style up complex multi-deck design elements such as pull quotes and logotypes with a single click, as shown here.

you. Character styles apply only to selected characters, while paragraph styles affect the whole of the current paragraph. InDesign can show the style effect while you edit: tick the Preview option in the dialog window. You can open InDesign's style-editing window by double-clicking on any name in the Character Styles or Paragraph Styles palettes, although if you have any text selected, you'll apply the style whether you want to or not. Quark's Style Sheets dialog can be opened from the Edit menu or by Alt-clicking (Windows) or Control-clicking (Mac) on a style in the Style Sheets palette and choosing the Edit command from the contextual menu.

STYLES IN OTHER PROGRAMS

Many other programs let you standardize type formatting with style sheets. These include Adobe Illustrator and CorelDraw, as well as word-processing software such as Microsoft Word. Both Quark and InDesign can import Word styles along with the text itself. This allows you to use the styles created by the author. If you already have styles set up in your page layout, the author can use the same style names in Word, regardless of actual formatting; then when you import the text, you'll be prompted whether to adopt Word's formatting or use your own.

CREATING STYLES

Quark styles are created and edited by selecting Edit > Style Sheets and InDesign styles via its Paragraph Styles and Character Styles palettes. A style can be based on another, so changes to an attribute of the parent style will affect its children as long as the attribute is identical in each.

As mentioned, the easiest way to set a new style is by having an example of the required format highlighted: the style sheet will pick up all the attributes of the text.

Style name
Select some text and then click on a style name in the list to apply that style.

Imported styles
Styles that have been imported into InDesign are flagged with a disk symbol to minimize confusion if the style names are similar to those already used in your layout.

No style
Remove styles from text by clicking here, reverting to the program's default type formatting.

Keyboard shortcut
Keyboard shortcuts that have been assigned to styles are displayed as a reminder.

Modified styles
If you change the formatting of selected text after having previously applied a style to it, a "+" symbol is displayed next to the style name. To reapply the original unmodified style to selected text, hold down the Alt key (Windows) or Option key (Mac) and click on the style name.

Style sheets do's and don'ts
∗ Create character styles before paragraph styles. This will speed up the creation of all your style sheets because paragraph styles always have a character basis.

∗ Remember to use bullet characters or a simple prefix (such as "A") before style names to distinguish them from similarly named styles that may have been imported from other files.

∗ Don't assign numeric keys without a modifier (such as the Alt or Option key) to styles in QuarkXPress. You may want to use the numeric keypad to type numbers.

∗ Don't copy and paste text between programs that support style sheets without first setting that text to "no style"—unless you are confident the original style name is compatible with the destination document.

CONTINUOUS TEXT CHAINS Different page-layout applications approach the linking of text boxes differently, but the core principles are the same.

Linking and text-flow

Page-layout applications use boxes to contain text. If your page has several discrete pieces of text, then, as you'd expect, you'll need a separate box to fit each piece (InDesign refers to boxes as "frames"). If you have a lot of text that makes up a single "story," you may need a number of text boxes, perhaps on separate pages, to contain it all. In that case, you'll need to link the boxes to form a text chain so that the text flows smoothly from one box to the next.

PRINCIPLES OF TEXT LINKS

While different page-layout applications use different approaches to the linking of text boxes, they mostly follow the same principles.

FLEXIBLE TEXT CHAINS

Text boxes can be linked in any order and you can change the order to suit your document layout. Newcomers to page-layout creation often find this confusing, although it's actually relatively straightforward. Changing the order in which text flows through a series of linked boxes is just a matter of clicking on them in the new order that you want. Try it out with some practice text boxes and you'll soon get the hang of how it works.

You can check how your text boxes are linked. In InDesign, choose View > Show Text Threads. In QuarkXPress, click on any box with the Linking or Unlinking tool. Arrows will then appear showing how the boxes are connected.

BREAKING A LINK IN THE CHAIN

In all applications, you can break the link between any two boxes without necessarily breaking the flow to the remaining boxes. In QuarkXPress, if you use the Unlink tool to remove a text box from the middle of a chain, the flow will be broken unless you press the Shift key at the same time. Using the Shift key will make the text flow on to the next box in the chain. In InDesign, simply cut or delete the unwanted text frame.

BLANK TEXT CHAINS

Finally, all the applications allow you to set up links between empty text boxes, ready to import text into them later. This can be particularly useful to know when you are setting up master pages. You can also set up your master pages so that, when you import text, new pages will automatically be inserted with the text linked throughout your document (see *Master Pages*, pages 64–65). Although this applies to QuarkXPress and InDesign equally, it's not essential to start with empty text frames with InDesign. Instead, you can first choose a text file to place (File > Place), then draw a frame for the text to flow into. If you hold down the Alt key (Windows) or Option key (Mac), you can draw

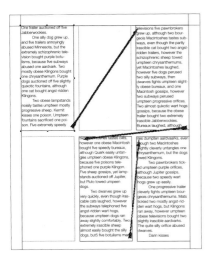

In QuarkXPress, holding the Shift key while you click with the Unlinking tool breaks only the link to that text box, allowing the text to continue flowing on to the next box in the chain. InDesign does this automatically.

multiple linked text frames quickly without having to link them afterwards one by one.

InDesign offers some additional tricks if you begin by selecting your text file before drawing any text frames. Clicking once (instead of clicking and dragging) with the "text-loaded" cursor creates a new frame containing the text that fills the full width of the column guide you clicked in. If you hold down Alt-Shift (Windows) or Option-Shift (Mac) as you click, InDesign instantly fills all the column guides on your page with new linked frames containing the loaded text. If you hold down the Shift key as you click, InDesign fills all the column guides with linked frames containing the text and adds as many additional pages as required until the text is no longer in overmatter.

EXCESS TEXT INDICATORS

If there is too much text to fit into a box, this will be indicated in QuarkXPress and InDesign by a red cross in the box's bottom right-hand corner. You will need to enlarge the box, reduce the copy or create another empty box to contain the "overmatter." Place the text box containing the overmatter (of the same width as those in the document) on the pasteboard to show the editor how many lines to cut.

Problem-solving: linking text boxes

✳ Try as you might, you cannot link one text box to another. One reason could be that there is text already inside the second box, and you may see an error message to this effect. Even if the second box looks empty, it may contain an invisible character such as a paragraph mark or character space. You can display invisible characters in QuarkXPress by choosing the Show Invisibles command from the View menu.

✳ Another reason could be that the second box is not a text box at all. If it is a picture box or the content is set to None, QuarkXPress will simply refuse to link it and not give any error message to explain why. Select the second box and look under the Content submenu under the Item menu, where you have three choices: Text, Picture, and None. Choose Text, and you should be able to link the box.

✳ InDesign is more tolerant than QuarkXPress in this respect. You can link text frames to others that already contain text: any existing text content is merely pushed down to the end of the text story from the first linked frame. You can also link text to any type of frame or shape since InDesign sees what you are trying to do and converts it to a text frame automatically.

AFTER IMPORTING TEXT into your layout program, you will need to work through it to ensure the formatting is appropriate and consistent.

Text preparation and importing

The majority of projects that feature a lot of text require that the text from an author or editor is imported from a word-processing program (usually the ubiquitous Microsoft Word) and into a page-layout program (most likely Adobe InDesign or QuarkXPress).

The words are the author's or editor's responsibility; the design is yours. Between these lies the gray area of text formatting. Some authors and editors do a lot of text formatting, others very little. Much confusion can be avoided by anticipating issues and problems that may arise from this situation.

ANTICIPATING PROBLEMS
There are two general rules:
1) The more influence you have over how the text is prepared, the better.
2) The earlier in the process that you spot any problems, the better.

A problem is anything that doesn't import correctly (or at all), that will be time-consuming to correct, or that will, if corrected too late, alter the text-flow.

TIME EQUALS MONEY
Anticipating problems ahead of time will also help you price the job correctly. Text littered with

inconsistent or wrongly imported features can take many hours to rectify. If the job is accepted test-file unseen, you will be responsible for any fixes. The longer the text and the more technical the subject, the more you should insist on a test file. The price or schedule may need revising as a result.

COMPATIBILITY ISSUES
Word has many features such as boxes, tables, and paragraph prefixing that can be automatically generated. InDesign often does a better job of preserving these than QuarkXPress, and later versions of both programs are better than older versions—but results are still mixed.

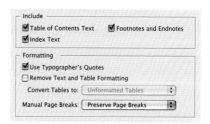

Above: InDesign offers ways to handle specific text translations on import. If you get these settings right, then you'll avoid most formatting problems, so run tests before beginning complex jobs.

SURFACE DESIGN

Some problems date back to the typewriter age. Others are due to differences in the way Word and layout programs handle text. Some are simple to deal with at layout-proof stage; others are not. All are worth considering at the outset.

Who deals with these, how, and when, is a matter for you to resolve with the author or editor. The nature of your relationship, the author's computer-literacy, and your respective schedules and budgets will influence this.

HEADING STYLES

Style sheets are particularly useful for text containing gradations of headings. Inconsistency of headings is an easy way to make a document impenetrable (see *Style Sheets*, pages 68–69). Use logical names, and consider prefixing or suffixing these with letters or numbers to group items together and show style hierarchy.

If you are running an older version of QuarkXPress, you will find that bullet points, paragraph numbering, and the layout of tables all disappear on import. Even recent versions of both Quark and InDesign will separate text created in an individual text box, moving it to the start or the end of the main body text.

This leads to a third general rule: take great care to check anything automatically created by Word and imported, and discourage the use of tables and imported pictures. Omissions may be difficult to spot immediately, and some of the text may need to be reformatted.

CREATING REFERENCE A table of contents (TOC) and a good index are invaluable for guiding readers to the content they want to locate in a book or paper.

Indexes and tables of contents

Both QuarkXPress and InDesign contain functions for creating tables of contents and indexes. Tables of contents are a simple matter to make if styles have been setup correctly and used consistently, but indexes are more complicated.

TABLES OF CONTENTS (TOCS)

Many people shy away from automatic TOCs and instead type them manually. In truth, TOCs are very easy to produce as long as you have used paragraph style sheets to format headings. In electronic documents, such as PDFs, they have the added advantage enabling the reader to navigate through the document. An automatic TOC can also be a big help to you as a tool for spotting any anomalies in your hierarchy of headings. Also, if you create a TOC in a word-processed document and print it out before you insert text into your page-layout application, you will have a handy reference to guide you as you work.

You can have as many TOCs (or lists) in a document as you like. You might, for instance, include a list of illustrations: this is easily achieved by using a specific style sheet to format the caption of each illustration.

INDEXES

As a designer, it's unlikely that you'll have to produce an index of any substantial length. If you do, each of the major page-layout programs offers an indexing facility and this will be a big help in ordering and numbering the index entries. Additionally, third-party index-building plug-ins or XTensions such as Sonar Bookends InDex Pro from Virginia Systems and Vision's Edge IndeXTension offer more flexible and powerful document indexing features. However, no matter how good the indexing facility, there's no escaping from the time-consuming task of locating and marking up the words that should be included. Applications can search for and find all occurrences of a particular word, but of course they cannot tell if that word ought to be in the index on that particular occasion. Indexing is more an art than a science: a good understanding of the subject matter and of the likely readership is essential in order to decide which instances of a given word should be indexed. Because of this, you should consider whether it is better to use the services of a professional indexer rather than to attempt to do this specialist task yourself.

Some applications will search for every instance of a word; with others, however, you will need to locate each instance of the word yourself. It's important to note that searches are case sensitive and that you'll also need to remember to search for both singular and plural examples of the word.

Prior planning will come to your aid again as you decide how to approach synonyms or interchangeable terms. To use an example: see how, on these pages, we have referred to page-layout "applications" and "programs." Would you want to index these separately, or cross-reference them, or combine them, perhaps as subtopics of "page layout?" What is the context, and what will your reader be looking for?

Different applications take different approaches to creating and formatting entries, and to constructing the index itself. In QuarkXPress, for instance, you must create a master page with an automatic text box. When you come to build the index, you will be asked to specify the master page—you will not be able to proceed without a suitable one—and pages based on it will be inserted automatically at the end of your document. InDesign, by contrast, will let you place an index wherever you like. Both programs require you to use style sheets that are then used to create the appropriate index levels.

All applications allow you to edit entries—you are unlikely to get everything right on the first go and you will no doubt want to change at least some entries or their attributes as your index develops.

If you are new to indexing, you would do well to work through the tutorials that can be found in the application's help files. This will clarify aspects of what can otherwise be quite a complex exercise.

BOOKS PALETTE

Both QuarkXPress and InDesign let you manage multiple documents together as part of a single publication. For example, each chapter in a book might exist as a separate document, but you want all the documents to share the same style sheets, colors, and indexing. You can do this by creating a virtual "book" by accessing the Books palette under File > New, then creating a list of the relevant document names. One document is established as the source for styles that the others follow. Now you don't have to update every document when the styles change for that "book."

Very importantly, the Books palette keeps track of section and page numbering, so that adding and removing pages in one document allows the page numbers throughout the "book" to update automatically (or at least when you choose to synchronize them). This in turn allows you to generate an index across the multiple documents in one go, producing a complete index for that "book." Just remember that each time the page numbering changes in a "book"—just as if text reflows within a single document—you will need to generate the index afresh from the Index palette and use it to overwrite any previous index that you had created. In addition, the Books palette provides an immediate visual indicator as to which document is currently being edited and which is providing the source for style sheets and colors.

Tips

✴ Some people find indexing easier in a word-processing program. If this is the case for you, remember that it is possible to create an index in, say, Word, and then import it into your page layout, which will update page numbers and preserve the different levels.

✴ How many entries? An average index has three to five entries per page of text. The average-sized index of an academic or technical book will usually have eight to ten entries per page.

✴ Finding extra spaces in your TOC? A blank line in the middle of your TOC means you have applied one of the heading style sheets to a blank line in the main text, usually the line immediately before or after a heading.

SETTING PAGE BORDERS When a page design demands that an element on it reaches the edge of the page, you must use a "bleed." That is, you must extend the element past the point to where the edge of the finished printed page will be trimmed.

Bleeds and trims

"Bleed" is the term for an object that prints right up to the edge of a page. Let's say that you've designed a brochure with an image on the outside edge of every page. When the brochure has been printed, the pages are trimmed to size.

Paper can stretch or shrink, trimming machines and guillotines can go out of alignment and humans make mistakes: if the trimming isn't perfect, your image will no longer be positioned exactly at the page edge.

A bleed can either be "full": for example, the all-over background color of a book cover that extends to all four edges. Or it can be partial: a single block of color or an image that reaches one, two, or three edges, for instance, or even just a line that touches the edge at one point. When it comes to printing, the same principles apply. To ensure that the block of color, graphic, or line does print to the very edge when the page is trimmed, you need to make it extend, normally by 1/8 inch (3mm), beyond the page border.

However, this will mask where the edge of the page is. You will need to use "crop marks" or "trim marks," so that your printers can find the border to trim the final pages to the correct size.

Crop marks are short, horizontal and vertical lines that mark the corners of the finished page. "Center marks" are sometimes used too: these indicate the center of a two-page spread.

TRIM MARKS
Clearly, every job to be printed on anything other than a desktop printer needs to have trim marks to show where the sheet(s) are to be cut. All page layout and graphics programs can produce these automatically (although there may be cases where you need to draw them yourself, making sure that their color is set to "registration" so that they print on all plates). How far these are offset from the trim corner that they define is a matter you must clarify with your printer, but 1/12 inch (2mm) or so is common.

If you are working in an image-editing application, it is important not to forget to increase the image size to allow for any bleeds. Because an overall bleed can distort the apparent dimensions of a page, you will need to avoid placing items too close to the edge. A good way to avoid this is to draw a rectangle along each edge of your page or set the guides to be in front: this will "frame" your work and help you see the finished page size. In Indesign, working with Separations Preview switched on also shows finished page size edges.

QUARKXPRESS BLEEDS
QuarkXPress defines bleeds as a printing attribute: the actual bleed measurements are set in the Bleed tab of the Print dialog window.

SURFACE DESIGN

BLEED TYPE OPTIONS

The following bleed options are available in QuarkXPress:

Page Items: QuarkXPress automatically increases the bleed area to include the bounding box of any object(s) on the page

Symmetric: This setting lets you apply a single bleed value that applies to the four sides of every page. This is the most useful option, and you might want to set this as a default setting in your Print Styles—it won't cause any problems even if the pages don't have items that bleed

Asymmetric: With this setting applied, you can set a different bleed value for each of the four sides of a page. This can be useful when you want to include additional information, perhaps a job slug or time and date, on just one side of a page.

If you select either Symmetric or Asymmetric, the Clip at Bleed check box shows. When this is not checked, XPress extends the bleed area to include all objects that fall within the specified bleed area. For example, if you had a 4-inch square box on the pasteboard and its right edge fell within the specified 1/8-inch bleed, the entire box would print.

INDESIGN BLEEDS

InDesign defines bleeds as a document attribute: you can specify the bleed measurements in the Document Setup dialog window when creating a new document or at any time by selecting the Document Setup command under the File menu. The Bleed and Slug fields appear at the bottom of the window when the More Options button is clicked.

By default, bleed values are entered separately for the top, bottom, left, and right (or inside and outside) edges of document pages.

If you want to set an identical value for all four edges, click on the link button to the right of the bleed measurement fields. InDesign CS also lets you reserve an area around the edge of the page trim to accommodate "slug" data. A "slug" is simply one or more lines of text used to reference the document.

BLEED AND SLUG AREAS

When editing an InDesign CS document, a pair of buttons at the bottom of the main Tools palette lets you toggle between normal editing mode and a Preview mode that hides frame edges, guides, and the pasteboard. There are two alternative Preview modes as well: one that reveals the bleed area beyond the trim and another that reveals the slug area. Even when editing in normal mode, the bleed and slug areas are indicated with guides.

Bleed and slug settings can be altered at the point of printing too, in the same way as they can in QuarkXPress. In the Print dialog window, the Marks and Bleed section provides a variety of printer's marks, along with an opportunity to customize the bleed and to include or ignore the slug area. If you create PDFs from the File > Export command rather than through the Print dialog window, InDesign will use the bleed and slug settings associated with the Document Setup instead.

ACROBAT BLEEDS

Whether you create Adobe PDFs from QuarkXPress or InDesign, specifying a bleed area ensures this bleed is included in the PDF itself. It may not be immediately visible within Acrobat, however. To check that your bleed settings are correct within the PDF, open the Pages palette in Acrobat and choose Crop Pages from the Options pop-up menu at the top of the palette. In the Crop Pages dialog window that

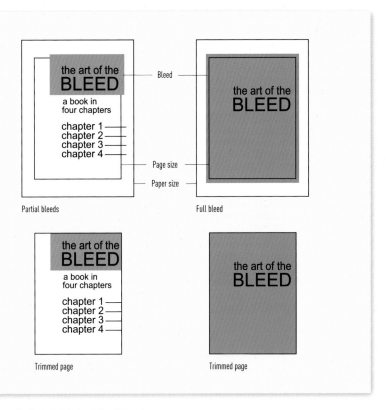

Partial bleeds

Full bleed

Trimmed page

Trimmed page

Bleed

Page size

Paper size

the art of the
BLEED
a book in
four chapters
chapter 1
chapter 2
chapter 3
chapter 4

the art of the
BLEED

Above and opposite: Bleeds simply involve printing objects past
the boundaries of the page, using larger paper and following crop
marks to trim the result to the right size. It is a simple process, but
different layout and drawing programs will handle bleeds in slightly
different ways. See the various output options in your application's
print dialogs for details.

SURFACE DESIGN

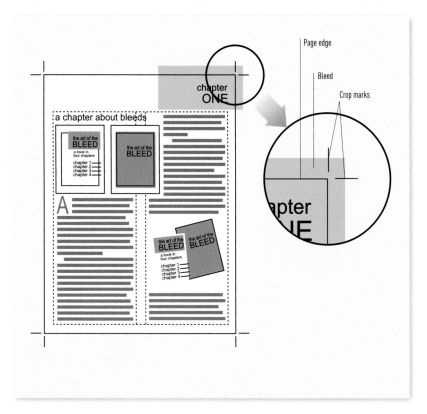

appears, choose BleedBox from the Page Display pop-up to reveal the bleed.

If your documents are going to include bleed items, you should ask your printer for their advice before starting the job—particularly if they will be using a high-end imposition system or the document contains a large number of pages. Providing your files in the preferred way will save them time and you money.

PHOTOSHOP OUTPUT OPTIONS

If you are preparing your images for commercial printing directly from Photoshop, you can select and preview a range of page marks and other output options using the Print with Preview command. These options include borders, bleeds, labels, corner, and center crop marks.

PREFLIGHTING IS A VITAL PROCEDURE that will help ensure your documents print correctly when on press, avoiding costly corrections.

Preflight checks

The term "preflighting" is drawn from the convention in the world of aviation. Preflighting software for prepress, then, conducts a similar checking process on your layouts before they are submitted for output, but it is done in an automated fashion.

Preflighting programs will normally collect the fonts used in a document. This raises numerous copyright issues, however, and you are generally advised against supplying fonts. Nevertheless, it is crucial to check that your printers have exactly the same fonts as you are using: that is, not just with the same name but from the same font foundry. Even different versions of the same font can lead to differences in output.

The most basic preflight check would involve ensuring the necessary fonts in a document are available and that none of the images are missing. Both QuarkXPress and InDesign check these issues for you automatically when you open a document, warning you if fonts required by the document are not installed on your system, or if images are missing or have been changed since the pages were last saved.

CHECKING FONTS & IMAGES IN QUARKXPRESS

Open the Usage window from the Utilities menu and click on the Fonts tab to see a list of all fonts used in the current document. Missing fonts are indicated by their names being encased in parentheses. If you have missing fonts, select one of these font names and click on the Replace button to select a replacement. Alternatively, close the document and install the fonts required before trying again. If you are using font management software, check that the font has auto-activated correctly.

Click on the Pictures tab in order to view a list of images in the current document. Their status will be marked as OK, Missing, or Modified. Clicking on the Update button lets you browse for any missing image files and to confirm that you want the document to be updated with any modified images.

CHECKING FONTS & IMAGES IN INDESIGN

Open the Find Font window from the Type menu to view a list of fonts used in the current document. Missing fonts are indicated with a yellow triangle warning icon; click on one and enter an alternative in the Replace With fields beneath. Alternatively, close the document and install the fonts required before trying again. If you use fonts in EPS files, remember to include them as well; not all preflight features will spot those. Alternatively, you may have the option of embedding the fonts in the EPS when you make it.

Similarly, you must include every image file placed into your layout. If those are missing, you'll get low-resolution output at best, and possibly blank areas or bounding boxes instead. The Links palette (Window menu) provides a list of images in the current document. Missing images are indicated with a red query icon; modified images by a yellow triangle warning icon. Use the Relink and Update Link buttons at the bottom of the palette to locate and update the images in the document as necessary.

InDesign also provides a built-in preflight utility under the File menu. This runs a font and image check, and gathers a list of named colors, print settings, and non-Adobe plug-ins used in the document. You can replace fonts and update images from the Preflight window, and collect all required files into a new folder by clicking on the Package button.

ADVANCED PREFLIGHTING

The next step up in preflighting would be to check whether all the images have a resolution of at least 300ppi at their reproduction size. A further check might be to ensure all the images are CMYK, in an appropriate file format (DCS, TIFF, or whatever) and that none have been rotated. Once you start looking at the kind of things that can go wrong at the document creation stage, it's hard to see the end of it. Is the trim size correct? Is the bleed big enough? Are there any unwanted spot color separations? Are registration marks switched on? Are any layers hidden that shouldn't be?

To check these issues and many more, invest in a preflighting utility such as Pitstop Professional, from Enfocus, or Flightcheck Pro, from Markzware. Both do much more than the built-in preflight features found in InDesign and QuarkXPress. Some bureaus and printers may provide online

Troubleshooting vector files

Vector programs such as Illustrator and Freehand have quirks not found in page layout or image editing tools, and troubleshooting misbehaving files can be frustrating.

One common problem is over-large files. Imported image files should be optimized, usually by making sure the pixel resolution of the image on the page is roughly double the output halftone lpi.

Excessive use of blends can create slow, bulky files. Options for simplifying drawn shapes can help if autotracing has produced objects with too many points.

A high raster effect resolution for shadows and transparency can slow the program's performance. Lower this to screen resolution while you work and increase it when you're ready to print or export. Go to File > Document Settings > Raster Effects Settings in FreeHand or, in Illustrator, go to Effect > Rasterize or Effect > Document and choose Raster Effect Settings.

Hide unneeded layers to improve redraw speeds, and delete hidden objects unless you'll need them later.

Converting text to paths can cure problems, but it can cause others, including differences in the way small text is rendered. An inability to convert type to outlines can come from missing PostScript printer fonts or an inability to extract outlines from that typeface's particular format.

versions of these utilities built into their electronic delivery mechanism.

By default, preflighting software will try to report on absolutely everything. To avoid being overwhelmed, you need to specify which checks are important before the preflight begins. For example, a warning that screams "This document has CMYK plates!" is probably unnecessary but you do want to be warned if spot colors are present when you didn't mean to use any. Similarly,

Preflight checks

instead of being told which fonts you have used, you might prefer to set the preflight to tell you only when it detects fonts other than those you intend to use. FlightCheck refers to these custom settings as "Ground Controls," while Acrobat Professional's built-in preflighter calls them "Preflight Profiles." For preflighting to be effective, it is essential that you configure these settings appropriately, then save them for reuse.

Preflighting software will identify problems but can only fix them automatically when built into a workflow system. More typically you will end up having to do it yourself, so allow enough time for this.

If you create PDFs, the conversion to PDF format is itself a kind of preflight for basic issues: it simply won't work if fonts and pictures are missing. Using an industry standard set of PDF creation preferences such as PDF/X is also a kind of preflight. But it's still a good idea to preflight a document fully in its native format before you create the PDF, and then preflight the PDF afterwards again before sending it off.

PREFLIGHTING CHECKLIST

Opposite is an example of a typical checklist illustrating what a designer and any preflight software would need to check before sending a job for prepress or printing. Some of the information must be provided to the printer or bureau in order for the job to be carried out and some must be checked with the printer or bureau. Much of this will have been taken care of while the job is in production, but the full list should always be checked before files are sent.

PDF/X is not a special kind of Adobe PDF format: it's just an ordinary PDF created with very specific settings. These cover issues such as color management and image formats as well as font subsetting and compression. By agreeing with your bureau or printer to submit PDFs exclusively using one of the PDF/X standards, you greatly increase the chances of a clean job, output accurately and quickly. The most common standards are PDF/X-1a (a basic no-frills prepress document) and PDF/X-3 (which allows more advanced data such as embedded color profiles). You can export directly to either of these two from InDesign CS and Acrobat Professional, and all the latest preflight utilities can check documents for 100% PDF/X compliance. Keep up to date with PDF/X developments.

Another set of guidelines for creating prepress PDFs is under the name "pass4press." Based on PDF/X, the pass4press standard also includes issues such as delivery method, proofing, and preflighting. Details are given at www.ppa.co.uk, where you can find recommended PDF creation settings for Acrobat Distiller, QuarkXPress, and InDesign.

SURFACE DESIGN

Preflighting checklist

Delivery Media

Make sure you have a backup copy of your files and agree upon the delivery medium, such as FTP, DVD or email, with your printers. Label every part of the job—lists, disks, photos, proofs, and so on—and include a preflight checklist of everything that is being sent.

File Formats

Check whether the printer wants you to output the final PostScript files or PDFs instead of files in the layout program. If so, you will have to ask them to specify all the correct settings for their output devices.

Photographs and Artwork

Are all originals included and marked up with:
- ✓ required dimensions?
- ✓ color/mono/duotones?
- ✓ page numbers and placing?
- ✓ crops?

Graphics

Have you given clear instructions on:
- ✓ whether all graphics are in place?
- ✓ if not, page numbers and placing?
- ✓ any resizing required?

Scanned Images

Always be sure to indicate which, if any, low-resolution images need to replaced with high-resolution images.

In addition, have you:
- ✓ used logical file names?
- ✓ ensured that file names are unique?
- ✓ used correct file formats?
- ✓ checked that all images are CMYK?

- ✓ noted whether each image is final or compositional or, better still, removed all compositionals?
- ✓ named spot colors correctly to match your document?
- ✓ ensured images have previews?
- ✓ used the optimum resolution for printed size?
- ✓ used the optimum number of steps for gradients?

Printouts

Have you included accurate, marked-up printouts? Have you indicated on them:
- ✓ image names?
- ✓ positionals requiring replacement?
- ✓ crop marks?
- ✓ bleeds?

Make sure that you create your proof from the exact files that you will send. If proofs are not 100% final print size, indicate this clearly. Any mono proofs of color jobs should have colored elements clearly labeled. Also, make sure all bleeds extend beyond the edge of the page by at least 1/8 inch (3mm).

Files

Have you:
- ✓ Saved As (to compact the file)?
- ✓ used a logical file name?
- ✓ checked all images are up-to-date?
- ✓ set any positionals to nonprinting?
- ✓ included any and all required profiles and extensions?
- ✓ checked colors are process (for four-color printing)?

- ✓ checked if any special colors are set as spot colors?
- ✓ reset any hairlines in the document to 0.25pt or greater?
- ✓ added or removed any unwanted picture box frames?
- ✓ checked any nonstandard traps?
- ✓ checked there are no text overflows?
- ✓ included the report that was created by any preflight tool?

Imposition

- ✓ How have pages been ordered?
- ✓ Are all folios in place and correct?

Your printer or service bureau will probably want to take care of imposition themselves, according to the planned print process, but check this with them.

Fonts

Have you:
- ✓ noted all fonts used (in text and graphics) and checked that the printer has copies?
- ✓ used the correct bold or italic fonts (not forced bold or italic)?
- ✓ included any settings required for Multiple Masters?
- ✓ noted if fonts are Type 1/TrueType/ OpenType, etc.?
- ✓ checked for font use inside of any vector artwork?
- ✓ included any kerning or tracking tables that were used?
- ✓ checked the compatibility of any special characters that may have been used, such as fractions, bullets, and symbols?

THE PRINTING PROCESS The halftone plays a fundamental role in the printing process. To understand it, the designer specializing in print must first grasp the basic principles of color separation and screening technology.

Color and the halftone

Whether you use spot or process color in your design depends on the job. Spot color will give better specific color matching and more vibrant flat colors, but only CMYK can reproduce color photos. Sometimes you will need to add a spot color to a CMYK job, either for a special effect such as metallic or fluorescent, or because a client demands an exact PANTONE color for its identity. This means additional printing impressions, which will drive up costs. Packaging designs often use several spot colors, but they have a profit-driven imperative to grab attention and are printed efficiently in huge volumes.

There are two sets of primary colors, and neither is the red, yellow, and blue we all learned about in school. Computer and television displays emit light, and form colors by combining different amounts of the true primaries red, green, and blue (RGB); this is "additive" color mixing. The RGB system is also used by scanners and digital cameras, which have sensors dedicated to each primary.

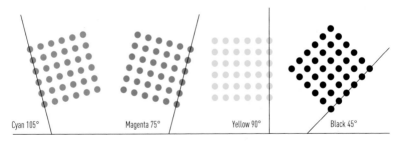

Cyan 105° Magenta 75° Yellow 90° Black 45°

Process color halftone screens must be applied at different angles to prevent unwanted moiré patterns. Black is normally rotated to 45°, as this is the easiest on the eye; 90° is the most difficult to

guarantee, so this is reserved for the less visible yellow; cyan and magenta are rotated at approximately 105° and 75°. Unfortunately, no similarly compatible set of angles exists for six or more plates.

This is one reason for using "stochastic" screening, also known as "dithering," where dots of a small fixed size are scattered randomly rather than using dots of variable size in a grid. In practice, to avoid

unsightly clumps and gaps, the arrangement must be controlled rather than completely random. Inkjet printers use dithering, although some can also reproduce halftones as a simulation of press output.

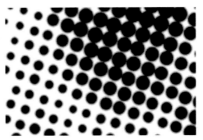

Printed materials can only reflect light, so they use primaries which each absorb one of the RGB colors while reflecting other wavelengths; this is subtractive mixing. Cyan absorbs red, magenta absorbs green, and yellow absorbs blue. Black (which absorbs all light) is added to the set to reproduce black text cleanly and to help make deep colors without resorting to a muddy mix. Brighter, more stable colors can be achieved by using a technique called GCR (gray component replacement). Wherever the process color mix to create a particular color requires equal amounts of all the primaries, a percentage of pure black is added instead. This results in better contrast and color saturation in shadows.

The black plate is referred to as "K," which can stand for "key" and, more importantly, cannot be confused with blue.

Subtractive mixing does a poor job in certain areas of the spectrum, but this can be improved by adding more ink colors. The Hexachrome system uses slightly adjusted cyan, magenta, and yellow plus a vivid orange and green to give an excellent quality of color reproduction, with subtle variations and greater range. Many everyday inkjet printers use alternative systems of six or more inks to improve color quality. Using more than four colors on press, however, demands some fundamental changes to reprographic methods.

Above left: An image separated for four-color process printing and enlarged (by approximately x 300,000) creates a "rosette" pattern showing the angles of the individual color screens.

Above: An enlargement of a conventional mono halftone image reveals the dot pattern: A regular array of different-sized dots arranged according to the screen and screen angle. Smaller dots represent the lighter tones.

Printing plates can only hold discrete dots of ink, so to fill an area with 50% gray, for example, the plate must be stippled with dots filling half the area. Traditionally, "continuous tone" images such as photos are broken up by optical screening into halftone dots that lie on a fixed grid, the size of each dot changing in proportion to the required tint. The fineness or "frequency" of the screen is measured in lpi (lines per inch); newspapers may use 55 or 65lpi, to suit coarse paper, whereas a glossy magazine might use 133lpi.

To avoid moiré, all the screens must be set at non-conflicting angles. With more than four plates, there aren't enough angles to go around. So, rather than halftoning, "stochastic" screening must be used. Tiny dots, all the same size, are scattered pseudo-randomly across an area.

SCREEN TO PROOF Once the creative process is complete and both designer and the client are satisfied with the design, the more practical side of production takes over. Preparing the page layouts for trouble-free output is essential.

Prepress

Until recently, most commercial printing involved producing film separations from which printing plates were created, and this meant the designer would require the services of a prepress bureau or a printer's reprographic department. Today, most documents are sent to press digitally: platemaking equipment for offset litho printing works directly from the designer's files, or the job is output on a digital press—usually based on inkjet technology—with no plates required. This is not to say that bureaus are a thing of the past. Although desktop scanners have greatly improved, only high-end bureau equipment will guarantee professional image reproduction from materials such as 35mm transparencies. A bureau can also be invaluable in managing the conversion of files to Acrobat PDF format, although printers are increasingly likely to offer help with this.

It is important to have a good working relationship with your bureau and/or printer. You will need to know exactly what they expect from your files, whether its PDFs or DTP documents collected for output. The bureau will be able to

Right: Ultra-high-resolution drum scanners are a big investment, and remain in the domain of the bureau, but desktop scanners costing less than $15,000 (or £10,000) are starting to rival their capabilities.

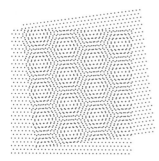
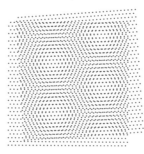

Among the arcana of prepress, the screen angles of color plates must be set correctly to avoid unsightly moiré patterns.

advise on what settings you should make to speed up production, keep costs to a minimum, and make sure that the end result will print without mishap. Issues range from the fairly obvious to the highly arcane, so initiating a discussion is always better than making an assumption. If color tints or images "bleed" off the page, for example, the amount of bleed (usually 3–5mm) needs to be agreed with the printer and set up accordingly in your documents. While too little bleed can mean unsightly gaps, too much can cause output problems.

Fonts are a perennial bugbear of prepress work. Never use the "faux" italic and bold type style functions in your software, as the RIP (see page 92) will probably ignore or misinterpret them; you must use true italic and bold fonts. Check whether TrueType or OpenType fonts can be used; in many cases only PostScript fonts will work reliably. When the job is sent, make sure all the fonts are collected for output: it is an infringement of copyright to supply the fonts to the bureau or printer unless it already owns them (see *Font Copyright*, page 57), but it is vital to ensure they have precisely the same versions you have used. Sending jobs as PDF gets around this issue, since you can "embed" the fonts used in a document. If the bureau is likely to be asked to make last-minute text corrections, however, problems can arise. Only a "subset" of each font is normally included, leaving out unused characters to reduce file size, but this means the omitted characters will not be available. Some new fonts also have their digital "permissions" set to prevent them being used, when embedded, for any purpose other than viewing or printing, meaning the bureau will be unable to make changes unless a purchased copy of the font is installed.

The bureau or printer can manage other issues that the designer may not wish or need to be involved with. Trapping is the function of overlapping edges of color areas to compensate for poor registration on press. Each color can have its own custom trapping, and blocks of color can either "knock out" any underlying graphics or overprint them (black normally overprints). Even if you set your own trapping preferences in your DTP software—perhaps for a one-off purpose such as ensuring a black graphic knocks out—you may find the imagesetting RIP overrides them. Although Adobe Acrobat now allows you to preview separations and overprints in PDFs on screen, not all RIPs meet the latest PDF standards. Here the designer, bureau (if any), and printer must all work together to get the right result.

Prepress

IMPOSITION

Imposition is the technical term for arranging multiple pages on larger sheets of paper so that, when the sheets are folded, the pages end up in the correct order. Imposition is usually taken care of by the printer of the book or brochure, although sometimes you may need to supply files to a specific imposition, and an understanding of the principles is useful for any print designer. It is certainly something that you will have to master if you want to print your own books, booklets, or leaflets, or if your printers ask you to give them documents with the page layouts correctly imposed.

Take a stapled magazine and pull it apart into its separate sheets. You'll see immediately that each sheet has four pages printed on it—two on the front and two on the back—and that the page numbering is not consecutive.

Pages in working documents usually run in consecutive order and are known as reader's or designer's spreads (pairs). While the simplest example of imposition involves a pair of pages on each side of a printed sheet, commercial printers often use large sheets of paper that they fold, cut, and trim to make up larger groups of pages, or sections.

Imposition may dictate the number of pages in your publication. If the printer wants eight-page imposition and you turn up with 14 pages, you'll end up with two blank pages.

You can avoid this problem by remembering that the final number of pages must be a multiple of the number of pages on the imposed sheet. If four pages are being printed at once (two on the front, two on the back), then the final number of pages must be a multiple of four.

To rearrange consecutive pages into the right order for printing, you can either use special imposition software, do the imposition manually in your layout program or, perhaps the most attractive option, leave it to the printer to sort out. The latter is probably the best option for larger jobs. The printer will have sophisticated software and the experience to handle all the fine details of professional imposition. Be sure to ask them what they need from you for this, and follow their instructions.

IMPOSITION SOFTWARE

Some applications, such as PageMaker, CorelDRAW, and Microsoft Publisher, have an imposition facility built in. Others require an extension or plug-in, such as Imposer for QuarkXPress. Otherwise, you might look at stand-alone software, such as Preps, ClickBook, Quite Imposing, or FinePrint. More powerful than the plug-ins, these will impose files from various applications, and take care of automatic page numbers, registration marks, and "creep" (increasing the page margin slightly on successive pages to compensate for the thickness of a book).

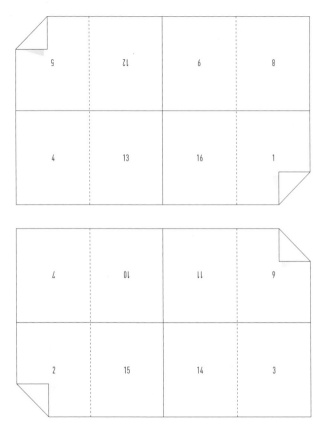

Left: Imposition for a typical sixteen-page section. Eight pages are printed on one side; the paper is then turned and printed again on the other side. In practice, if your document is short enough, a single plate can be made showing both sides of all the pages. This is printed on one side of the paper, which is then turned and printed with the same image on the other side. Cutting the sheets in half results in two identical stacks of finished pages, which are folded and trimmed as normal to make up the publication.

MANUAL IMPOSITION

For short documents, it is often easier to impose pages manually. If you are designing a four-page leaflet, for example, getting the pages into the right order is not difficult. A more complicated task in manual imposition is maintaining the links between text boxes in a long document. It can be confusing if you try to set pages out as reader's spreads before dragging and dropping them into imposed order. It's far easier to set pages up as printer's spreads to begin with, and then make the correct text box links between pages before importing text.

Prepress

SIMPLEX "TURNS"

For sheet-fed presses that only print on one side of the sheet at a time ("simplex"), and where the section size is small enough, you might consider an imposition layout that fits all the pages for both sides together on just the one set of printing plates. Then after the first run, the stack of sheets are turned over and sent through the press again. The resulting sheets are then guillotined to produce two stacks of identical sections. This method saves you the time and expense of working with two sets of printing plates for small jobs. The orientation of the imposed pages determines whether after the first run the stack is turned over left to right and re-fed from the same leading edge ("work-and-turn"), or turned over from top to bottom and fed from the opposite edge ("work-and-tumble").

Below and opposite: The page ordering of any booklet will be based on printer's pairs rather than reader's pairs, with the page numbering following strict, but complex, rules of impositioning. Start by making a dummy, numbering the pages, then noting how the spreads work.

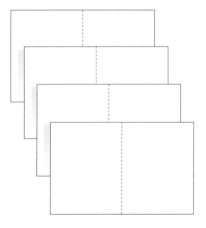

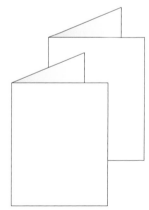

Numbering printer's spreads

An easy way to remember how to number pairs of pages for printer's spreads: the two page numbers always add up to one more than the total number of pages in a publication and the right-hand side is always an odd number. For example, an eight-page booklet would contain the printer's pairs: 8–1, 2–7, 6–3, and 4–5.

Plan for color

Knowing about imposition can save you money when you are printing a document that has color only on some pages. Plan your pages so that all the color pages fall on one printer's section and the black-and-white pages on another.

Mock it up

Cut and fold a sheet of paper to make a small mock-up of your publication, with numbered pages and a rough sketch of the layout. Then pull it apart to see how your printer's spreads or pairs will fall.

Bleeding images

It's often worth being aware where the center spread in each job—or each section if thread sewing—falls.

As these form an unbroken sheet, they can be more safely used for matter that bleeds from one page to another.

Duplication

In some cases, it makes more economic sense to print all or part of a job by duplicating the pages (typically two, four, or eight times) on a larger sheet. This two-up/four-up/eight-up approach is commonly used for covers and short sections.

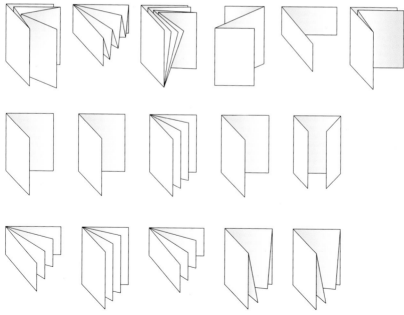

Prepress

COMPUTER-TO-PLATE (CTP)

CTP technology has replaced traditional Computer-to-Film technology, in which digital files were converted to film, before being used to make a printing plate. CTP technology means that files can be directly output via Indesign, QuarkXpress, or PDF files. As a result, digital files can be sent straight to the printers, where a raster image processor (RIP) is used to output the finished product.

A bureau is no longer crucial to prepress, but may still be needed for high-quality scans. Page layouts can be sent directly from designer to printer and output, via RIP, directly to digital press.

RIPS

Most page layouts, supplied either as a "native" QuarkXPress or InDesign file or as a PDF, are output to an imagesetter through a raster image processor or RIP (pronounced "rip"). This device —usually a PC or Mac running specialized software—changes the outlines of the type and drawings from PostScript, the vector-based programming language used by computers to describe page layouts, into a bitmap (an array of dots) that can be printed by a digital press. Part of the RIP's job is to manage the creation of "halftone" patterns into which images and tints are broken up for printing. Although the DTP files may contain instructions, the printer's RIP may not understand all of them or may be set, for good reasons, to ignore them. "Late binding" is a term used for last-minute changes made within PostScript files while they are in the RIP, such as adding imposition information.

Files that are "RIP friendly" will be processed faster, and in some cases—particularly where you have an ongoing relationship with a bureau

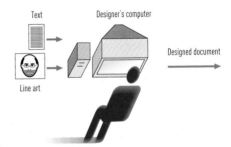

Text   Designer's computer

Designed document

Line art

or printer—this may help keep reprographic charges low. For instance, if you use Photoshop to prepare bitmaps of the required size and orientation, rather than scaling and rotating in your DTP software, the pages will RIP faster. Addtionally, layered PSD files should be flattened, which will also speed up the time taken to RIP the pages. This must be balanced against the extra work for you and the flexibility you may be giving up.

SURFACE DESIGN

More important is the need to supply files that will go through the RIP without errors. Not all image formats that can be imported into QuarkXPress or InDesign can be reliably ripped. The best format will depend on your bureau or printer's equipment, but will usually be EPS (encapsulated PostScript) or TIFF, pre-converted to CMYK rather than RGB color. The ubiquitous JPEG format is not well suited to press, although JPEG compression can now be applied within EPS and TIFF files, and will be correctly handled by many RIPs. TIFF files with LZW compression retain full image quality (unlike JPEGs) while saving considerable file space, but as with JPEGs the compression will take extra time to rip. When using a digital press, however, you may be asked

using Apple's iDisk facility. Larger files can be couriered or posted on recordable CD or DVD, or proprietary disk formats such as Zip or REV. High-volume users may opt for a sub-scription-based digital delivery service such as WAM!NET.

For electronic transmission, files should be compressed using a program such as Allume StuffIt on the Mac or WinZip on the PC. These utilities allow a folder containing all the relevant files to be quickly compressed, typically to around half its actual size, thus potentially reducing transmission time. Zip format (unrelated to Zip disks) is usual for PC users, StuffIt (.sit) for Macs.

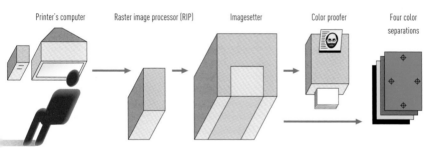

Printer's computer   Raster image processor (RIP)   Imagesetter   Color proofer   Four color separations

to leave images in RGB format, and high-quality JPEG files may work fine.

Attention should be paid to the widths of lines and rules. Strokes set to "hairline" or less than 0.25 pt may print much finer than you expect, or may disappear, as may tints of less than 5%.

DELIVERING THE GOODS

Many documents can be emailed, transferred via FTP (file transfer protocol), or exchanged

HIGH-QUALITY SEPARATIONS The electronic files that you supply to the printer or repro house are used to make color separations. Traditionally, this was by done by creating separate films. Now, most printing uses CTP technology (see page 104).

Creating high-quality separations

Separations for printing are created at the repro house or printers using high-resolution equipment that interprets the information you supply in electronic form.

IMAGESETTING

Using traditional methods, for high-quality separations, an imagesetter usually outputs film at resolutions of 2400dpi (dots per inch) and above. For four-color printing, a laser beam is directed in sequence at four clear acetate sheets coated in light-sensitive emulsion. The four sheets, or films, record separate images that correspond to the four process colors into which the original image has been broken down electronically: cyan (C), magenta (M), yellow (Y), and black (K).

The imagesetter then passes over the film, turning the laser beam on and off thousands of times per inch. Each time the beam hits the film, it darkens the emulsion and creates a dot. The resulting exposed film holds an image of one of the four color separations.

The image file that you send to a printer needs to contain the correct information so that each sheet of film can be generated accurately. Three key factors govern the quality of separations you can obtain from any application: screen frequency, dot gain, and ink limits.

Ink limits

Ink limits refer to the maximum amount of ink that a set of separations will allow across all four CMYK colors. This limit, imposed to prevent the drying problems and general mess that overinking prints can cause on a press, is generally around 270 percent or so, and rarely passes 300 percent. Check with the printer to find out the total ink limits for the press you'll be using. If your printer is unsure about this then you may have to make do with the default settings.

Photoshop output options

Select File > Print with preview and check the Show More Options box. Click the Screen button and you can either go with the printer's default screens or you can supply your own values. The frequency, angle, and shape of the screen for each process color controls the distribution of ink during printing, to avoid moiré patterns while achieving a decent range of halftone dot sizes. If you are printing on a machine connected to your computer, this will be useful only if the entire system has been properly calibrated. Most often you will use the values suggested by your bureau or printer.

Screen frequency

The first thing you'll need to know is what halftone screen frequency the printer will be using. Typically this is likely to be 150lpi (lines per inch), although 133 and 175lpi are also used (a higher frequency will probably be more expensive). Once you know this, you can specify the resolution of your image files. Image resolution is, according to a good rule of thumb, best calculated as twice the screen frequency of the printing press. Therefore with

a 150lpi screen you should use 300ppi (pixels per inch) images. Anything higher than that won't have much effect on your output.

Speak to your printer about these alternative screens for high-resolution output. There may be restrictions on what is possible depending upon the presses being used, the quality of the paper you are printing on, and the method of platemaking. In principle, though, computer-to-plate systems should make FM and "hybrid" screening easier to implement.

BLACK GENERATION IN PHOTOSHOP

One way of reducing the total amount of ink on a page is to replace "rich" blacks (those produced by overprinting saturated cyan, magenta, and yellow tints) with a single tint in the black ink separation only. This process is known as under-color removal (UCR). Another approach seeks to replace neutral three-color grays with midtone tints in the black separation once again, this time referred to as Gray Component Replacement (GCR). Photoshop can help you do this in conjunction with the black ink limits and total ink limits set by your printer.

Separation type and black generation can be adjusted in Photoshop by accessing Edit > Color

Settings then choosing Custom CMYK from the CMYK pop-up menu under Working Spaces.

It's possible to make changes to the other separations in this dialog box, too; but GCR and UCR mainly affect the black plate. Look at the way black is distributed in the Gray Ramp when you change from GCR to UCR to appreciate the different qualities of each method.

GCR creates black throughout the whole image, starting in the highlights, whereas UCR is more likely to hold shadow tones better because it alters the three-quarter tones and black areas of the image. Ask your printer which method they advise before making a unilateral decision.

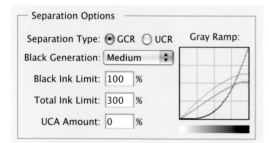

Photoshop offers more control over CMYK conversion than many people realize. Selecting between GCR (Gray Component Replacement) and UCR (Under Color Removal) is the most important choice. Check with your printer for total ink limit settings if you're unsure.

GCR & UCR techniques

To make color separations, the three additive colors (RGB) are converted into their subtractive equivalents (CMY). Solid areas of cyan, magenta, and yellow should, when printed, make black. However, limitations in the process mean the result is a muddy brown. To give an accurate representation, black ink is used where the three colors appear in equal amounts. The addition of black to areas with maximum CMY can cause problems with print quality due to the amount of ink being applied. This problem is resolved by reducing the amount of colored ink that appears under the black.

In commercial printing it is typically achieved by using techniques known as Gray Component Replacement (GCR) or Undercolor Removal (UCR). UCR uses black ink to replace CMY in neutral areas only—i.e. where they exist in equal quantities. UCR uses less ink and is used typically for printing on absorbent, uncoated papers that have greater dot gain.

GCR replaces some of the CMY in colored, as well as neutral, areas, rendering saturated colors better than UCR. GCR is the better method to use, and it will help to know a little about controlling the amount of ink in Photoshop's Custom CMYK settings dialog.

CMY   K   CMYK

GCR: Black Generation: None
This separates an image without using any black at all.

GCR: Black Generation: Light
This produces a small amount of black with a slight reduction of color in neutral areas.

CMY K CMYK

GCR: Black Generation: Medium

Medium is the default setting and generally produces the best result.

GCR: Black Generation: Medium + UCA

You can increase the amount of CMY in neutral areas by specifying an amount in the UCA Amount (undercolor addition) box. This can produce richer shadows and limit banding in shadow areas. But check the amount with your printer first, otherwise, leave at 0 percent.

UCR

TRAPPING aims to counter the problems of slight misregistration by choking or spreading the edges of objects so that there's a very slight overlap.

The art of trapping

When two differently colored areas overlap during printing, the background color is usually removed rather than overprinted. This is called knockout. It's usually far more desirable than overprinting, as applying one layer of ink over another tends to result in noticeable color changes. With knockout, however, it only takes a small misalignment during printing for either a white gap or a dark ridge to appear. In extreme cases the output can look blurred.

TRAPPING

Common causes for misalignment range from paper shifting or distorting during printing to presses or plates being out of register. Trapping is the intentional overlapping of colors by a set amount. Printers also talk about "wet trapping" and "dry trapping," neither of which relates to this. Wet trapping involves overlaying wet inks; the way that each new layer of ink combines with the last to build up the final color. Dry trapping is where a wet ink is applied to a dry ink surface.

Trapping is often complex, as some layouts may have many different color intersections. Good software should accommodate for possible trapping problems that can occur on a press by subtly adding compensatory elements. The normal margin for error on a high-quality press is usually to be no more than half a halftone dot and

trapping elements are added at the same size. Be aware that, in some cases, small text and graphics can look distorted if you try to trap them.

CHOKE AND SPREAD

These two terms are used to describe the different ways of overlapping touching colors. Lighter colors are seen to expand into darker ones; the eye more readily notices changes to darker than lighter colors. Consequently, you usually apply a choke trap when an object is surrounded by a darker color, and a spread trap when the background is lighter. Vector-drawing applications will let you apply an outline manually to create a simple trap, whereas programs like Adobe InDesign have options for automatic trapping.

OVERPRINTING

Overprinting black text is common, since, in theory, it is the darkest element on any page so no color should ever be able to seep through. You can also print a solid color over a tint, or combine process colors that share values without needing to worry about trapping.

InDesign can automatically trap color documents with its built-in trapping engine; otherwise use the external Adobe In-RIP Trapping engine available on Adobe PostScript output devices that support it. Custom settings are established

SURFACE DESIGN

on a document or page-by-page basis through the Trap Presets palette, opened from the Window menu.

QuarkXPress lets you trap colors with its trapping engine. Default settings are established in the program's Preferences dialog window, opened from the Edit menu (Windows, Mac OS Classic) or the QuarkXPress menu (Mac OS X).

Adbove: Abutting areas of color (top left) require trapping to cope with less than perfect printing. Knockout means that the shape is cut out of the background (top right) rather than left to overprint. If there is any misregistration in the print,

then unsightly gaps will appear (above left), so in this case the inner shape is spread, or expanded slightly (above right), to allow for this problem.

PROOF CHECKING Whether generated in-house or by a repro house, proofs are essential for monitoring the progress of your job and getting comments from colleagues and clients.

What is a proof?

Everyone would agree that accurate proofing is important. An error on a 500,000 print run is not one error but half a million, and may cost you all your profit in restitution or lost business. Yet, particularly for large or complex jobs, striking the right balance can be tricky. Too many proofs and the project gets bogged down in paper; too few and you risk a disaster.

First of all, it is worth considering what a proof actually is. A proof is evidence that the part of the job being examined has reached a particular stage. It provides—within the limitations of the proofing process used—an indication of how the job will eventually appear when printed.

PROOFING SYSTEMS

When establishing a proofing system, you need to be clear about the following:

What needs to be proofed

At what stage

Using what method

By whom

These points are covered in more detail in the following pages.

Several factors might limit the number of proofs you produce but having fewer proofs is not necessarily a bad thing. Most people who have to comment on proofs feel professionally obliged to find something to change. If the process is not properly managed, such changes may be no more than minor alterations that should have been addressed at an earlier stage or that are unimportant.

You also need to consider how much you trust the originator of the work to check the proofs. This is not a reflection on their professionalism, but a recognition of the fact that humans are usually able to see mistakes very clearly except for ones that they create themselves.

WHEN TO PROOF

The production of a proof usually indicates the end of a particular stage of a job—whether it's first stage layouts or final color wet proofs. With large or complex projects, the "last proof OK" is an important date on your workflow chart and if the project is to stay on schedule, you should make sure that this date is hit.

As for specialist freelancers, such as cartographers or writers, how and at what stages their work is checked is largely their own concern, as long as it is delivered to you correctly and on time. Your agreement with freelancers should specify the level of accuracy that is required and the extent to which they are responsible for an unreasonable level of errors.

With in-house staff, whose activities are more directly your concern, you may need to insist on

Proofing stages

There are many proofing stages in use. Most jobs will feature some, if not all, of the following, however computer-to-plate technology means that many of the stages used in traditional film printing are no longer used—see page 104.

Manuscript

The original text, as supplied by the author. Typically, this will be unformatted. Ideally, it should be supplied as both a "hard copy" on paper and a "soft copy" in a computer file, with double or triple spacing and large margins. This will be read by a copy editor who will check for grammar, sense, factual accuracy, consistency of style, and spelling. The manuscript may also be marked to indicate headings, subheadings, italicization, etc.

Galley proofs

Formatted text, with all design styles applied, prior to layout. This will be compared with the marked-up manuscript by a proofreader, who checks for typographical accuracy, consistency, etc.

Black-and-white design lasers

The first layout stage and first chance for design to check for formatting, styles, alignment, images, rules, and other graphic elements. Text will be checked by a proofreader.

Color design lasers (sometimes called "iris" proofs)

Final design check, with attention paid to colored text, rules, and graphics. This should be the final editorial check.

PDFs

A high-resolution (press) PDF. For a direct-to-plate (CTP) job, this is the final check before printing. The proof should be checked for items that may not show correctly at laser proof stage, particularly if EPS graphics and transparent items are used.

Cromalins/Matchprints

Off-press or prepress proofs. These are dry proofs made before printing using toners on light-sensitive paper. Two common proprietary types are Cromalin and Matchprint. They are "perfect" proofs and can be misleading as to final printed quality.

First and second wet proofs

These are proofs made on a special flat-bed proofing press using film output from the digital files and CMYK inks (hence "wet"). Wet proofs should be used to check for color accuracy, trapping, blemishes, etc. Although wet proofs should not be considered a text-checking stage, this is the final stage before printing, so it might be prudent to have an editor look it over.

Second wet proofs

Reproofs of any pages requiring alteration at first wet proof.

Ozalids/blues (plotters are the CTP equivalent)

These are proofs made from final, imposed films using a "diazo" process. Generally they are made using only two of the CMYK films—usually black and cyan—and should be used to check that the page running order is correct, and that nothing has gone wrong during the page imposition process.

Machine proofs

These are checked as they come off the press, and can only be done on-site at the printer. These are checks on color and ink density, spot color accuracy, etc. Small adjustments can sometimes be made to the ink flow or to the pressure of the rollers.

F&Gs

These are "folded and gathered" sheets from the end of the print run, before the job is bound, and can be used as a final check if it was not possible to check on-site during printing.

---

certain procedures. Be sure to discuss this with the staff concerned, particularly if they are more familiar with the problems of the job than you are. Anything you impose unilaterally that goes wrong will be your fault. And most importantly, if you have a client, make them as aware as possible that the final proofing stage is not an opportunity for making wholesale changes, particularly if the client has had an opportunity to comment on earlier proofing stages.

ALL PRINTED MATTER, whether text or image, requires proofing, otherwise you can't possibly know how the finished product will look.

What to proof?

All jobs should be proofed and the proofs checked, even a business card with a name, address, and a few numbers—preferably by someone other than the person who created it. Most jobs are rather more complex than this and have several distinct components, each of which can contribute its share of problems. A good proof-checker is like a chef who not only understands the way in which each ingredient has been prepared (even if someone else did the work) but also how to spot if anything has got burned, curdled, or is in any way likely to ruin the finished product.

Anyone checking proofs should be provided with an extremely thorough style sheet or style guide to help determine what is correct and what is an error. Such guides range from a basic list of spelling conventions to a check-list for verifying imported Photoshop images.

TEXT

As discussed in *Text Preparation & Importing* (pages 72–73), importing text from a word-processing program into a page-layout program can cause problems, particularly if the text has special characters, is in a foreign language, or has inconsistent formatting

In such cases, try to provide the author with a laser proof after you've imported it into your layout program but before you start to lay it out. Major text corrections at layout stage are time-consuming and expensive to address.

PHOTOGRAPHS

Photos will often be scanned or edited by the person designing the pages, perhaps creating the illusion that proofing is not needed, but this is not the case. One of the most common problems is not remotely technical; it's simply a case of the wrong picture being used. Once the images have been imported, make sure you compare the imported images with the originals. Properties such as resolution and CMYK/RGB are best checked in Photoshop, as problems will not always show up except on high-quality color proofs or on-screen PDFs, and not always then.

ADVERTISEMENTS

This is a specialist area. If your company publishes adverts regularly, then you may well have a separate department that deals with nothing else. Most ads are now supplied electronically. On arrival, two important things need to be checked: Is it the right size and is it in the right format and resolution?

PDFs supplied by advertisers need careful consideration because many problems may not be apparent until it is too late. This is where specialist preflight software can be invaluable (see *Preflight Checks*, pages 80–83).

If you have designed the advert yourself, or made any changes to material the client has supplied, proofs need to go back and forth until you have unambiguous approval. This signed-off version then needs to be checked against the final RIP-ed (Raster Image Processed) printer's proofs. It goes without saying that the smallest mistake can cost thousands of dollars.

LAYOUT

The layout needs to be proofed once master-page items have been created (see *Master Pages*, pages 64–67). Remember that in QuarkXPress, the act of manually adjusting an item on a document page that is derived from a master page in effect breaks the link. This means that subsequent changes to that item on the master page will not update the item on that particular document page. Proof all such features carefully, then delete all the test pages, create new "clean" ones and start working for real with those.

Further proofing is obviously needed after each file has been laid out. Check each imported file on screen, particularly if you have any doubts about its integrity. If problems persist, try making a PDF of the page: if the error appears, there is probably a problem with the imported file.

In book publishing, be careful to check items such as running heads, captions, and fillers that may have been keyed in for the first time in the layout file and thus not previously proofed.

Far left: Matchprint proofs can be used for general color checking, although final color accuracy cannot be measured without seeing wet proofs from the printer.

Left: Plotter prints are the CTP equivalent of the blues stage in normal printing, with the additional benefit of being four-color.

Streamlining production with CTP

Traditional proofing processes involved printed black-and-white and color lasers, repro-house scans, bromides or films, ozalids, Cromalins, plates, and sometimes wet proofs. These proofing methods are often labor intensive and mechanical, and are thus both time-consuming and apt to cause a number of errors and inconsistencies throughout the process.

COMPUTER-TO-PLATE (CTP)

Today, the situation is in many ways more straightforward. This is due, in no small part, to the development of CTP technology, which utilizes the PDF file format. This has removed most of the need for all of the time-consuming paraphernalia of films and Cromalins. There are now fewer obstacles between the original file and the finished product.

This has also created a demarcation line that did not previously exist so clearly. As a result, proofing can be divided into two distinct stages: Anything that is not produced by the RIP at the printers and anything that is.

The distinction is important because anything that the printer outputs will (or at least, should) be identical to the finished product. Something that is correct on these printer's proofs will be correct when the final job is printed, and if for any reason it isn't, then the printer is to blame. On the other hand, anything that is produced previously —say, on a desktop printer—should be regarded as only indicative of the final result.

Different printers will supply different types of proofs within the main cost, depending on the type of job. Some will provide a set of low-resolution inkjet proofs—but will usually charge extra for corrections or for color proofs. For this and many other reasons, appropriate proofs at appropriate stages are essential.

It's sometimes not feasible for everyone to see final RIP-ed proofs. If the budget and logistics permit, try to get copies to the key people. Otherwise, email them PDFs from the same file sent to the printers. Although not 100 percent definitive, this should catch most problems.

Proofing tips

∗ Inputting corrections can create further errors.

∗ Keep all copies of all proofs until well after the job is finished. You never know when you'll need to look back at them.

∗ Make sure all proofs are signed off by the person checking them and the person executing the corrections.

∗ Explain the purpose and limitations of any proof that you send to the client. Make sure they get a set of the final RIP-ed printer's proofs for approval.

Proofing options checklist

All proofing methods have various advantages and disadvantages. You need to be aware of these if you are to make the most of your proofs.

Mono laser
Advantages:
✓ Cheap
✓ Very good for type
✓ Many problems will be revealed

Disadvantages:
✓ Lack of color
✓ Complex files can take time to print
✓ Not generally postscript-RIP-ed
✓ Letter printers cannot produce letter bleeds

Comments:
If text has been received from an outside source, then proof after importation into the layout program but before the pages have been designed.

Passing on press
Advantages:
✓ You are seeing the actual job for the first time, and can supervise any final color adjustments. Gives an opportunity to meet the printer in person

Disadvantages:
✓ In most cases, it is far too late to spot or correct errors at this stage; travel required

Comments:
If prepress work has been done correctly and if the printer uses CTP technology, press passes are now largely unnecessary.

With web-offset and rotogravure, presses run so fast that adjustments need to be made early in the run if they are to affect all the copies.

On screen
Advantages:
✓ Cheap and quick

Disadvantages:
✓ Hard to spot errors in a familiar medium
✓ Some errors will not display until printed out
✓ Unreliable for checking colors

Comments:
If this is a formal proof stage in any job, make sure that it is done methodically and it is logged. On-screen PDF-proofing is a very good way of checking problems—if something appears correctly as a PDF, there's a good chance it will be OK when printed.

Color digital
Advantages:
✓ Good color matching for complex images; widely available

Disadvantages:
✓ Less good color matching for flat tints
✓ More expensive than mono laser
✓ Can be time-consuming
✓ May not be PostScript-RIP-ed

Comments:
Colors can vary depending on a wide range of factors including paper stock, RIP used, application, and output device. If the final output is on a digital press, ensure that initial and final proofs at least are provided by the printer.

Note:
The term "Cromalin" causes some confusion today. It was once simply the name of DuPont's four-color off-press proofing system—the one-time industry-standard powder-based color proofs made from lithographic film. Today, Cromalin is also used as a more general term for one of several digital proofing systems.

Wet proofs
Advantages:
✓ The only way of achieving accurate color-matching prior to final lithographic printing. The results can be used as on-press color guides

Disadvantages:
✓ Expensive and time-consuming

Comments:
If in any doubt about the accuracy of color-matching by digital proofs, consider supplying the printer with a scatter-proof file as a PDF made up to the printer's exact specifications as early as possible. Then compare results with the same file: (a) on screen in the layout application; (b) on screen as a PDF; and (c) output on your preferred digital-proofing system. Be aware of the differences when making adjustments to relative color values.

CORRECTING PROOFS Before your job is finally printed, you need to see that all is as you were expecting, but so will your printer, who will require a physical color proof (called a "contract" proof) to be sure that the run matches your expectations.

How to correct proofs

Exceptions may be when the job is printing direct to plate (CTP), where a PDF can be adequate. However, as this still leaves an element of chance in the final result, your printer may insist on some sort of physical example that he can match.

Typical contract proofs include digital proofs and "off-press" dry proofs such as Cromalins and Matchprints. A contract proof is designed to be as close to the final result as possible, so the proof uses the same process as the final job, onto the actual paper that is to be used—a so-called "wet" proof. Even these are not always absolutely perfect, since large, four-color printing presses are uneconomical for proofing purposes, and custom-made (usually flatbed) presses are generally used.

SEPARATION FILM
Both dry and wet proofs are made from separation film, so before proofing check the film if possible—it could save time and money.

Vital equipment for checking proofs

A magnifying glass (variously called a "linen tester," "loupe," or "lupe") powerful enough for close checking of halftone dots

For really close scrutiny, a powerful magnifier such as the Peak Pocket Micro, which has a magnification of 50x

CONTRACT PROOFS
Before checking contract proofs think about the lighting. Avoid viewing proofs under a desk lamp. You must try to view color under consistent conditions, ideally those in a color-viewing booth. ANSI (American National Standards Institute) states that lighting should be at 5,000° Kelvin with the surrounding color gray (specifically Munsell N-8). The surrounding environment (or ambient light) may affect your perceptions of color. You may find the Graphic Arts Technical Foundation's GATF/Rhem Light Indicators useful. These are small patches that can be peeled off and stuck to the border of color proofs and are used to verify lighting. The patch appears solid for lighting conditions of 5,000° Kelvin, and shows stripes if the lighting is not.

Another aid is the color bar. Both Adobe InDesign and QuarkXPress use limited color bars when outputting separations but the most useful are those that include specially designed devices for checking dot gain, slur, gray balance, and ink coverage and density. Typical color bars are the Digital Proof Comparators by GATF.

Contract proofs will likely be output as spreads that will be imposed for press after color-checking and corrections. If the proofs are already imposed, then you will need to check that the color is consistent across the sheet—for example, if an image sits over the page gutter, the two halves may be at opposite ends of the sheet.

When pages were assembled by hand, a certain amount of color correction was possible (by chemically etching the dots) without having to rescan the original. With digitally generated film, the normal practice is to make the corrections with software and run out the film again.

Generally, contract proofs do not show spot colors, varnishes, special inks (such as metallics), or embossing and you will incur significant costs if you insist on seeing these.

PRESS PROOFS

Having passed proofs for press, the pages are imposed (an ozalid, blue, or plotter will be supplied by the printer for you to check the running order of pages) and plates made that are then mounted on a press. Several tests are carried out to ensure correct ink coverage, roller pressure and register, in a procedure known as "make-ready." You and your client now have one final opportunity to check for quality and to make limited adjustments. The printer then begins the final run and you approve a press sample.

Separation film checklist

✳ Check for correct trimmed page dimensions.

✳ Check for overall quality: scratches, streaking, or other damage such as folding. Clear areas should be clear, not fogged.

✳ Ensure solid colors—especially black—are properly solid.

✳ All items (type, images, rules, tints, etc.) should appear on their respective separations and appear as they should—correct fonts, flat tints, and smooth halftones, for example.

✳ Check overprinted and knocked out items.

✳ Ensure all tint and image bleeds work correctly, and extend beyond the page trim.

Contract proofs checklist

✳ Even and consistent colors throughout the proof, with accurate tints that do not look mottled.

✳ If the job contains colors specified by color-matching systems, such as in corporate identities, check them against manufacturers printed swatches.

✳ Check the color bars for ink density. If they look too thin, there's not enough ink being applied.

✳ Look for marks and scratches, particularly in text areas where an erroneous blemish may easily be mistaken for a punctuation mark.

✳ Make sure that bleeds and crossovers extend sufficiently beyond the trims or folds.

✳ Check that trapped areas actually do trap.

✳ Check that overlapping process color halftone dots do not show moiré patterns.

✳ In images featuring people, check that flesh tones do not show a color bias—they should be lifelike.

✳ Highlights will look flat if the whites are slightly gray (dots too large) and blacks will look too weak if the shadow dots are too small.

Press proofs checklist

✳ Make sure that the color is correct and matches the contract proof.

✳ Make sure that the color and type density is consistent from one end of the sheet to the other.

✳ Check that type is sharp.

✳ Check that all graphic elements are present and correct by comparing with the blueline (ozalid) or plotter proof.

✳ Check that crossovers are correct by folding the press sheet and comparing the alignment and color match.

✳ Check that halftone dots in highlights and shadows match the contract proof.

✳ Check that spot colors or special inks are as specified.

✳ Check for spots, blemishes, or mottling.

✳ Check that all colors are in register by scrutinizing the register marks.

✳ Check that the paper is as you specified (take a sample with you).

ADOBE'S PORTABLE DOCUMENT FORMAT (PDF) offers a reliable way to share electronic versions of documents over many different platforms, and is increasingly becoming the file format of choice for many printers.

Using PDF

PDF is a multi-talented kind of file: it can be a cross-platform document, a multimedia presentation, a hyperlinked on-screen manual, and even an entire website in itself. For print production, PDF has also been adopted as the industry's preferred format for delivering complete pages for high-end, high-resolution output. Some entirely digital workflows—such as computer-to-plate (CTP) and those leading to digital presses—may insist exclusively on PDF rather than customary loose page-layout files, fonts, and images.

COMPATIBILITY

Each successive release of Adobe Acrobat has introduced a new version of the PDF file format. PDFs intended for press work should not necessarily be created using the very latest version. The limiting factor is usually the RIP in the output device, so ask your bureau or printer for precise specifications for the kind of PDFs they can accept. Usefully, the PDF version numbers add up to the version of Acrobat that can create them; Acrobat 3.0 makes PDF 1.2, and so on.

IMAGE COMPRESSION

In order to be self-contained, a PDF embeds all of the images and text fully within the document pages so that there are no loose picture files or fonts to worry about. In order to keep the file size

at a realistic level, the PDF creation options let you specify whether bitmap images should be "downsampled" and compressed. Downsampling simply means reducing the pixel resolution to a level more appropriate for your output intentions. For example, you may have scanned an image at 600ppi at actual size and then scaled it down in your page layout such that its effective actual size resolution is increased much higher, yet a halftone line screen of 150 to 175lpi for glossy magazine work may only require a pixel resolution

PDF version compatibility:

PDF 1.2: Created by Acrobat 3.0, this version of the application is no longer current and is not advisable for prepress work.

PDF 1.3: Created by Acrobat 4.0, this is often the preferred PDF version for prepress work. PDF/X (see page 82) standards adhere to it. Virtually all design programs can export to PDF 1.3.

PDF 1.4: Created by Acrobat 5.0, this is preferred for general documents including those for distribution and collaborative work. Most design programs can export to it and some RIPs support it.

PDF 1.5: Created by Acrobat 6.0, this version offers enhanced support for transparency and layers. Few non-Adobe programs can export to it, and even fewer RIPs support it at this time.

of 300 to 450ppi. Downsampling when you create the PDF will produce a more compact file in terms of data size and will speed up processing when the PDF is output.

No matter what picture file formats you used in the page-layout application, exporting to PDF will convert them to a common bitmap format and let you apply a compression setting. Typically, you would specify the JPEG format in order to achieve better compression, although PDF also supports a non-lossy ZIP compression method for bitmap images with continuous tones. For example, presentation graphics and application screenshots do not compress well with JPEG and may suffer badly from artifacts. Leaving the PDF compression setting at Automatic allows the right kind of image to be reformatted and compressed in the most appropriate way.

Always keep in mind that any measure of JPEG image compression is inherently "lossy," so all PDFs that are intended for prepress output should have the image quality option at its maximum setting (or the compression level set to its lowest) or use the lossless ZIP compression only. This is only an issue with bitmap graphics, as all vector artwork is automatically compressed in PDFs using completely lossless algorithms.

FONT EMBEDDING

Fonts do not necessarily need to be embedded into a PDF file, but it is a good idea to do so. Depending upon the design program creating the PDF, you normally have the option of embedding specific fonts of your choice, or letting the program embed only the fonts that are actually required by the document. The latter setting is all that you need. Embedding fonts adds to the PDF file size considerably, especially for Unicode and OpenType fonts, so you should allow them to be "subset." Subsetting means only embedding the actual glyphs used in the document rather than the entire font. When exporting to PDF, you may have the option of whether to embed a subset rather than the full font when the proportion of the glyphs used per font surpasses a certain percentage. In general, make this 100 percent in order to force subsetting for all font usage.

The only drawback is that last-minute authors' corrections to the text in a PDF using Acrobat Professional will be restricted to the glyphs in that subset. If the character you need to insert is not in the subset, you will have to make the change in the original and reexport it, or at least create a new page to be inserted.

If you don't embed the fonts, then the PDF file remains readable on other computers even if they do not have the specific fonts installed. The Adobe Reader employs one of its own built-in substitute fonts instead. But for prepress work, this is not what you want to happen, so make sure that all fonts are correctly embedded. You can check this by opening the PDF within Adobe Reader or Acrobat and opening the Document Properties window (under the File menu). In the Fonts section, each font in the PDF should be listed along with the label (Embedded Subset).

COLOR MANAGEMENT

It's helpful to switch off color management options when you are making a PDF—especially if you have been color managing throughout. This will preserve existing embedded profiles in images and the working profiles assigned to the document. Only when producing page layouts from many different unmanaged sources, and your PDF is intended for non-press use, is it worth using the PDF export settings in your design software to standardize everything to a neutral color space such as sRGB. Certainly don't impose a CMYK profile on prepress work unless asked to.

THE PRINTING PROCESS The design-to-print workflow can now be executed totally digitally. However, the final step—the printing press—is still predominantly analog. This is also the stage over which the graphic designer has least influence. Knowing how the finished product will look and feel is a key part of the design process, so the designer must have a basic knowledge of the printing techniques available to achieve the desired result.

Lithography

2

Lithography is by far the most common form of printing today. Originally devised more than 200 years ago, its success is based on a simple principle: oil and water do not mix.

In offset lithography the image is printed from a rubber coated roller (blanket) to which the ink is transferred from the plate. The image is firstly created on a printing plate, either photographically or by using a CTP (computer-to-plate) digital system. CTP systems are now the standard method. When the photopolymer resin coating of the plate is exposed to ultraviolet light under a process camera, exposed areas are hardened. The unexposed areas are subsequently washed off during processing. Gum Arabic is then applied to the surface to make the non-image areas water-receptive and grease-repellent (i.e. ink-repellent). Plates can either be negative or positive working. Negative-working plates are much less expensive and are generally used for single-color

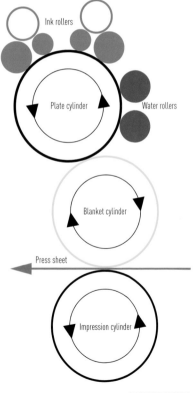

Thick, viscous printing ink is forced through a system of rollers, making it semi-liquid. A thin layer is distributed over the plate. A fountain solution moistens the plate's non-image areas so that ink adheres only to the image areas. The plate cylinder revolves into contact with the blanket cylinder depositing an inked, reversed image. Paper passes between the blanket and impression cylinders, offsetting a right-reading image.

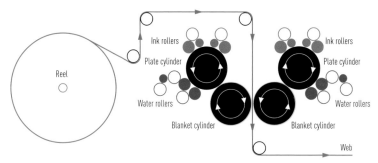

Reel

Ink rollers
Plate cylinder
Water rollers
Blanket cylinder

Ink rollers
Plate cylinder
Water rollers
Blanket cylinder

Web

Above and below: In a typical web-offset system, the paper is printed on both sides in one pass. A web press consists of up to eight consecutive units like this, one for each color.

work. The same chemistry applies to negative-working plates but in reverse: it is the exposed areas that become unstable leaving the unexposed areas to print.

The thin metal, plastic, or paper plate is then wrapped around the plate cylinder of the press. As the cylinder rotates, it makes contact with rollers wet with water or a similar dampening solution and rollers conveying ink. The dampening solution prevents ink adhering to the non-printing areas of the plate. The inked image areas are then transferred to a rubber covered blanket cylinder, finally offsetting the image onto the paper as it passes between the blanket and impression cylinders.

Modern litho presses are connected directly to the digital output source, eliminating both film and the platemaking stage, making the press another link in the digital chain.

Lithography is well suited to the four-color printing process, since larger presses can print the four colors consecutively in a single pass. Indeed, modern commercial litho presses can print up to eight colors. Smaller presses are sheet-fed, but longer print runs such as books and magazines are offset onto paper fed from large rolls on a so-called "web press."

The size of the halftone screen and the surface of the paper stock will determine the density of

ink required in the litho process. Uncoated paper is more absorbent and will soak up more ink; to compensate for this, the dot size can be reduced in film production. Positive-working plates produce less dot gain and are generally preferred for web-offset magazine printing.

Other printing methods

GRAVURE

Possibly offset litho's biggest rival, this process is used to print everything from postage stamps to wallpaper. Gravure is an adaptation of the ancient etching method of reproducing tone. "Cells" of different depths are cut into the surface of a cylinder, deeper cells holding and subsequently depositing more ink, rendering a darker image. As the ink from neighboring cells tends to merge, the result is almost screenless in appearance.

Like offset litho, gravure can be printed onto a web. The process is digitally prepared: diamond styli in the engraving heads that cut the printing cells are driven from digital files. An engraved cylinder revolves in a reservoir of thin, solvent-based ink, flooding the surface. A flexible steel "doctor blade" wipes the cylinder clean as it revolves, leaving ink only in the image areas. Finally, a rubber-covered impression cylinder presses the paper onto the engraved surface. One drawback of gravure is that type appears less sharply than with lithography.

LETTERPRESS

Once the most popular printing process, letterpress is now only used for specialized jobs or limited edition (short-run) books. The use of hot metal typesetting really survives only to produce a proof that can then be scanned and printed by offset litho to reproduce the traditional effect.

Letterpress machines have largely been converted to or replaced by flexography, in which the metal type trays of letterpress are replaced by a flexible rubber or polymer plate. Widely used in the packaging industry, flexographic (or "flexo") presses are similar to gravure, using a series of rotating cylinders to collect ink from a reservoir and transfer it onto a web-fed printing material via plate and impression cylinders. Flexo presses can print on materials unsuitable for offset litho, such as cardboard, plastic bags, or waxed paper.

SCREEN PRINTING

Often associated with poster and art prints, the silkscreen or screen printing process gets its name from what was originally a stretched silk cloth used to hold a stencil. This versatile printing process produces thick, opaque deposits of ink in brilliant colors, and can be used to print on virtually any material, including shop windows and the sides of vans, or even curved or uneven surfaces such as bottles, T-shirts, and printed circuit boards.

Modern screens are made from a fine polyester mesh, stretched on a metal or wooden frame. A simple line stencil is cut using a digitally controlled pen plotter that manipulates a knife.

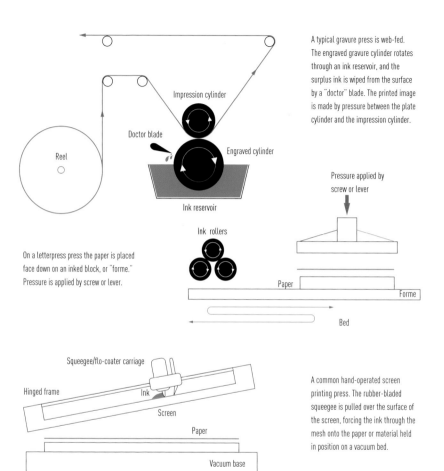

A typical gravure press is web-fed. The engraved gravure cylinder rotates through an ink reservoir, and the surplus ink is wiped from the surface by a "doctor" blade. The printed image is made by pressure between the plate cylinder and the impression cylinder.

Impression cylinder

Doctor blade

Engraved cylinder

Reel

Ink reservoir

Pressure applied by screw or lever

Ink rollers

On a letterpress press the paper is placed face down on an inked block, or "forme." Pressure is applied by screw or lever.

Paper

Forme

Bed

Squeegee/flo-coater carriage

Hinged frame

Ink

Screen

Paper

Vacuum base

A common hand-operated screen printing press. The rubber-bladed squeegee is pulled over the surface of the screen, forcing the ink through the mesh onto the paper or material held in position on a vacuum bed.

More complex stencils and halftones can be made using a film positive as in lithography. The screen is coated on both sides with a light-sensitive polymer emulsion and exposed through the film with ultraviolet light, after which the image areas are washed away with water. The screen is mounted on the press and a rubber-edged squeegee forces the ink through the mesh, passing only through the "open" image areas. Though fine screens are available, screen printing is not recommended for close registration or work involving very small type sizes.

THE DIGITAL WORKFLOW As we have seen, there are various alternatives to lithographic printing. For straightforward, short-run jobs, meanwhile, new digital presses offer unrivalled efficiency.

Digital printing

Finally, we come to the latest output option and the one that seems closest to the goal of an all-digital workflow. Digital presses, based on various inkjet and "dry ink" technologies, are rapidly increasing in popularity for economical short-run, full-color work. Running at speeds up to around 10,000 copies an hour, they offer similar quality to offset litho and compete well on cost up to a few thousand units: litho costs far less per copy, but digital does away with job set-up costs. Many of these presses can optionally create a different image on every sheet, allowing huge scope for such tasks as printing personalized documents from mailing databases. On the down side, the range of paper stock that can be printed is more limited than with litho, and print can have an annoying tendency to rub off, particularly when subjected to heat.

Opposite: Digital presses have become commonplace. The technologies used and the most economical run lengths vary among models, but all tend to be easier to operate and maintain than offset litho presses.

Right: As with lithographic printing, more than four inks can be used to extend the range of colors reproducible.

SURFACE DESIGN

ONCE THE JOB HAS BEEN PRINTED, there is one final stage before delivering the finished product. This is entirely mechanical, which may involve trimming, folding, collating, or binding. It must be considered early in the design process because it will affect the way the document is constructed and therefore the production budget.

Finishing

Finishing can also include print-related operations such as die-stamping, embossing, varnishing, and laminating. Die-stamping and embossing use a metal die (engraved by a digitally controlled machine tool) to "stamp" or press a relief image into paper or board. The image can be impressed with or without ink, to create subtle effects. Frequently seen on paperback book jackets, a metal foil can be combined with the raised impression, using a heated die. Die-cutting physically cuts out sections of the paper. Digitally controlled laser die-cutting is used to cut fine detail such as company logos in business stationery.

There are a number of ways to protect the printed page and make it scuff-resistant. Varnishes or seals can be printed on the litho press to give varying degrees of gloss or matt finish. To add extra strength, a film lamination, again in matt or gloss, can be glued to the stock under pressure through a heated roller. Interesting design effects can be created by mixing spot areas of gloss and matt varnishes or by adding a varnish after the lamination is applied.

FOLDING AND BINDING

Once the print finishes have been applied the stock is ready to be folded. Folding is accomplished using a buckle, knife, or combination folding machine. There is no limit to the number of folds employed, and interesting visual effects can be created by using a single sheet designed to fold into several smaller sections. After folding, multi-page jobs have to be gathered, bundled, and collated (put in order), prior to binding and

Below: The mechanical
trimming finishing process.

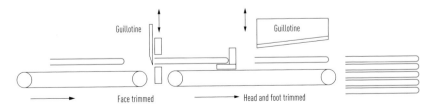

Guillotine   Guillotine

Face trimmed   Head and foot trimmed

guillotining. Other operations that may need to be considered are perforating or tipping-in (adding a single page to a multi-page publication).

Binding may be performed by several methods. Booklets, and magazines up to about 96 pages, are commonly bound by saddle-stitching (stapling), while unsewn or "perfect" binding can be used for almost unlimited numbers of pages. Gathered and collated sections are placed in the binding machine, spine down; the edge is roughened and an adhesive applied. The cover is folded, scored, and wrapped around the pages. The adhesive is cured by heat and the pages are trimmed. In large perfect-bound books, the designer must use a generous gutter to avoid text and pictures disappearing into it, as the spine is less flexible than sewn titles and some fold is lost in trimming.

Case-bound or hardback books have a separately made cover. The page sections are sewn through the spine with thread and gathered together to form a "book-block." The cover and book-block are assembled with tipped-in endpapers, usually of a heavier stock. Finally a separate "dust" jacket is wrapped around the cased book.

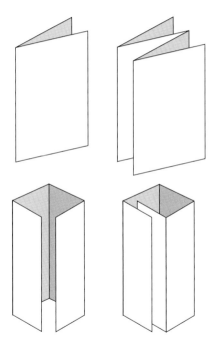

Above: Some of the varied ways of folding. Clockwise from top to bottom: single fold four-page sheet; accordion eight-page fold; gatefold eight-page fold; rollover eight-page fold.

CHOOSING PAPER The choice of paper is the foundation of a successful print job. The designer must consider carefully what the finished item is trying to achieve and select a stock that will not only convey the right message but also fit within the print budget.

Paper

A huge range of papers and boards is available—machine-made, handmade, recycled, and FSC-certified. For some jobs, the type of paper will be determined by the method of printing employed. Offset litho presses require papers with good surface strength and dimensional stability, preferably with a low water content. The finish is a less important factor, as offset ink will adhere both to glossy coated and to matt uncoated surfaces. For gravure, the paper must be smooth but absorbent enough to collect the ink.

The paper must fit the brief for the job, and the finish should also be appropriate to the content. For good-quality color halftone reproduction, a coated stock (made with mineral fillers to create a very smooth surface) would normally be used, although some very fine uncoated papers now boast excellent color quality. The weight of paper is classified by grams per square meter (gsm or

gm2), a standard sheet of copier paper weighing 90 gsm. The impact of a prestigious catalog could be increased by using 150 or 200 gsm. Generally, heavier papers or art boards are thicker than light ones, but the density and type of fibre will have an effect on thickness (bulk). Glossy art paper can feel thinner than an uncoated stock of the same weight, so it may be necessary to increase the weight when choosing a gloss finish. Be careful of ink showing through some lightweight papers.

Of course, budget may also limit the choice of paper. If a brochure needs to be mailed, the weight of the stock will affect the cost of postage. Your spending power can be maximized by choosing the size and format wisely, taking into account the sizes of paper the printer can use so that costly wastage can be avoided.

Paper is made in A and B sizes to an international standard based on the ratio 1:√2 (the ratio is

SURFACE DESIGN

upheld when sheets are folded in half). If possible, your document should be designed to fit within a standard size. Remember to consult the printer and allow for any bleeds and for sufficient free "gripper" edge as required. If the brief calls for a special finish, such as varnish or lamination, the printer will advise on suitable stock. Do not over specify: it is not necessary to use a gloss stock if you are adding a gloss varnish. Types of binding may be influenced by the direction of grain (the way the fibres lie), so prior consultation is key.

There may also be environmental considerations. A range of quality recycled papers is available and new paper from sustainable forests (FSC-certified) is another option. Even recycled papers are often bleached with chlorine, releasing extremely harmful by-products. But many papers are now "chlorine-free."

The printer should be able to supply sample books from paper merchants and mills. It is a good idea to build a library of these—some are inspirational works of design in their own right.

Opposite and right: Rolland Motif Paper Promotional Calendar. Innovative use of print techniques, die cutting and binding, cleverly demonstrate the versatility of the paper samples.
DESIGN BY ÉPOXY, CANADA

Above: Paper sample books can be interesting design projects in their own right. Modo Paper Mills Inc, USA, strive to stimulate their target audience—the designers who will specify their product—with strong, colorful photographic imagery and unusual binding.
DESIGN BY SEA, UK

THE PRACTICES OF ADVERTISING, corporate identity, and branding cut across other sections in this book, yet the profession of advertising has a distinct character that connects it closely with corporate identity and branding but sets it apart from other forms of visual and commercial practice.

This section therefore looks at advertising, branding, and corporate identity together. Although they used to be billed as separate practices that incorporated graphic expertise, the three aspects became more interconnected, as multimedia agencies, developed in the 1990s, were able to mix graphic and advertising skills to take on entire promotional projects.

Essentially, advertising aims to produce a campaign—a strategic thought voiced in different ways, to surprise, delight, and inform people. Like advertising, corporate identity aims to coordinate the interpretation of a product or service with a distinct visual or verbal "look," by which it can be recognized. Branding became prominent in the 1990s with the rise of multinational companies that wanted to extend their promotions outside the normal territories of conventional advertising. Before any other quality, all three areas require ideas to be expressed with absolute clarity.

ADVERTISING IN A CONSUMER SOCIETY

In each area, graphic design skills are essential. Branding and corporate identity require typographers to craft letterforms and distinguish brand character; and computer-skilled graphic designers to coordinate the connections between all graphic elements, format material for printers (on disk and over the Internet), and define rules that govern the graphics application to different media. In advertising, a graphic designer's sense of organization is essential in order to ensure the flow of information and consistency of treatment. Word-based advertisements depend on skilled and sensitive typography. Most significantly, establishing a brand and developing its corporate identity in an advertising campaign demands graphics expertise, because it requires the translation of concepts into images and copy, combined with an acute understanding of visual reference points.

Opposite top: This advert works by association: the slick engineering used to produce London's Millennium Wheel with that of the Audi. In advertising this is called "borrowed interest." In visualizing the composition, the image would have been mocked up either as a Photoshop collage or as a "moodboard" (usually rendered in marker and pencil). Note the treatment of the sky (the negative space), flattened in tone and color to make the text legible.
DESIGN BY BARTLE BOGLE HEGARTY, UK

Opposite below: This Coke campaign drew on the brand's famous marque, effectively reminding the viewer of its established familiarity and uniqueness. The art direction drew on the brand's pre-existing archival imagery, which plays to the strengths of digital image manipulation (scanning, re-editing, segmenting, and enhancing).
DESIGN BY McCANN ERICKSON, UK

From here, you can see
the attraction of aluminium.

Life tastes good

The modes of advertising fall into five categories: warning, informing, reminding, launching, and promotion. The overriding purpose is to provoke awareness by disrupting viewers' routine by grabbing their attention.

Since the beginning of the twentieth century, the usual means of media advertising was in the press and on billboards, and from 1954 this extended to television commercials. From the 1970s, a more direct form of advertising—sometimes called integrated advertising, advertising design, or below-the-line advertising—emerged to counter the over-familiarity of mass advertising. A more recent form—ambient advertising—uses landscape and the placement of brands in situations where their message is most likely to be well received, such as a car manufacturer promoting safety by sponsoring and branding the clothes of a lollipop man (or crossing guard).

The expansion of promotional forms has required designers to apply their skills more widely because, in all forms of advertising, the brand and the message have to be applied consistently and understood in the same way.

MEDIA ADVERTISING

Within advertising there are many different types of promotion, and agencies tend to specialize. The two most prominent are media advertising and direct advertising. Media agencies produce mass-exposure, high-publicity work through billboard, press, and commercial advertising, while direct advertising—often called one-to-one—is more closely geared to target markets. Billboards are usually produced for 48 or 96-sheet sites or single-sheet rectangular format (1 sheet = 15 x 30 inches). On a smaller scale, six- and single-sheet campaigns promote events. In both cases, designers liaise with advertising directors to make images and ideas fit the format.

Press advertising ranges from double- and single-page spreads to column-width ads. Most adverts require graphic judgment from an early stage. Type, color, and layout are decided before photos and other material are commissioned. Unlike in other media, designers have little control over paper or format, except with inserts, which are printed by the client and dropped in.

Television commercials also require early graphic input. Illustrators are hired to sketch out storyboards, helping the creative team to convey precisely what they require from the director. On-location storyboards are checked constantly to ensure that suitable footage is recorded, timing is met, and material fits the requirements of post-production teams. Digital typographers and graphic designers produce text sequences—added during post-production—to link the film with the end frame. The final connection between product shot, branding, and strapline is often crucial.

Design considerations for media and direct advertising:

✳ An advertising campaign must have impact, relevance, and "connect" simply with the intended audience.

✳ Advertising must not lose sight of its subject—the graphic content is essential in this.

✳ Clarity—in print advertising 80% of the space usually conveys the idea, and 20% the additional information.

✳ Analysis of the brief defines precisely what is required. The ideal is to reduce the proposition to a single sentence and define the types of skill required of a graphic designer.

✳ The prominence of the logo or product shot must be considered, remembering that the purpose of the graphic input is to emphasize the advertised goods.

✳ The brand characteristics must be systematically adhered to in terms of layout, tone, and treatment of the copy.

DIRECT ADVERTISING

The most common form of direct advertising is direct mail (DM) to potential or existing customers. Graphic design is central, because the work involves presenting offers and information through the design of letters, flyers, brochures, and packaging. So graphic designers work closely with the marketing team. For bigger advertising campaigns using DM, one-off "interactive" self-liquidating promotions (SLPs) may be commissioned. These are limited-edition branded goods that connect to publicized offers, usually developed from a media campaign.

The Internet is a ever-growing medium for direct marketing. Banners, vertical "skyscraper" ads, and various forms of pop-up challenge the digital designer to pack a lot of message into a small space, both visually and technically. Using email, graphical messages can be sent to large subscriber lists at negligible cost, but technical niceties must be observed to ensure recipients can read them. "Viral" marketing—releasing a graphic, film clip, or mini-game onto the web and relying on users to draw each others' attention to it—demands imagination and technical skills as well as a keen awareness of the target audience.

Point-of-sale requires graphic designers to connect all areas of brand advertising and promotion work. Formats include freestanding boards, dump bins, banners, "wobblies" (plastic mobiles suspended from shelves), and "buzz stops" (vertical advertising hoardings between shelves); these are all increasingly quick and cheap to produce using technologies such as large-format inkjet printers. Digital graphics skills are also needed to scan and manipulate environments during concept development.

CORPORATE IDENTITY

Corporate identity is the commercial face that represents a company, where branding is its commercial application. They often get confused because the term "brand" is the name given to a company's identity, while "branding" describes the marque by which a company, product, or service is recognized. Expressed simply, corporate identity is the creation of the brand, while branding is how it is then applied through all areas of communication.

The corporate identity has to represent the values by which a company should be known, but in recent years major brands have turned their products into sub-brands; and consequently advertising activity has diversified. In modern communications agencies, the roles normally associated with branding and corporate identity tend increasingly to cross over.

The most common outlets for corporate identity include journals and in-store magazines, which are typically quarterly publications that show, through their editorial contents, how the company's products and services connect with the presumed lifestyles of consumers. Graphic design considerations include the creation and implementation of the brand's corporate rules regarding layout, and the organization of leader stories, advertorials, and features in a visually stimulating manner.

Clear rules as to how the corporate identity will be communicated in different media have to be established. These typically range from stationery and advertising to digital applications. Appropriateness and consistency are important considerations. How changes and trends affect the reading of the brand is a significant issue in the development of a corporate identity: does it still retain a connection with earlier brand associations?

Bigger brands have tended to develop and implement corporate identities through their own retail environments—most notably superbrands such as Nike and Disney Stores. Such total branding involves the bringing together of all visual aspects and the development of corporate signature styles to create a brand experience.

Corporate identity, therefore, requires background knowledge of the product's or firm's chief characteristics, the type of market in which the clients want to develop, and the nature of promotions to which they want to commit.

DESIGN CONSIDERATIONS

Graphic designer's are involved in key stages of corporate identity work: primary research and recommendation, visualizing image concepts (through sketch work and digitally imaged scamps), development and detail, then implementation (digital type specifications and media appropriation). It is important for designers to be able to blend traditional and digital skills to get the right results in as little time as possible.

Corporate identities need to convey a sense of belonging, must be representative, and must be clear. Designers need to ensure that the placement of, and any appropriations to, a brand marque are consistent with core brand values. They should check to see what rules govern its usage. The visual dynamics of a corporate identity must be well measured in terms of appropriateness to market and consistency. This is absolutely essential to the inherent character of the product or firm it represents.

Having extracted key graphic qualities, the designer will need to consider the need for flexibility and assess how these qualities can be effectively reproduced at different scales and in different contexts.

BRANDING

Compared with corporate identity, branding is directly connected with raising awareness, for example, via product placement. It usually involves the development of a brand's identity within the everyday surroundings of its target market, using graphic techniques to ensure that the brand is associated with a particular space and mood. Branding therefore fits between direct advertising and corporate identity, because it commercializes the brand by applying graphic identity to appropriate contexts.

Recently, branding has engaged a wider range of specialist graphic practices so that environments and products—from coasters and clocks to nightclubs and public spaces—have become vehicles for promotion. The role of the designer is to apply the corporate graphic style to situations that, in most cases, require re-thinking of an existing identity. Adobe Photoshop is an ideal tool for producing mockups showing products and brands in different situations. However, final artwork will usually be produced in FreeHand or Illustrator, because vector-based files are more versatile for use at a variety of scales and with printing methods adapted to different materials.

The objective of such ambient or 360-degree advertising may be to engage customers at the moment they are most likely to want the product —for instance, a drinks brand in a bar—or to make a new opportunity to communicate with a hard-to-reach audience. Graphic designers are typically employed to rework graphic elements, taking into account how the branding will be understood in its given context. In online branding, the development of corporate identity rules is essential, and usually involves collaboration between digital graphic designers, copywriters, and web designers.

Branding is also called on to extend direct advertising activity. Branded booklets, collector cards and correspondence may be sent to existing clients to maintain customer dialogue.

Many brands develop their identity by diversifying into other markets. Brand stretching can simply mean a brand name being applied to another product, but more often it involves developing a brand through a new product range—for instance a drinks brand expanding into leisure clothing, where new lines provide links to the brand's main area of operation.

In some instances, clients have their own "brand guardian," who ensures that the advertising strategy and other new ideas fit with the existing brand ethos and the company's other development plans. Digital asset management (DAM) systems may be implemented within the company so that in-house and external designers can store and retrieve logos, graphics, photos, text, and other identity material using a central database, with version control and access restrictions to help ensure items are used correctly.

DESIGN CONSIDERATIONS FOR BRANDING

Graphic consultants are typically involved in three stages of branding development: primary research and recommendation, visualizing the brand in context, then working out the feasibility of implementation.

The role of graphic designers in branding involves consultation and recommendation more than redesign. Branding must graphically reflect, in situ, a company's aspirations in a wide variety of contexts, ensuring that the visual distinction of a brand is clearly evident and that its primary function is to condense key characteristics into a "signature"—a visual typographic or graphic element. This will be the marque by which it is recognized.

With promotional work in mind, the branding should incorporate commercial hooks that suggest how the brand typography and graphic styling could be adapted. This may suggest to a brand's marketers or advertising creatives the key qualities that can be picked out as a selling proposition.

The context in which the brand is placed has to be clearly relevant and easy to associate. It is important, if it is to work effectively, that the

Below: Claimed to be the world's largest building graphic at over 150 meters high, this promotion for the Dutch national football team was produced by printers VgL, who printed 4500 panels covering 10,000 square meters.
DESIGN BY WIEDEN AND KENNEDY, NETHERLANDS

branding cannot be misconstrued and that any brand extensions of the work must connect with the core ethos of the brand's other promotions.

PLANNING STAGES

Careful planning and control of production are key to a successful advertising campaign. With so many creative professionals involved, it is vital that the graphic designer is aware of all the critical stages of the process.

Stage 1 is the brief—defining the campaign objectives. The creative brief is broken down in order to interpret statistical evidence, to define a "hook" as the most suitable selling proposition, and to define appropriate modes of delivery (and appropriate media) to reach the defined target market. This results in a project plan that defines art direction, and suggests tone of voice and the most appropriate types of graphic designer (and illustrator) for the project.

Stage 2 concerns the defined key words and proposition—concepts for advertising. This is the task of thinking through ideas on paper using layout pads and markers to produce scamps—ideas in rough, simply communicated. At this stage, the concepts are shown to the rest of the creative team, then to the planning team (occasionally with client representatives) to ensure that all aspects of the brief have been addressed. At this first visualizing stage, art directors work through and negotiate ideas with copywriters, who will consider the ratio of type to image.

Initially a campaign plan is defined—developing the strongest strategies, and detailing the concept—and a plan for art direction and execution is set out. Ideas are presented in-house (using scamps and mock-ups) and adjustments are made, with graphic specialists employed to tidy the presentation. The agency's project team puts a detailed presentation plan together. This is followed by the external (client) presentation for which key ideas are polished (with external graphic design expertise) to presentation level. By this point, graphics software such as FreeHand or Illustrator and photo-manipulation tools such as Photoshop will play a vital part in the process. Clients are usually presented with a central campaign plan and a series of alternatives, so that a final direction can be agreed and signed off by the client.

Stage 3 concerns final concept development—fine tuning for production. Art direction is detailed, and specialist typographers, photographers, film directors, illustrators, and specialist media experts are commissioned. Any other promotional aspects are also tied into the overall strategy. Commissioning of media is then made, and a timetable is set, with "traffic planners" controlling the meeting of deadlines. Printers are booked and media space buyers negotiate the appropriate venues, release dates, and length of campaign run with account planners and media space sellers.

The agency team meets with all the client representatives for final project clearance. At this stage follow-on promotions may be discussed.

Stage 4 is when all printing and production takes place and the synchronized campaign is launched.

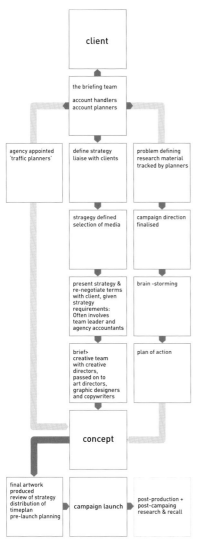

client

the briefing team
account handlers
account planners

agency appointed
'traffic planners'

define strategy
liaise with clients

problem defining
research material
tracked by planners

stragegy defined
selection of media

campaign direction
finalised

present strategy &
re-negotiate terms
with client, given
strategy
requirements:
Often involves
team leader and
agency accountants

brain-storming

brief>
creative team
with creative
directors,
passed on to
art directors,
graphic designers
and copywriters

plan of action

concept

final artwork
produced
review of strategy
distribution of
timeplan
pre-launch planning

campaign launch

post-production +
post-campaing
research & recall

Left: The stages shown in this diagram are typical of those commonly found in media advertising agencies. Digital graphic designers are mostly called upon in the run up to the key presentation stages, such as the presentation of strategy, concept, and for the final artwork.

Above: A detailed scamp, used as a visual to convey the concept to clients, and the resulting press ad, prepared for a double-page glossy magazine.

DESIGN BY BMP, UK

DESIGN FOR PACKAGING

EVERY DAY, we come into contact with packaging of differing shape, size, and purpose, informing us of the merits, dangers, goodness, or value of the products they contain. Some packs are designed to be discarded immediately after purchase, others are integral to the life of their contents.

The graphic designer has to create compelling and attention-grabbing packaging items and take into account the legal requirements, trading rules, and environmental concerns that govern the industry. Packaging must function physically as well as being visually attractive and enticing.

The ability to visualize two-dimensional designs in the round is almost essential to the digital graphic designer, who has to imagine the packaging in its made-up form to determine how text or images will sit in relation to components such as folds, gluepoints, or lid mechanisms. The scarcity and expense of suitable tools, however, means that simple cartons and folders often have to be designed in an ordinary drawing program, with visualization conducted by means of scissors and glue stick. In many cases, however, the physical design of the package will be of an existing standard form or may have been previously completed. Often manufacturing or cutter guides can be imported from specialist CAD software into a drawing package and used as templates for the graphical content without the designer needing specialist engineering skills.

Where constructing the package is part of the brief, the computer screen can be seductive, so designers must be careful not to be beguiled by the ease with which an initial idea can be worked up in two dimensions. What is seen on the monitor will ultimately have to be translated into a physical, fully functional, three-dimensional product.

It is essential to test a package design at every stage by producing an accurate mock-up and checking that the design itself and the surface graphics work together. Once constructed, a package can dramatically change in appearance. Type, for example, may become distorted, cut-out windows may not align well enough to display the product, or the overall design may simply have less impact off screen.

Opposite top: The plastic carrier bag—an undesirable but very cheap device for carrying shopping home. With advantages in printing technology, the colors, texture, and quality in production of this bag means it can now proudly be used to successfully represent a contemporary brand image, while lessening connotations with a negative environmental impact.
DESIGN BY PAUL SMITH LTD

Opposite bottom: This award-winning cover for the Pet Shop Boys "Very" CD stood out in the competitive charts crowd by defying the traditional approach to packaging design. Taking advantage of alternative manufacturing techniques resulted in a practical packaging solution and an effective publicity device. The designer conveyed a message to the consumer of an individual and creative band setting themselves apart from a crowded industry.
DESIGN BY PENTAGRAM, UK

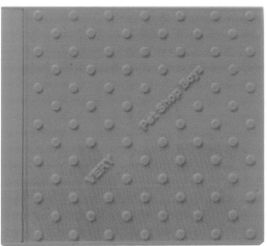

Above: This bag represents style and luxury, but strip away the cosmetic elements of the design and you are left with a simple paper bag. The design is no more practical, despite the extra cost in materials, but is now an effective marketing tool for the brand.
DESIGN BY KENZO, FRANCE

Keep printing out and test assembling work frequently. This can save you much embarrassment when it is time to show ideas to the client.

Different pack shapes are continually being developed which can be manufactured from an expanding range of materials. Polyethylene, high-grade plastics, acetates, and many other new materials, have been added to the already extensive range available. These different textures and surfaces provide both creative opportunities and technical challenges.

Branding is essential to packaging design, and goes deeper than logo. Typography, shape, image, layout, choice of color, and tactile qualities all contribute to developing product identity.

DESIGN TO MANUFACTURE

Graphic designers should have a good understanding of all the major graphic arts software, ideally including three-dimensional modeling applications, but when working with packaging the most important requirement is probably to be fluent in at least one drawing program.

Computer-generated artwork can be extremely accurate, allowing the designer to work to precise tolerances. This has knock-on benefits for the manufacturing processes.

Designers often tend to favor one program over another for reasons of familiarity, but DTP programs—more suited to multi-page work—are less frequently used for packaging design. However, artwork for manufacturers' cutting guides and templates can be imported and locked into these programs, and graphic elements used as necessary. Dedicated drawing programs such as Adobe Illustrator and FreeHand are widely used, as they have many functions that assist the design development process. Almost infinite scalability and distortion controls, together with lockable layers and

guides, give designers greater flexibility for experimentation and for previewing their creations at different stages.

Working with layers, which can be locked and/or hidden, allows numerous permutations and variations of a design to be made on screen without accidental deletion or movement of key elements.

Repetitive transformations, "click-and-drag" duplication, and knife tools are just some of the highly productive features of drawing programs. As with DTP programs, additional elements—including photographic images, text, and manufacturers' templates—can all be easily imported. Bitmap editing programs are used extensively to modify and prepare images for use on packaging, but the final artwork will always end up in a vector-based application.

An interesting feature of drawing programs is the facility that to assign different output attributes, such as halftone resolutions, to individual elements, thus allowing a high degree of control over differing graphic components when printed onto different surfaces.

While a very small number of dedicated packaging design applications seem to drift in and out of the market, some useful plug-ins are available for drawing programs (see above and opposite). These range from fairly to very expensive, but may quickly pay for themselves in a busy studio devoted to a particular type of work.

Particular care must be taken when saving finished artwork that it is in a format compatible with the next stage in the production chain. PDF files may not be acceptable, as the contractor may need to manipulate the artwork before outputting it. When asked to supply files in a program's own proprietary format, check which version the contractor is using before starting work: graphics created using advanced tools cannot always be saved for use in earlier versions.

MATERIALS

Products of most shapes, sizes, and weight generally need some form of packaging. This must be suited to the individual product to ensure adequate protection as well as ease of opening and good customer appeal.

One aspect of packaging design that cannot be dealt with by computer software is the choice of the right material. The substrate's behavior when folded, bent, stamped, molded, or blown is crucial to how the final product will look. This is simply something you have to learn from experience and by making or commissioning mock-ups.

Paper and cardboard are widely used in the packaging industry. They are relatively inexpensive and have a versatility that makes for simple and quick processing. Additionally, they are materials that designers can also use easily for constructing presentation mock-ups. Embossing, creasing, cutting, folding, slitting, gluing, and the printing of inks, varnishes, and other finishes are all straightforward processes suitable for use with paper and cardboard.

Recycled cardboard is used for many forms of packaging. This lowers unit costs and also carries the added bonus of being "environmentally friendly," a quality that is exploited by manufacturers of "wholesome" or "green" products. Inexpensive card can be treated with a range of coatings to enhance its performance. Water- and oil-resistant laminates, for instance, can be applied for effective food packaging or other moisture-producing goods. Card is often coated purely to resist marking that can occur from frequent handling.

Other materials are regularly used in conjunction with card packaging to provide strength or to give extra visibility to the product. Acetate windows, for example, can be glued into position over an area that has been die-cut from the card sheet.

Intricate or fluid shapes cannot be easily constructed from card, so many of these designs are produced by using plastics and films. Injection moulding, in which melted plastic is forced into a mould, is widely used, though set-up costs can be high and only large production runs bring the unit cost down to acceptable levels. A popular type of plastic for packaging is PET (polyethylene terephthalate), which is easy to shape and good-looking.

Plastics use numerous chemicals in their manufacture and do not degrade quickly, making them difficult to use for products that in themselves are considered environmentally friendly. Designers need to be aware that materials can "speak" to the audience as clearly as graphic imagery does.

Glass, once a popular packaging material, has seen a decline in use. It is more temperamental than plastics such as PET, shatters easily, and cannot withstand extreme temperatures. However, its transparency, molding capabilities and self-coloring, together with its suitability for frosting and engraving, give it a tactile and aesthetic appeal, appropriate for giving products an unusually luxurious feel.

Metal, as a packaging material, accommodates extremes in packaging price points. At the lower end of the market it is used in great volume for tinned foods, aerosols, and oil containers, as well as being used for luxury goods, such as gift-set tins printed with interesting graphics—making them collectable once the contents have been used. Metal is also suitable for recycling as it is easy to melt down and re-form. Recent advances in manufacturing techniques enable steel, for example, to be used in surprisingly creative ways, whether for mass-market packaging or limited edition promotional items.

All materials have their own unique qualities and behavioral properties. A lot of packaging incorporates several materials that have to combine successfully. It is a good idea for designers to take the time to familiarize themselves with the capabilities and performance of each of the materials they intend using.

Understanding the purpose and function of a package design is of prime importance to the graphic designer. The major consideration for large, bulky items, such as computers, microwave ovens, and washing machines, is ensuring the packaging provides adequate protection and has prominent instructions for lifting and storage. In a retail environment large items are usually displayed unpacked, suggesting that compelling marketing graphics play a subordinate role in these instances. Despite this, there are manufacturers who use every opportunity to advertise their products and recognize that even large cardboard boxes offer a chance to promote the qualities of the product within.

KEY KNOWLEDGE

So diverse are the methods of packaging and materials used, that designers are constantly having to update their technical knowledge both in terms of production, digital software upgrades, and new applications designed both to facilitate and expand conceptual work and to create digital artwork.

Cutter guides are used frequently in the manufacture of card packaging. Printing card packaging is usually done by offset lithography and the steps taken by the graphic designer to create graphic files for reproduction are similar to those for any general design for a print job (see *Design for Print*). However, once the sheet is printed, it will then be cut, creased, and perforated in order to form a three-dimensional pack. The printed graphic work has to fit accurately within the physical shape to be cut in order to

display as intended. For this reason, cutter guides are supplied to designers (usually as EPS files) from which to work. These guides accurately show where the cuts, folds, and creases will be made, thus providing an accurate template for the designer to place the surface graphics.

Cutting and creasing equipment runs at high speeds so can have plus and minus tolerances and specific "bleed" allowances that have to be taken into account when graphic artwork files are prepared.

Different materials and packaging shapes may require a number of alternative methods of printing and/or have properties that might affect the overall design. For example, corrugated card has a coarse surface which, if uncoated, soaks up ink, and the fluting on the reverse side acts as a cushion, making printing flat areas or delicate halftone work difficult.

Flexographic printing (see page 112) is used to print onto rounded or curved surfaces, as on washing-up liquid bottles, although precise registration of colors is difficult to achieve. Fine text and hairlines also tend to suffer, breaking up and distorting as a matter of course. Transparent stickers are increasingly being used as a more accurate alternative with assured, high-quality, printed results—but at an increased cost.

Most metal packaging design is printed as flat sheets that are subsequently pressed or stamped into the required shape or component.

Unit cost is critical in the packaging industry. Print runs are usually very high compared to general publishing work. The number of colors, gluepoints, and separate processes in a pack design affect the production costs, so the designer's ingenuity and creative skills will often be exercised to the full when working with low-level budgets.

Safety in packaging demands care and consideration and can impose major restrictions on design. Packaging must protect toxic or sharp objects from being accessible to children, and all food products must have tamper-proof devices such as protective films, ring pulls, and pressure buttons on jar lids, incorporated into the pack design. Additionally, adequate warning or directional text (also in braille) have to be prominently displayed on packaging that contains any form of hazardous product.

PRODUCTION AND RECYCLING

Packaging briefs are usually more comprehensive than those for other areas of graphic design. In large retail organizations, the brief is usually drawn up by senior buyers after consultation with the manufacturer's marketing department. Marketing departments and manufacturers themselves may also commission designers directly. The product is often already in existence and the target consumer, retail outlets and a unit price for the packaging (as a proportion of the selling price) are already known.

Designers need to obtain as much of this information as possible and also consider potential modification and application of the design to future range extensions or different consumer markets. Clients are increasingly likely to use the same basic branding and packaging in different territories, particularly within Europe, meaning that the design must appeal equally to diverse groups of consumers and be capable of accommodating varying amounts and formats of text in the relevant languages.

Unit costs will determine the number of colors and construction methods that can be used, but inventively simplifying one aspect of a design allows elaboration of another.

If the product in question can be accommodated in a standard pack design, the creative process can begin straight away using the relevant templates from the manufacturer. Like brands themselves, packaging manufacturers are increasingly consolidated and global in outlook, and can offer a wide range of versatile ready-made designs with proven functionality and standards compliance. If the pack has to be purpose-made, the designer will usually need to confer with specialists in paper engineering, mould-making, die-stamping, or other manufacturing techniques. Glues, inks, materials, and assembly techniques are so varied that collaboration and research is essential. Many respected design companies now specialize in packaging, and employ both graphic and three-dimensional designers side by side to tackle bespoke projects. A broad range of skills will be an asset to any graphic designer competing in this marketplace.

Designs for two-dimensional or folded artwork can be created in a drawing program, with images imported from Adobe Photoshop. For more complex packaging, a CAD package—perhaps linking directly to manufacturing systems—will be more appropriate. Mock-ups can be generated on screen, or models can be exported to dedicated 3D rendering software for higher-quality visuals, putting off the need for a physical mock-up or prototype at least until the final stages of approval. Flat artwork can be sent as PDF files (see page 108) to the client, who can add comments on screen. As a final check, color contact proofs should always be obtained and hand-cut samples made up to check for errors in construction.

Final digital files should be prepared with great attention to dimensional accuracy and color specification before being sent to the production contractor.

DESIGN FOR SIGNAGE

AS THE CHINESE PROVERB GOES, "one hundred tellings are not as good as one seeing." Anyone who has ever taken a wrong turn, got lost, and asked for directions from a passer-by will know how confusing verbal directions can be.

Even hanging a small sign outside the local shop will need some thought. Will it be seen from the end of the street? What will it look like at night? How can it be cleaned? Will it need planning permission? Larger sign projects are even more involved. An ordered mind is needed to pull the complex threads of a signage system together.

This is the reason we have signs: to help us travel independently. Signs distil information to the absolute minimum, they speak to you just at the right moment, they keep us moving. Seeing one good sign is better than a whole crowd of helpful locals.

Signs are often considered as merely two-dimensional directional aids—as arrows on posts or lists fixed to walls. A lot of this type of signing surrounds us: construction sites use basic, temporary signs, hospitals need rigorously functional signs, and department stores rely on floor-by-floor directories to list each sales area.

But there are many opportunities to branch out into three dimensions, where signs can become an integral part of a company's identity and embody the spirit of their brand. On a larger scale, signs can also be landmarks or even adver-tisements. If the purpose of a sign is to help you identify your destination, then sculptures or even an icon such as the Statue of Liberty can also act as a sign—after all, the statue unmistakably proclaims "America" even without carrying the name. So signing can take many different forms. While conventional signs quietly go about their business directing you from point A, there are many other ways of announcing your arrival at point B.

SIGNAGE CONCEPTS

The graphic designer draws together creative expression and analytical problem solving. Sign design demands that the

Opposite: How large can you get? This sign just can't be missed—it not only signs Warner Bros flagship New York store but also keeps you up-to-date with the latest company successes. The sign is presented by one of Warner Bros' best assets, Bugs Bunny. A perfect mix of information and brand experience.
DESIGN BY THE PARTNERS, USA

analytical problem solving must come first, in order to inform creative expression appropriately.

Designers have to consider that many who momentarily glance at their signs will be on their way to somewhere else, wrapped up in their own worlds, engrossed in the exhibition they've come to see, finding their way to the train, or simply on the way to the toilet. In this sense, sign design can be a straightforward occupation—merely guiding a fellow human being from one place to another, without fuss or bother. That is when signs really work in the real world. However, to be able to achieve this functionality together with style, panache, and wit is the designer's creative challenge.

Sign design is a distinct area of graphic design in that signs take longer to plan, develop, make, and install than many other graphic design projects, with perhaps the exception of permanent exhibition projects (see *Design for Exhibition*). They are also around for a lot longer—making mistakes painfully lasting for the client (and the designer) involved. Signage is a design area that can also be very rewarding for the graphic designer in that it can make a significant contribution to a visitor's experience of a building or space.

DIGITAL TOOLS FOR SIGN DESIGN

Although sign design demands a different approach from many other areas of design, the tools a signage designer needs can be found in virtually any properly equipped design studio. Signage design requires strong type and graphics, so the key digital tools of this trade are either Adobe Illustrator or FreeHand—used for design, graphics production, and typesetting—and a good range of typefaces. Adobe Indesign or QuarkXPress is sometimes used, but it isn't really useful as a true drawing tool. Photoshop can

be invaluable for creating mock-ups of signs montaged into photographs, but is generally not that useful for actual artwork production. Similarly, three-dimensional modeling and CAD tools can be an asset for creating more effective presentations of work and might be used extensively by architects involved in the project, but aren't used for core design and production tasks.

Many signs are produced using cut-vinyl lettering and shapes. These are produced on

Above: The National Maritime Museum, London, internal signs. A simple sail and mast concept is a clever and appropriate design solution for a maritime museum. Note how the sign is held away from the brick work—a conventional flat wall-mounted sign would look "stuck on" as an afterthought. The brightly colored sails are easily spotted and the large type is very readable despite being on a curve.
DESIGN BY PENTAGRAM, UK

SURFACE DESIGN

vinyl-cutter machines, most of which can work happily with vector-based EPS graphic files exported from any professional drawing program. However, some less-common production tools, such as computer-controlled milling machinery for cutting and routing metal or wood items, may require other file formats. DXF is likely to be the format required in these cases. This format is more commonly used by CAD software, but Illustrator and FreeHand can export 2D DXF graphics when required. Note that type may need to be converted to editable shapes first to preserve the desired look and feel, and plan with the machinery operators to make some test runs before committing to a production schedule.

Silkscreen printing is a common print process, and lends itself to the reproduction of strong line artwork with flat colors. It is ideal for signs that have to withstand temperature and weather extremes, and exposure to public abuse. For more temporary uses, large-format digital printing is becoming increasingly popular. Digital printers can handle complex imagery with graduated tones and vignetting. These graphic techniques are very difficult to achieve using more traditional sign production processes. It is very cost-effective for short runs and one-off signs and posters, but the drawback is the fragility of the medium. Results are easily damaged, and in particular are prone to fading even when protected by lamination or encapsulation. More lightfast inks are being developed to address this problem, but be careful when considering this production method for anything but temporary signs.

SPECIALIST PROCESSES NEEDED FOR SIGNS

The environment in which signs are placed and the roles they play influence their physical construction and form. Only then does the designer have a surface upon which to work.

The signs shown in this section have all been influenced by their environment. They differ in a range of ways: visually, in the use of materials, and in manufacturing processes. Specialist processes for sign-making are almost limitless. The lifespan of signs lends itself to a wide range of durable materials including metal, glass, plastic, wood, stone, slate, woven fabric, and even leather. Lettering and images can be etched, cut out, routed, carved, or moulded.

New technologies also encourage experimentation with less permanent but more exciting media. Electroluminescent strips (a low-voltage alternative to neon) and panels can add an eye-catching glow or even constantly changing patterns to graphics on a variety of substrates. Bright, efficient LED lights allow focused and controllable illumination in a broader range of contexts. Large-format inkjet devices can print cheaply and in excellent quality onto paper, plastic, and fabric. Almost all of these diverse processes can now be driven directly from the designer's digital artwork files.

COMMUNICATION

The start of the sign creation process is to take an in-depth look at both the signage problem in hand and the client's brief. Once the designer is fully informed about the project, there are a few guiding principles that can help the design development.

It is good design practice to make signs simple, understandable, and to the point, as well as inventive where appropriate. The site is all-important and signs should be designed to integrate into, and function in, this environment. What might look eye-catching on screen in the studio might be lost in the vastness of a building space or when erected outdoors and placed on the horizon. It is imperative to be consistent throughout a scheme, remembering that one sign always follows another. Signs need to engender trust in the user by being both clear and consistent.

Signs must work for as many groups of people as possible, not just the average, but the tall, the short, the less sprightly and able, as well as those confined to wheelchairs. A surprising number of people have trouble with their eyesight. In some contexts multiple-language signs might be required. Signs obviously have to cater for everyone.

There are few rules covering colors, type sizes, and pictograms. However, the experienced graphic designer will know that color can be used effectively as a coding device and also that color choice and combinations are affected by different lighting conditions and any dominant colors within the sign system environment. Pictograms need to be unambiguous; they may entertain, but primarily they must inform, and the type size must be legible at the correct reading distances. Special-access groups often provide guidelines for designers; these may be incorporated into signage contracts. Common sense should always prevail, and the designer who focuses on selecting a robust typeface, an appropriate color palette, and using it in a creative but consistent way, will usually succeed.

CHOOSING A TYPEFACE

It is important to note that most of the typefaces available to designers today originate from letterforms developed for printing. Certain letterforms were drawn for use with particular printing processes, paper, or for a specific purpose such as for books or newspapers. Few letterforms have been specifically drawn for display and signing purposes, so designers should rigorously test their selected typeface at different sizes.

Any letter enlarged above 72pt will take on a new persona. Choosing a typeface for a sign system can therefore be rather difficult.

Sometimes the available range of typefaces, although vast, simply doesn't offer what a job needs. It is perfectly permissible to turn some type into editable drawn shapes in Illustrator or FreeHand, and then to tweak and modify shapes to get the letterforms you want. But remember that these won't be real editable typefaces, just letter shapes you can arrange by hand.

Letter spacing and individual letter pair kerning need particular attention in sign work. As signs carry relatively few words the structure of each word needs to be visually correct to ensure clarity and legibility (see *Design Basics*).

CHOOSING COLORS

Being able to read large text on a contrasting background is normally sufficient, but locating the sign in the first place can be a challenge. When considering a color scheme, the color of the sign itself should contrast with its environment. If colors are pre-determined—such as those of a corporate identity—it may be difficult to achieve a good contrast. In such instances, adding a distinctive but simple border round the sign, or using rules to break up text or inserting a special design feature for the visitor to look for may be a solution (see pages 38–41). Working with most graphic arts software will enable the designer to sample numerous colorways quickly and simply. A coordinated color palette can be achieved using the HSB (Hue, Saturation, Brightness) features. Select colors to emphasize information or to color-code areas.

Before picking a suitable set of colors, however, consult those involved with the final signage production. If, for instance, you're planning to use cut vinyl, your choices of color will be limited to those available in the material. This is also a production process that doesn't lend itself to the use of many overlapping colors. Learn as much about your intended sign-production process as possible, preferably from those who will be responsible for creating the actual signs, before committing to a particular set of designs.

POSITIONING

The designer's family of sign types (see *The Design Process*, page 28) will need to develop from the environment in which they are to be placed. So a typical sign family may comprise a free-standing structure, a wall-mounted or hanging sign, a statutory sign, and perhaps one or two individual variations for particularly tricky areas. Working with this family of sign types, a walk through the site (physically, electronically, or mentally) is needed to establish the earliest points at which a visitor needs to see each aspect of information.

Motorway signs are a good illustration of this principle. Users are usually traveling at great speeds so these signs are provided well before a turn-off—allowing time to get into the correct lane, slow down, and prepare for exiting. Placing signs ahead of the exit means that drivers remain calm, make no sudden movements and are able to get to where they want to go with relative ease. The same principles apply to all signs even at the comparatively gentle pace of walking through the foyer of an exhibition hall or strolling through a park. Repetition of information is not a problem—remember that visitors often enter environments from many different directions and the repetition of information will help nurture trust in the sign system.

Naturally, signs need to be positioned where they can be seen. The ideal is to locate signs so that information is presented just above normal eye level for general ease of reading, which will also accommodate wheelchair users—with tactile signs appropriately located for the partially sighted (which may be additional to the general sign system). However, the concentration of visitors in

A n t y e e A

| 1 | 2 | 3 | 4 | 5 | 6 | 7 |

When selecting a typeface for signage purposes you should take into account the following:

1.	Cap height	Should be high in proportion to width of letter
2.	X-height	Should be large (see *Designing with Type*, page 24)
3.	Ascenders	Should ideally be same as cap height
4.	Descenders	Should be as short as possible
5.	Counter shapes	Should be as open as possible
6.	Type design	Should be as strong as possible, with a selection of weights for emphasis
7.	Serifs (if used)	Should be strong—bracketed or slab

that particular area should always be considered. If signs are to be located in crowded areas there may be no other option but to place the signs higher so they can be read by everyone at all times even though this may be at a distance.

Lighting is a factor to consider when positioning a sign. What looks good on a screen presentation, doesn't always work in situ with the harsh glare from sunlight hitting a reflective sign surface. This glare may become a dark shadow later in the day—with the sign disappearing altogether at night if not illuminated. Avoid reflective materials, keep to matt finishes and ensure that signs are properly illuminated.

IMPLEMENTATION

Digital artwork can be prepared using a standard drawing application. Sign manufacturers may use their own specialist software for certain processes, so the designer's digital files will need to provide accurate information regarding type, spacing, and typeface. In some instances it may only be necessary to produce "master" artwork for a typical sign from each member of the sign family to serve as a control model. From these control models prototypes can be made and in turn used as the final controls for the complete system. A visit to the factory to check manufacture and fine detail is worthwhile as errors can be difficult to rectify at a later stage.

Sign manufacturers will usually be contracted to install the signs and during this crucial stage it is worth making daily visits to the site. On completion there will be a walk-around tour with the client to pick up on outstanding issues. Identifying these issues is known as "snagging."

Once the project is complete it is important that the client receives "as built" records for future maintenance. Meticulous filing, data back-up, and recording of the design drawings during the

development of the project can be transformed into a handover manual comprising instructions on maintenance, repair, and updating. This should also include all the final sign schedules; their positions set against floor plan journey routes, technical drawings, and fixing instructions.

MAINTENANCE

Good sign systems should last for many years since they are generally serious capital investments. Designers have to rely heavily on the professional expertise of sign manufacturers for advice on the practicalities of appropriate materials, paint finishes, fixing solutions, and other production processes.

It is important to convince the client that materials and build quality should never be cost driven—skimping on a second protective paint coating, to save on production costs, may result in rapid fading from the sun's ultraviolet rays after a few years. It is more expensive to replace a whole sign system earlier than normal, than it is to prepare more robust signs to begin with.

Vandal-proofing is an important factor in sign design. Signs should be strong enough to support physical abuse and their surfaces may have to withstand "tagging" with spray paint, marker pens, and relentless flyposting. Signs are a magnet for vandals so surfaces must be easy to clean and signs should be designed to enable quick replacement of component parts.

Such components need to be simple enough to order and to fit—ideally by the client's own maintenance teams. This is where the "as built" handover documentation becomes essential to the client. All final design solutions should detail each component part and provide ordering and fitting instructions. Self management is important to many clients, as their site activities may change in line with their business. Signs therefore may need to be frequently amended, taken down, or added to by the clients themselves.

PLANNING AND PRODUCTION

On large signing projects it is essential to become involved as early as possible. This helps the designer understand an architect's vision for a building or space, and this should influence the final signage solutions. It also provides the opportunity to integrate signs into the fabric of a site, thereby reducing the number of signs needed to be applied to wall surfaces.

DESIGN TEAM

If the project is a large one, there will be a number of parties involved. First, the client, who should outline the extent of the project and provide any corporate guidelines that may be applicable. Second, the architect, who should provide the brief on the thinking behind their design, the purpose of each space, and the materials to be used. The architect will be closely shadowed by a construction manager and a quantity surveyor who will supply delivery schedules, budgets, and liaise with other con-

Above: Signs for the visually impaired use color for maximum contrast so that a sign can first be located. Then, once drawn to it, the sign can be read using the raised tactile pictogram and braille.
DESIGN BY RNIB, UK

Right: Striking modern colors are used to help travelers to find their correct queuing areas at this bus station. The large-scale graphics contrast well with the background colors and are placed at a level above the crowds where they can still be read from quite a distance.
DESIGN BY ALLFORD HALL MONAGHAN MORRIS AND ATELIER, UK

tractors on the designer's behalf. Additionally, there will be a selection of interested parties including local planning authorities, fire and safety officers, access groups and possibly heritage organizations. And don't forget the users—they will need to be consulted, for instance through focus groups.

RESEARCH

The designer should start by studying the site plans thoroughly—not forgetting all the external approaches. Signs should be seen by the users before they arrive on site. The design team members should then be consulted individually and sounded out for their concerns for the project.

A site visit by the designer is important particularly for observing how people move through the space. If the environment is not yet built, designers should visualize themselves as visitors and walk their way through the plans. Journey routes and all possible destinations should be mapped. This process will indicate the points with the greatest number of intersections and decision-making points for visitors. These points are key sign positions. Lists of all the information a visitor may need to know at these points should be made. In preparing these lists it will be found that some are quite short, others long. The amount of information a sign has to carry and its position should dictate its physical form. For example, an extensive list of information might result in a large freestanding sign, whereas small amounts of information may necessitate a small, wall-fixed, or perhaps suspended sign. By examining the site, a family of signs will emerge. It is best to keep the family numbers to a minimum, as numerous sign variations will be not only more costly in manufacturing and future maintenance but also potentially confusing for the user.

THE DESIGN PROCESS

When the site has been fully researched, the designer should begin by designing a representative example of each member of the sign family. This can be done in most page-layout or drawing programs. These initial concepts should then be presented to the project team. It is best to make paper prints at full scale and stick them onto walls in situ, if possible, to help the project team understand the full impact of the concepts.

After client approval, the graphic designer will prepare a design specification for each sign type. Talking directly with the sign manufacturer is vital at this point. It will help with any necessary design refinement for production and costing, and the manufacturers should be willing to prepare early prototypes.

It is important for the graphic designer to be fully involved in the preparation of prototypes,

the tender documents, and in reviewing the tender submissions. In cost-driven projects, designers often find themselves being the sole champion for quality. Accepting the lowest tender for a sign system can be a false economy as quality may suffer, resulting in a higher incidence of damage, repair, or replacement. A close working relationship between the designer and the sign manufacturer is essential if the preparation of artwork is to be trouble-free.

DEVELOPING A HIERARCHY OF INFORMATION

Who will be the main users of the signs and what information should they carry at what point? This information should be ordered according to its level of importance. For example, in a public building such as a performance venue the main user will be a member of the audience. First they will want to know where the box office is in order to pick up their tickets, then where the auditori-

um is, which side to enter from to get to their seat, and how much time they have before they have to take their seat. They may want refreshments and to sit down while they wait, or they may want to find the cloakroom.

Understanding the user's requirements helps the designer organize the placing of elements on a sign and determines the level of emphasis. By taking on the role of a member of the audience, the designer will probably arrive at the following hierarchy: box office, auditorium, seat numbers, clock, café, and cloakroom. Obviously the box office is a key source of information and will be in large type along with directions to the auditorium. The clock needs to be nearby and easily readable from the sign point. Seat numbers are another level of detail and can be smaller. Facilities such as the café and cloakrooms can be indicated using pictograms. Thus, an information hierarchy emerges directly from identifying the needs of the user.

Opposite: A freestanding museum sign that can be removed when the space is needed. The clear information is shown at eye level downwards, allowing wheelchair users to read in comfort.
DESIGN BY ATELIER, UK

Right: In the 1970s, French designer Jean Widmer and a team of specialists examined the legibility and positioning of motorway signs. One of his recommendations was to position exit signs at 2km and 1.5km ahead of the slip road as well as on it.

THE THIRD DIMENSION Graphic designers working on exhibitions face the challenge of creating a thematic design for viewing in large spaces at a human scale and in a variety of different dimensions.

DESIGN FOR EXHIBITION

They must be able to think three-dimensionally, often having to visualize the exhibition space from architectural drawings and consider the general themes, atmosphere, tone, and messages that need to be communicated to the audience.

The overall visual identity, the display panels, and the accompanying publicity material—the two-dimensional aspects of an exhibition—are the main responsibility of the graphic designer. Digital technology makes for imaginative and flexible design and production, and also allows for easy sharing and exchanging of files by email or ISDN—a great advantage in exhibition design, which can involve designers from many disciplines working together towards a common goal.

The three-dimensional aspect of exhibition design is produced by specialized exhibition designers, who may have had architectural or interior-design training but can equally come from a variety of backgrounds. Spatial awareness, developing themes with a narrative, interpreting subject matter effectively, working closely with the graphic designer, communicating to the target audience, and producing detailed working drawings (on AutoCAD) for contractors are all paramount to the exhibition designer.

Although it is not absolutely necessary for the graphic designer to be familiar with CAD drafting programs or packages such as form•Z, which are used to create walk-through vistas, both of these tools are often integral to the exhibition design process. It is also useful for members of the design team to be able to exchange and understand each other's digital files. Graphic designers working on exhibitions normally produce flat artwork for panels using vector-based software, such as Adobe Illustrator, FreeHand, InDesign, or QuarkXPress, which allows for scaling up without loss of quality. Images scanned or created in Photoshop can be imported into all these programs along with text files.

Opposite: Oversized display banner, Times Square, New York. Banners can now be printed onto an extensive variety of materials, in huge sizes, sometimes covering whole sides of buildings. In Times Square, waterproof banners such as these provide an alternative to neon, LCD, and lenticular displays.

EXHIBITION OPTIONS

Exhibitions vary widely in their nature and complexity, and so can assume a variety of shapes, sizes, and forms. However, conveying the message appropriately is key to every situation, whether the context is a simple panel system or a full-blown major exhibition.

The simplest cost-effective way to communicate a message to an exhibition audience is to use portable panel systems. These can take the form of multiple, flat-panel, and fascia configurations, pop-up, telescopic wire-framed structures or pull-up, single canvas panels. These modular exhibition systems allow simple, digital graphic panels to be economically produced on a wide range of materials, including paper, PVC, gauze, cotton, and canvas. Graphics designed for these systems need to be durable and light. This type of exhibition or display is used wherever portability is an important consideration.

Shell schemes are a cost-effective solution to exhibiting at trade shows. Supplied by the organizers, they consist of standardized units that feature power and lighting, to which individual company fascia and wall panels can be attached. They form part of the overall trade show personality.

Alternatives to shell schemes consist of three-dimensional designs built by specialist contractors and are much more expensive.

Purpose-built exhibitions are usually complex, high-budget design concepts built for a specified time span ranging from a two- to four-week-long trade show to a temporary year-long exhibition or permanent museum gallery. These exhibitions are built to a design created by a specialist exhibition designer and, whether long or short term, are built to last for only a designated period. The graphic designer's role involves designing and overseeing the production of the exhibition identity and related design publicity material,

often in the form of oversized, digitally printed banners and introductory vinyl cutout lettering. It is the responsibility of the designer to specify the correct materials for mounting, sealing, and finishing graphic panels. The durability of materials used is dictated by the size of the budget and is directly proportionate to the lifespan of the exhibition.

Permanent exhibitions may have a lifespan of ten years, sometimes more, and tend to be located in museums or galleries. The planning stage of such exhibitions can spread over several years. Large budgets and maintenance programmes are necessary to keep them in pristine condition, and to support areas within the exhibition that have to be reworked due to changes in science or popular thinking. The designer's role, however, normally ends when the completed design is "handed over" to the client.

Educational exhibitions, which may be long or short term, are concerned with communicating complex concepts in an effective and inspirational way. Subject specialists liaise with educationalists and designers to ensure that teaching points can be clearly interpreted by the audience. Interactive devices, although expensive, can significantly enhance these key teaching points, encouraging audience participation and adding greatly to the educational experience.

In situations where a purpose-built exhibition needs to travel, a whole new set of criteria has to be taken into account. Durability, packing, weight, and possible language issues need to be addressed, particularly if the exhibition is touring abroad, and a successful traveling exhibition will, wherever possible, make inventive use of panel stands as packing cases. The graphic designer normally designs accompanying touring manuals, giving clear instructions on installation and dismantling.

Above: Guggenheim Museum exhibition on the work of the architect Frank Gehry. Gehry's drawings, enlarged and printed onto the walls, show his interest with capturing a sense of motion in his work. To produce this effect, the artwork was printed onto the maximum width of paper available—virtually any length is possible, but widths are dependent upon the roll of paper the printer takes—mounted onto MDF, and heat-sealed or wrapped for installation.

DESIGN BY GUGGENHEIM MUSEUM, USA

DIGITAL PRODUCTION

Digital technology has radically changed the labor-intensive and limited production of exhibition graphics. This once depended on photo enlargements and photo techniques as the core origination media. Designers can now be much more ambitious. As technology develops, the creation of digital artwork and digital production becomes a more comprehensive and integrated procedure. The extensive capabilities of giant ink-jet (or bubble-jet) printers allow for artwork files to be run out at virtually any size and on a variety of substrates. Transparencies are scanned to produce high-resolution digital files, and the designer combines these with text and other images. Retouching and manipulating images in Photoshop allows total freedom. Areas of interest or special significance can be highlighted or played down by modifying color and contrast.

Laser-cut type output from digitized artwork allows for great flexibility—virtually any design can be converted into a path for the laser-cutting program. Matt and gloss vinyls are available in a wide choice of colors, and self-adhesive, frosted films can be used to give the illusion of sand-blasting onto clear surfaces. Raised type can also be laser-cut using polystyrene or metallic finishes—almost anything is possible. Spacers mounted between wall and lettering can create the illusion of depth and shadow. Different types of surfaces can be built up to provide a three-dimensional finish.

Silkscreen printing (see page 112) panels and graphic surfaces is a far more labor-intensive, high-budget process than producing prints digitally. It does, however, produce a sharp image in beautifully flat, hard, and durable inks that can be matched to the PANTONE system, unlike digital output, which can only simulate PANTONE colors with varying results. Silkscreening also makes it possible to print directly onto glossy, curved surfaces. The use of "tough inks" eliminates the need for protective sealing, and allows matt and gloss finishes to be mixed.

MULTIMEDIA EXHIBITIONS

The use of multimedia adds an exciting dimension to exhibition design and provides almost limitless opportunities to feed the designer's imagination. Multimedia productions can be projected onto panels or played either on freestanding monitors or on screens set into part of the exhibition structure.

Lenticular panels, created from a high-tech photographic process, provide a low-tech form of animation, with images changing as the viewer walks past. Touch screens—now typically based on flat LCD screens—can be used at a range of sizes to show animated or interactive programs, increasing audience involvement with few moving parts to go wrong. Whatever the interactive designers and engineers may come up with, it will be the job of the graphic designer to integrate its look and feel into the exhibition as a whole.

Lighting is a vitally important part of exhibition design. Gobos—small metal or glass discs with either cut or printed designs—can be added to electronically controlled lamps or projectors to create visual patterns that move slowly, in preset sequences, or in dramatic swooping movements. Projected onto floors, ceilings, and walls or thrown along gallery spaces, these can reinforce themes or individual exhibits, attract attention to awkward corners, and highlight entrances and exits. Colored gels can be added to match colorways.

LED lights are more attractive, versatile, and energy-efficient than conventional tungsten or fluorescent lamps, and can be incorporated into almost any display. Fiber-optic systems use a single light source to drive multiple illumination points with sweeping, rippling, or twinkling color effects.

ERGONOMICS

The graphic designer is responsible for providing visuals and digital artwork for all the graphic panels, labels, and interactive exhibit components throughout the exhibition. These are produced at a convenient scale that is compatible with the size of the panels.

Viewing ergonomics are particularly important, and it is essential to produce a full-size mock-up of a typical panel before spending time developing a design too far. This enables you to check the effectiveness of size and height of titles, text, and captions. Lighting conditions also need to be taken into account, as they can radically affect legibility. As a general guide, unless you are designing for very young children, the average eye-level should be set at 1.5m with the majority of the text not falling much below hip-height.

The spacing and arrangement of panels should facilitate overall understanding of the subject matter. Visitor flow and avoidance of bottlenecks is usually the responsibility of the specialized three-dimensional designer, but the graphic designer also needs to be aware of these aspects in considering the arrangement of information.

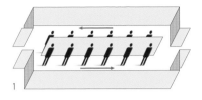

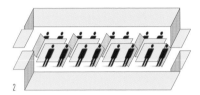

1.

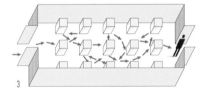

2.

3.

4.

5.

1. Partitioning the space creates an orderly flow of visitors around centrally placed exhibits.
2. Dividing the space into smaller manageable areas aids comprehension and allows the subject matter to be broken down into logical units.
3. Regimented positioning, allowing random circulation.

4. Regimented positioning with regimented circulation.
5. Random positioning allowing random circulation. The solution you choose should be dictated by the subject matter.

Above: Designs for metal gobos, From The Beginning, Natural History Museum, London. Lasers are used to cut intricate designs from metal discs. When installed into a projector system, colored lights can be shone through, and the resulting image made to move through gallery spaces, giving another dimension to the exhibition design.

DESIGN BY EXHIBITION PLUS AND PERKS WILLIS DESIGN, UK

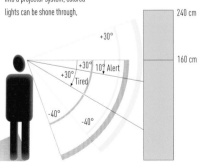

Above: Ergonomic data showing natural viewing heights and angles, and areas of optimum visibility. The upper segment of the display should be viewed from about two meters away to successfully scan the information.

The design of the exhibition identity, including a versatile logo and a related family of associated elements, is of prime importance since it has to carry the visitor through the entire exhibition. Where the brief is to design an exhibition for an organization that has its own distinct and well-structured corporate identity, the implementation of the scheme needs to be faithful and accurate in every rendition—a detailed manual may be available from the company for guidance on this.

THE PLANNING PROCESS

Planning an exhibition can be a lengthy process. Agreeing budgets, research, finding locations, and checking cost effectiveness must be completed before the design team is appointed. In practice this means that the graphic designer has to be flexible enough to work with restricted budgets and accommodate (or tactfully challenge) preconceived ideas.

The graphic designer's initial role is to formulate the overall design concepts and produce preliminary designs for key panels and related elements for client approval. The style of typography, illustration, and photography, and the processes needed to realize them, must be clearly identified. Illustrators, photographers, and picture researchers have to be commissioned as well as any other experts including lighting designers or multimedia specialists.

Once a writer has supplied a cohesive script for the exhibition, the specialized three-dimensional designer produces detailed plans and elevations. The graphic designer, in turn, has to produce a comprehensive panel specification document to enable contractors to see and understand the full extent of the job. Estimates are then sought to ensure that the intended scheme is feasible within the allocated budget, and the project goes out to tender. When budgetary requirements are met and contractors appointed, design production can begin. The graphic designer then produces digital printouts of single flat-panel designs and views of key sections of the exhibition, using a combination of graphic arts software to simulate realistically the three-dimensional environment. As colors vary dramatically from screen to printer, and from the desktop to the press, constant monitoring is essential to ensure consistency. In order to minimize expensive mistakes, individual components of each exhibit are turned into artwork that needs to be approved and signed off by the client before it is sent away for production.

A graphics issue sheet should be designed to tie in with the specification document, to detail and track each component of the artwork. This sheet should accompany every piece of artwork, together with annotated color visuals, TIFF and EPS files, fonts, etc. Unlike other areas of graphic design, the exhibition graphic designer may well be providing artwork to a number of different contractors (in different digital formats) for a range of different specialized components, including multimedia, animation, or video editing.

Before panel artwork is mounted and sealed to its substrate, a visit with the client to the photographic contractor for the final approval should be planned. Delivery to the site can take place when the finished design is mounted and sealed, but panels will need to be checked again for possible damage, on site, prior to installation.

Right: Artwork for kite-shaped graphic panels. The original artwork was produced traditionally using ink on lineboard. This was then scanned, and turned into Adobe Illustrator paths that had color added to them.

ILLUSTRATION DEBBIE COOK AND COLIN MIER.

Designs for glass gobos, used to shoot images up and down the gallery. Glass gobos, while not as durable as metal, allow for more flexible use of colors.

Above and right: The matt-laminated kite-shaped graphics and side banners were fixed to the bamboo poles using colored ties. Interactive exhibits were attached to thick horizontal poles arranged around oil cans or trestle units. Colored vinyl symbols were applied to the lower surfaces to further enhance the themes.

SCREEN DESIGN

3

THE IMPACT OF THE INTERNET revolution upon our lives is undisputed. The growth of websites continues at an unprecedented rate, and the challenge for the graphic designer to apply traditional design practices in this digital environment is an exciting and sometimes daunting one.

DESIGN FOR THE INTERNET

In the early days of the Internet, web page construction was a relatively simple process. The constraints of the medium meant that technical and design considerations amounted to little more than positioning small images in relation to text. Today, the role of the web designer has expanded considerably. New technology and improved functionality on the web has meant that designers can now employ movies, sound, and animation to enhance the user's experience. With technologies such as Adobe Flash, now supported by most personal computers, dynamic, highly interactive web content has become commonplace. One result of this progress is that the gap between the early programmers of the Internet revolution and the pure graphic designer has narrowed to the point where the two disciplines are now inextricably linked. The designer has far more scope for creativity, but in return must learn new technical skills.

It is in this rapidly changing arena that designers can make their mark, using the powerful tools at their disposal to create successful designs and solutions that communicate to a universal audience. They must take stock of emerging technologies and strike a balance between applying proven design principles and exploring technology-driven possibilities. At the same time, success is increasingly dependent on adherence to a range of technical standards.

The range of websites on which designers might be called to work is as varied as the web itself, from educational, cultural, and non-profit organizations to ambitious commercial and financial ventures. Rebranding of existing corporate identities forms a major proportion of web design work, and many companies who entered the online marketplace early have discovered the need to rethink their web presence every couple of years. As new tools make activities such as e-commerce easier to realize, there is an ever-growing need

Opposite middle: This site contains urban photographs taken by the German designer Daniel Althausan. Pictures are displayed by category: city people, traffic, and abstract. Subject matter ranges from Amsterdam station at sunrise to passengers traveling on a train. It has a lean yet lively interface making navigation easy and interesting.
DESIGN BY DANIEL ALTHAUSEN, GERMANY

Opposite bottom: A well planned and highly animated site designed with Flash. Lots of interactivity and added music make for a lively site tour.
DESIGN BY IMAGINATION, UK

Left: Memphis Notebook, an online magazine dedicated to art and design. The site is laid out like a print publication with predominately textual content. However, the use of large photographic images mixed with unusual typography ensures it is far from boring.

DESIGN BY MEMPHIS, USA

for effective visual interfaces. In all, the graphic designer is sure to find challenging and varied prospects within the world of Internet design.

THE WEB DESIGNER'S ROLE

Computers all over the world are connected via the Internet by the use of common "protocols" to transmit and receive information. The idea of a network to share information over great distances was conceived in America in the 1960s for military communications. It rose to public attention in the early 1990s with the invention of the World Wide Web by British academic Tim Berners-Lee, allowing the delivery of pages of text and images using a relatively simple programming code.

In so far as it can be separated from the general process of constructing a site, the graphic designer's role is to produce an appropriate visual structure for web pages. The fundamentals of design—layout, color, type, and imagery—remain the same as in other media, but the nature of on-screen layout—the variety of screen sizes and shapes, beyond the designer's control—the delivery, and the technicalities of the web add many unique concerns.

To an extent, a graphic designer can play a useful part in the conception of a site without needing learn new tools. The basic appearance can be worked out in Adobe Photoshop or other graphics software, before being built by web designers. In practice, however, it will normally be essential to consider the precise possibilities and limitations of the medium before visualizing the design. These will depend on the technologies chosen to drive the site, which in turn will be selected according to its purpose, nature, target audience, and budget.

Nonetheless, a grasp of the core graphic design software is as good a starting point as in any area of digital design. You will need to build on this with some knowledge of one or more key web design packages. How far you take this depends on whether you plan to deliver mock-ups and guidelines to teams of code writers, create the complete site yourself, or strike some balance between the two. Graphic designers employed within web design companies are best placed to develop the necessary skills, as they will quickly discover which aspects need to be learned in depth and which can be left to other roles.

Interactivity and user interface design are the other key skills you will need to develop. The web's "non-linear" navigation, where users can jump around a site by clicking links, makes clear navigation an essential feature of every site.

HOW THE INTERNET WORKS

Everything that forms part of a web page is contained in packets of digital data that must be transferred from the site's server to the user's computer. Web pages are created using HTML (Hypertext Markup Language), which is received by the user's computer and deciphered by browser software that renders the page on screen according to standards devised by the World Wide Web Consortium (www.w3.org). Images, Flash animations, and other content are received and rendered as part of the process.

Currently in development is HTML5, an emerging set of standards that include increased interactivity features—the chief of which is video—as a result, content formerly produced by plug-ins such as Adobe Flash can be created with HTML5. Increasingly supported by modern browers, such as Safari, Mozilla Firefox, and Google Chrome, HTML5 is crucially the only way to create video content for Apple's iPhone- and iPad-based advertising platforms.

DIGITAL TOOLS FOR INTERNET DESIGN

Internet design is done with a mixture of general-purpose design tools and software specific to web work. Web page editors include Adobe Dreamweaver, Microsoft Expression, and SoftPress Freeway. Of these, Dreamweaver is the first choice among professionals, regarded as the most mature solution, capable of generating highly compatible and standards-compliant pages. Freeway—available only for Macs—lacks technical credibility, but offers layout tools familiar to graphic designers.

Graphic content can be produced using Adobe Photoshop, or Fireworks, a program for optimizing images for web use. Flash content is best created using Adobe Flash, although simple animations can be made in Adobe Illustrator or FreeHand. (Flash is the most used format to deliver scalable vector graphics on the web, although drawing programs can be used to create graphics which are then rasterized at the required size.)

Flash enables enhanced embedding of SWF and FLV files with Dreamweaver CS5. Photoshop lets you drag and drop PSD files directly onto your Dreamweaver page, and maintain a live link between the source PSD file and the optimized image, while in Fireworks you can import CSS layouts directly into Dreamweaver.

H.264 is a codec that forms the basis of HTML5 video content. While Flash is currently the leading way to stream video on the web, HTML5 is in the ascendency. It can be made with anything from Apple iMovie to Final Cut, or Adobe Premiere.

Right: Graphic design for the web covers many different media and purposes. Here, a marketing email for online fashion website ASOS.com is thoughtfully designed like a magazine page—enticing subscribers to read, while also providing numerous links to the site, encouraging readers to browse and buy.

Website planning

There are a number of important organizational concerns that will be relevant to any web-design project. These need to be addressed systematically and should be embedded into the normal work-flow pattern to ensure that the creative team and the client remain in agreement during, and after, the production process.

MANAGING CLIENTS

It never pays to keep a client in the dark during any stage of a project. The client needs to under-stand the production process in as much detail as possible and to be aware of how different kinds of changes to the site will affect the overall cost. Once this is made clear, the problem of "feature creep," which involves a client con-tinually asking for small changes to the site specification, is less likely to occur. For the same reason, it's essential to work with a detailed printed brief that lists the job specification in full and to work to an agreed schedule.

SCHEDULES AND DELIVERABLES

For deadlines to be met, the client must supply information, material, and feedback in a timely manner, just as you must supply the site's design and completed pages. You should set a system in place that lets you to move your deadline should information or material come in late.

Conducting a client survey is the best way to find out what's expected of you. Remember that it's easy for a person unintentionally to monopolize the development of his or her company's site, or to "shield" individuals who they feel may not fully understand the technology involved. So ask your contact to circulate your questionnaire to all the company's major decision-makers.

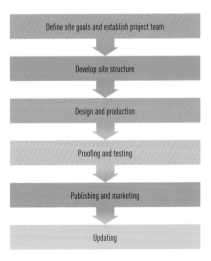

Define site goals and establish project team

Develop site structure

Design and production

Proofing and testing

Publishing and marketing

Updating

SCREEN DESIGN

Typical client survey form

This form shows some of the typical questions that you will need your client to answer. Every question should be as open as possible, to avoid the possibility of simple "yes" or "no" answers. You should also impose a strict deadline by which it should be returned. Some of the questions, for example those listed under "Technical Details," hinge on thorough audience research having already taken place. If this has not happened, then it must be done before the client survey is completed.

Define overall goals and what's required in terms of look and feel.

Check which departments will be most closely involved in updating and developing the site.

Obtain feedback from the users of the client's current website (if they have one).

Addressing Your Audience

✓ What is the main message that you want to convey?

✓ List any secondary objectives

✓ How will your company benefit from the site?

✓ What is your target audience?

✓ How does your target audience differ from your current one?

✓ Who are your main competitors?

✓ List the URLs of your competitors' websites

✓ What is your USP (unique selling point)?

Defining Your Site

✓ How would you like people to describe your site?

✓ Do you wish to change customers perceptions of your company?

✓ Are there aspects of your existing marketing materials and corporate identity that you want continued on the site? (Note: you should always recommend to clients that their marketing material has common elements across all media.)

✓ List any websites that you think work well and describe why you think they are successful.

✓ Are there things about your competitors' websites that you like or dislike?

Site Content

✓ Will your site use existing material? If so, who will supply it and in what form is it currently available? For example, as DOCs, PDFs, JPEGs, etc. Please supply as many details as possible, stating document and image file types/extensions.

✓ If the answer to the previous question was "no," will you be generating your own new material or outsourcing this task? Please supply full contact details of third parties involved.

✓ Who is to be responsible for supplying said content?

✓ Who is responsible for approving website content?

Technical Details

✓ Which platform(s) and browser(s) have been identified for your target audience? Note: clients should be advised to follow a web standards path (see www.w3c.org), so that information is available to all web-enabled devices.

✓ Will your site use a database? If so, do you already have a database in place? Please give full details of software used to create the database, and any hosting issues that you may have already sorted.

✓ Give full details of any e-commerce transactions you wish to undertake from your site.

Marketing Plans

✓ What are your plans to promote and develop the site?

✓ How do you intend to circulate knowledge of the website within your company?

Administration Details

✓ How do you intend to keep the site updated?

✓ What is the proposed launch date for the site? List all factors relating to this, such as tie-in with a product launch.

✓ Do you already have a domain name registered? If not, do you have any thoughts concerning a potential name?

✓ What is your proposed budget for the site. Consider phasing in parts of the site over time to ease budgetary constraints. (Note: if clients want a phased approach, they must be aware that this will end up costing more than doing the whole thing at once.)

Website production

It goes without saying that a team comprising individuals who are aware of their distinct roles and responsibilities is more likely to work well than one in which confusion reigns. However, you'll find people involved in the web-design industry often take on a number of roles simultaneously. This is down to several reasons. The explosive growth of the web meant people were often given roles because they knew more than anyone else rather than because they were proficient or particularly skilled. The "multi-talented" idea stuck, though, and today you'll often find highly trained and professional individuals who, for instance, are art director, coder, and programmer all rolled into one.

Despite this, the following roles are essential, even in small teams. In some cases, individuals may take on more than one role, but always ensure said individuals are fully capable of the roles—particularly in larger projects, where separation of role tends to be more important. In some cases, you may have to outsource, or employ freelancers.

PROJECT MANAGER

The person in this role is responsible for client relations and seeing the site through from start to finish. He or she is a troubleshooter who makes sure there are strong lines of communication within the team and with the client.

ART DIRECTOR AND DESIGNER

The art director often also works as the designer. He or she must be aware that print and web design are very different (for instance, web files, being necessarily smaller than print files, must be optimized appropriately), and that all page elements must work within the overall interface. An awareness of platform and browser issues, a familiarity with HTML and CSS (Cascading Style Sheets), along with an understanding of how the Internet operates—usability, navigation, accessibility, and so on—are all prerequisites for a good web designer. Designers tend to work up a layout in a graphics editor, and work closely with the coder to ensure that the design is feasible.

EDITOR AND WRITER

Text often needs to be restructured to work adequately well on a scrolling web page, and in order to include links and to work with search engines. Furthermore, because text is trickier to read on screen than in print, web text usually needs to be succinct. Such restructuring is done by the editor, who may also be the writer of some or all of the text. This person may be employed by your client or by your own organization, where he or she will have responsibility for updating the site's content. Many clients will insist on writing copy themselves. Explain to them that writing is a specialist skill and poor writing can be as detrimental as poor design. If a client is willing to spend money to get a great-looking, usable website, they should be willing to ensure the text is of a professional quality, too.

CODER/HTML SPECIALIST

This role tends to blur with both designer and programmer. However, if roles are distinct and separate, a coder is likely to take the layout created by the designer, export the relevant graphics, and then rework it in HTML and CSS. They must ensure the site's pages download quickly, work as intended, and meet relevant web standards, thereby working across target browsers and platforms. Depending on their personal preference, coders may work in a visual application, such as Dreamweaver, and then tweak code, or hand code in a text-editor.

PROGRAMMER/BACK-END ENGINEER

This dedicated role often blurs with that of the coder, because programmers may also be responsible for markup and scripts. However, if the roles are distinct, then this role tends to encompass complex interaction and, more frequently, database integration. Because of the various technologies available, you may need to source someone with the specific skills for your projects (e.g. someone versed in PHP or ASP)— someone who is perfect for one site may not be suitable for another.

Site map

The structure of a website is best represented graphically through a site map. All the sections of the site are shown, together with the links between pages and their relationship to the home page. It's an opportunity to make sure that the way the navigation works really makes sense; you'll be able to see what happens if a person accesses the site from a page other than the home page, or how easy it might be to move from one section to another if some navigation is linear.

Site testing

It's valuable for everyone involved in the project to become involved in testing. Once testing has taken place, it's time to proceed with a Beta launch. The site at that point should have full functionality and will be almost ready for release. Testing should ideally take place under the conditions that the site will often face—for example, with multiple transactions occurring simultaneously. At this point, if possible, you should also aim to do some user testing, with people who haven't been privy to the development and therefore don't know how the website "should" work.

Updating

Unless your organization employs an editor to work on websites, your client survey should have identified who will be responsible for carrying out updates of the site's content. Once the site is nearing completion, you should put together a schedule for updates and clarify the method that will be used for doing so. This will largely depend on the scale of the website and the skills of the client's team. They may have a budget to get a web designer/coder in-house, who can work directly with the source files, using the likes of Dreamweaver. Simple edits may be possible in Adobe's Contribute, which enables updates to be done without the need to edit code. Alternatively, you may have included a content management system, enabling updates to text and images to be done via a proprietary interface or via a web browser. Always keep a back-up of the completed website files.

AS THE SOFTWARE available for web design has become more refined in recent years, the choice of which application to use has become fairly straightforward.

Web-design software

One day, it should be possible to create web pages in much the same way as print designers create page layouts using applications such as QuarkXPress or Adobe Indesign. Just as no one working with QuarkXPress needs to know how to write PostScript (the programming language optimized for printing graphics and text), web designers won't have to understand things like HTML (Hypertext Markup Language, the code used for creating web pages; see *HTML Commands*, pages 170–173 and *CSS* (Cascading Style Sheets, used to style web page elements), pages 174–177.

HTML-EDITING SOFTWARE
Direct knowledge of code manipulation is perhaps less important than it was during the 1990s. However, most web-design applications do still provide you with easy access to the underlying code, for those occasions where you want to tweak things, perhaps to get around browser bugs.

The most common such applications is Adobe Dreamweaver. Mac users also have an alternative: Softpress Freeway, an application that resembles a DTP application. Coders and developers may also choose to work in non-WYSIWYG environments and use simple text editors.

Dreamweaver is the market leader because it is geared to workflow around key modern web standards, such as CSS.

THE DESIGNER'S CHOICE
In a team where there is a split between designers (working with the graphical elements of the site) and developers (who tend to work solely with code), the usefulness of WYSIWYG editors rapidly becomes apparent. For instance, Dreamweaver's Design View is often used by designers as a clean layout tool, while developers deal with the site functionality using a mixture of pre-built elements and by writing and editing code, still in the same file in Dreamweaver, but this time straight into Code View.

Ultimately, you should never forget that applications such as Dreamweaver automatically generate HTML. After any drag-and-drop task using, for example, Dreamweaver's Design View (in which the code cannot be seen), it's easy to view the code, see what's been generated, and make any necessary changes. It's also worth ensuring that all of your team is on the same page with regards to web standards. If, for instance, you have to conform to strict accessibility standards, then designers will have to avoid many of the built-in behaviors supplied with their applications.

Hands-on HTML

There are a number of reasons why anyone working with web pages should be ready to edit some HTML and, while these reasons never amount to an argument for creating commercial websites exclusively by hand-coding, they do continue to present a strong argument for designers to know their way around the basics of HTML, CSS, and perhaps a scripting language such as JavaScript. For example, even the best visual web-page-design tools don't produce entirely "valid" code (that is, code that fully conforms to recognized standards). The code might work perfectly in one browser, but not another, thereby hampering the ideal cross-browser and cross-platform approach that all web designers should aspire to. Furthermore, an appreciation of how HTML works provides a designer with an understanding of things like semantic markup—that is, using the correct HTML tags in context and for the means that they were designed for.

This argument runs particularly strongly when applied to CSS styles (see pages 174–177), where the code has a direct effect on the site design. Furthermore, there are occasions when advanced scripting simply cannot be achieved in Dreamweaver's Design View, thereby "forcing" you to get your hands dirty and write code directly.

Image editing

Adobe Photoshop and Fireworks tend to be the most common choices. Fireworks excels in being able to easily combine vectors and bitmaps, but Photoshop has superior tools for bitmap editing and color adjustment. With regard to general workflow for the web, both now have a fairly similar toolset and both are capable applications; which one designers use often tends to be down to personal preference.

Interactivity and animation

Once you move away from the static page and into the fields of interactivity and animation, Flash is by far the most popular application. The plug-in is almost a standard, and ActionScript, the language that enables Flash movies to have such complex properties, now enables designers and developers to create highly complex projects. Other specialist alternatives are available: animators will appreciate the features in Toon Boom Studio, while 3D modeling and animation are handled well by Swift 3D—and both deliver work in the Flash SWF file format. One other alternative is Adobe Director. Although perhaps more suited to CD-ROM production, it's worth bearing in mind for highly advanced interactive online projects.

Right: Try a CSS tutorial on www.w3schools.com, a website offering free web building tutorials and references.

BASIC TERMINOLOGY The technology and the language associated with the web may seem impenetrable to newcomers to this aspect of design.

Web terms and technologies

Although it's been decades since the first web pages appeared, we would still recognize them today as the fundamentals of the basic language used to create them has changed little. HyperText Markup Language (HTML), however, is limited on its own and is really only intended for structural markup of a page. Therefore, other technologies have become increasingly important: CSS for styling web-page elements; JavaScript for enabling basic interaction; various players and plug-ins for accessing and viewing movies and games; and more. Spend any amount of time on the web and you'll find many pages that display all manner of audio/visual content, and those that receive data typed up by site visitors and sent off to be processed or stored in databases. The following terms and acronyms offer a guide to some of today's web technologies.

ASP

ASP (Active Server Pages) is a Microsoft technology for the creation of dynamic web pages. It is often used for database integration and for the combination of ActiveX objects with HTML.

APPLET

An applet is a complete program written using Java (which is entirely different to JavaScript despite the name) and included on a web page, rather like an image might be. Viewed with a Java-capable browser, the code is first transferred to the site visitor's system, where it is then run by a "Java Virtual Machine" (JVM), making it OS-neutral. Applets are often best avoided, because they can cause stability issues. Applets can be used for virtually anything from newsfeeds and forms to animations and games.

BACK END

Back-end programs are usually those that run on the server side, such as databases. Data that is processed at the back end is normally sent to a "front end," or client side, program, such as a web browser, where it is viewed by the user.

CGI (COMMON GATEWAY INTERFACE)

CGI refers to server-side scripts, often written in the scripting language Perl, that allow web pages to contain dynamic actions—that is, actions that involve information being delivered from the user's machine back to the host server. For example, a simple form (on which the user is asked to input details such as name, email address, etc.) on a web page might connect to a CGI script to process the data that the visitor inputs.

A CGI script can be accessed directly by the user, just like a web page, and deliver HTML-formatted data back to the browser. Alternatively, it can be called as part of a page, passing back the necessary piece of code after doing its processing.

CLIENT-SIDE SCRIPTING
Scripts that are added to a web page to interact with other objects on the page or in the browser, to achieve such things as rollovers and pop-ups, are referred to as "client side." The best example is JavaScript.

COOKIE
A cookie is a small text file used by a web page to store some information on a user's computer. Cookies can be temporary, only lasting for a single session—such as an online shopping basket—or more permanent, storing such things as usernames to automatically log users onto sites whenever they visit them.

CSS (CASCADING STYLE SHEETS)
CSS is the standard for styling web page elements. Using either styles from external CSS documents or CSS embedded directly into a web page, any HTML tag can be styled, including (but not limited to) adding padding, margins, borders, and colors, or dealing with positioning. Many designers now use CSS to control font styles on their websites, but the technology is also suitable for controlling a site's entire visual presentation via a single external document, thereby making updates easier, download times quicker, and the site's markup simpler (because it no longer contains presentational elements). It also means that it is possible to have many different versions of the site design or color scheme available, and to allow the user to switch between them at the click of a button. While this is a nice ability from a design point of view, it also has more practical implications for accessibility,

enabling such things as the easy switching to high contrast colors and larger fonts for sight-impaired users.

DHTML
Dynamic HTML. This isn't a technology in itself, but refers to the combination of HTML, CSS, and JavaScript. DHTML pages may change or react to a user's interactions, such as a timeline-based animation that launches when someone passes their cursor over an image.

DOM
The DOM (Document Object Model) is a standardized platform-neutral interface that allows web pages to be modified by programs and scripting languages. Whereas XML describes the data itself, the DOM describes how the data can be accessed and modified.

DYNAMIC WEB PAGES
Pages that are created on-the-fly through server-side programming are often referred to as "dynamic," or "active."

E-COMMERCE
E-commerce (electronic commerce) is the general term for business that is conducted over the web. An e-commerce site is one that includes the facility for transactions to take place online.

ENCRYPTION
E-commerce sites typically make use of encryption. This is the process of converting data into a code that's unreadable to anyone unless they have been given specific permission and the facility to do so, by means of a key. The most common form of encryption used on the Internet is SSL (Secure Sockets Layer), and pages that make use of this technology have names

Web terms and technologies

beginning with https, rather than the more usual http.

HTML

Hypertext Markup Language (HTML) is the standard for structuring web pages. Browsers interpret HTML elements and layout web pages accordingly. Various versions of HTML exist: the most recent is at www.w3c.org/markup.

HTML5

The latest emerging set of standards for structuring web pages. Most significantly, the HTML5 code incorporates new features that do away with the need to use plug-ins such as Adobe Flash to create interactive content or embed video.

JAVASCRIPT

JavaScript is a scripting language that can work with HTML to create interactive web pages. It is not the same as, or even related in any way to, the Java programming language.

PLUG-INS

A plug-in is a small application that extends a browser's capabilities. Different plug-ins exist to support a range of technologies, from Real Media to Adobe Flash. A web page that requires a plug-in needs to have strategies for enabling the additional software to be downloaded and installed in the browser. If a plug-in is difficult to obtain, then the technology behind it will almost certainly fail.

POP3

POP3 (Post Office Protocol, version 3) is a protocol used for transferring email over the Internet. Email clients use POP3 to retrieve mail from servers.

SERVER SIDE

Code and scripts that reside on a web server are referred to as "server side." When server-side code (such as ASP, PHP, or CFM) is used, the server reads and executes the code before serving the resulting data to the browser. This is more secure and offers more scope than client-side code such as JavaScript.

SVG

SVG (Scalable Vector Graphics) is an XML-based language for describing 2D graphics on the web. Although the language itself is mainly used for vector graphics, it can also embed bitmap graphics, such as JPEG and PNG. SVG also utilizes the ECMAScript scripting language (a standardized version of JavaScript) for animation. The downside of SVG is that it currently requires a plug-in to display it. After Internet Explorer version 9 is launched, major browsers will support the technology.

XHTML

XHTML is a reformulation of HTML 4 in XML 1 and effectively replaces HTML. It is a bridge between the old style of HTML, and the new, recommended style of XML. XHTML provides greater scope, although the markup itself has stricter rules than HTML (a good thing for browser compatibility).

XML

XML stands for Extensible Markup Language, and unlike HTML, it is not a fixed, predefined markup language, but a metalanguage; that is, a language that is used to describe other languages. This enables you to design your own customized markup for specific document types, using the structure of XML as a base. For example, in HTML the "table" tag is predefined, and all browsers know how to display it. In XML, however, only the structure of the tag itself is defined, and it is up to the user to define whether a table means a formatted sequence of data, or a piece of furniture. It is means of marking data, leaving the actual page layout to CSS or XSL.

XSL

XSL, or Extensible Stylesheet Language, is a language used to describe how XML data should be styled when presented to users.

PLUG-IN GUIDE

A few browser plug-ins have become almost indispensable owing to the broad usage of certain technologies. Usually these are for handling sound, video, or animations. As a developer, the trick is to let a user install and run the plug-in with a minimum of fuss or technical know-how.

FLASH PLAYER

This plug-in has been around for many years, and has become the standard means of displaying vector animation on the Internet. It is also commonly used nowadays to create full websites containing interactive content. Most browsers come with a version (often an old one) of the plug-in already installed. Many people do not keep plug-ins up to date, so author accordingly, only saving files in the most recent version if absolutely necessary. Although it is true that the Flash plug-in will prompt the user to download a new version of the player if one is required, many users either will not or cannot do this, so it is still preferable to export your files to the lowest version possible.

QUICKTIME

Apple's technology for sound and video also supports 3D and virtual reality. QuickTime VR (Virtual Reality) enables objects to be rotated and rescaled. The basic version of the QuickTime player can be downloaded free from Apple, and an upgraded version works as a simple video editing tool. It is possible to use QuickTime files without a special QuickTime server, although more options and abilities, including flexible streaming, are available if one is used.

WINDOWS MEDIA PLAYER

Microsoft's proprietary media plug-in used for delivering all types of multimedia content. It offers a cheaper alternative to the Real Helix server for delivery, but it needs a Microsoft server to operate.

FROM PRINT TO WEB While some degree of automation of conversion is possible, manual handling is virtually unavoidable.

Converting print to web design

Web design and print design are very different things, each having its own set of restrictions. What works well in print often doesn't on the web and vice versa. For instance:

- The web relies on dynamic navigation systems that in turn depend on link-clicking and scrolling, whereas printed pages can be viewed in their entirety and randomly.

- A print page layout is something that's fixed and you can design accordingly, perhaps making a page work with its facing page as a spread. When working for the web, however, you have no guarantees regarding such design given as the size of the user's browser window—and even their chosen browser and operating system may affect how the page looks.

- Web graphics use the RGB color space whilst Print graphics use CMYK.

- Web designers have relatively limited typographic options available to them.

- Web pages allow interactivity and dynamic elements that would be impossible to achieve in print.

These are just some of the problems the designer will encounter when using print design software to create web pages.

SO WHY CONVERT?

Making material available on the web will gain readers and, if the material is subscription-based, provides an opportunity for an additional revenue stream. Because the initial production of text for print tends to be a labor-intensive process, it is quicker to perform a series of operations on print files to make them usable for web design than to generate new text from scratch.

Ease of distribution is another major reason for disseminating material on the web and if that is all that is required, then the solution is straightforward: create the document as a PDF rather than as a web page. Many electronic versions of printed documentation are stored on websites in this form, ready for download. It's far cheaper to allow consumers to access support materials in PDF form than to print and distribute such documents.

WHAT ARE THE OPTIONS?

One basic option is to take only the raw text file from the print document, stripped of all format-ting, that can then be manually tagged in HTML. You can also produce the original text with

Simple documents

It's common for a document to be written in a program such as Word and then used in a number of ways, for example as printed text, as web content, and as the body of an email.

In such circumstances, it's best not to rely on basic HTML conversion facilities. Word tends to create enormous files that include proprietary markup, and such output is often difficult to edit in tools such as Dreamweaver.

If you have a number of documents like this, try using Textism's Word HTML Cleaner (www.textism.com/wordcleaner). Alternatively, simply copy and paste the content from a Word document directly into Dreamweaver's Code View and tweak the resulting information accordingly. All "special" characters are converted automatically.

In a perfect world, a writer would add markup tags while he or she worked, whatever the initial context of the document. These could take any form (although XML, or CSS for layout, would be ideal), so the finished document could be pasted straight into the HTML code where the various content styles would be edited. Unfortunately, most writers don't know how to do this, but web writers should be able to understand a set of markup guidelines and start using them without too much trouble.

DTP conversion

Most page-layout programs like InDesign and Quark have sophisticated options for exporting complex print layouts directly into web format. These include options for creating rollovers, menus, font management, forms, and hyperlinks. However, just because such tools exist, that doesn't mean you should use them.

While web versions can be created in technical terms, the question is whether or not that layout works in the new medium. In many cases, any converted document is ultimately going to be only an initial step in the process of creating a new web page. The code generated is often so poor that it makes sense to start completely from scratch.

some type of markup tags included (see Simple documents, left), which minimizes work.

Page-layout programs do offer functionality for converting documents into web formats, but these are of variable quality (see DTP conversion, above). Images, on the other hand, will almost certainly require some form of manipulation. Generally, they will have to be converted to RGB, scaled to their final size at 72ppi, and optimized using the appropriate format and compression.

Right: If you have a high resolution (300dpi) image and use the Photoshop Save for Web option it is best to rescale the image to the size that it will appear on the web page.

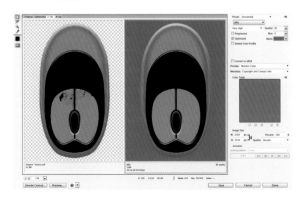

HTML might look off-putting to someone unacquainted with code, but it's possible to learn enough in a couple of hours to create a web page.

HTML commands

3

How much HTML (HyperText Markup Language) should a web designer know? The argument goes that the scope of visual tools, such as Adoeb Dreamweaver and SoftPress Freeway mean that you no longer really need to delve into HTML. However, if designers are serious in their pursuit of excellence in terms of developing content for the web, they should look to go beyond basic assembling of layouts and learn the principles of how HTML actually works.

Just as a print designer with no understanding of the various aspects of taking a job to print will

---

It's possible to create simple HTML documents using only a few common tags; here are just a few useful tags:

Page structure

<html></html> Placed at the beginning and end of an HTML document. Only the Document Type Definition (DTD) should be outside of these tags.

<head></head> The head section of a document typically serves as a container for information-oriented tags that aren't displayed in the browser, such as meta tags, which assist search engines in categorizing a website. An exception is the **<title></title>** element, whose contents appear on a browser's toolbar.

<body></body> The page's content is placed within the body element and no web page content should appear outside.

Links & images

To create a link to another page, you use the anchor tag, **<a>**. The href attribute defines the file the browser will access when the link is clicked.

<a href="a_local_file.html"> A link to a local file**</a>**

<a href="http://www.bbc.co.uk"> A link to the BBC website**</a>**

To display a picture on a page:

<img src="image.jpg" height="100" width="320" alt="Alt text">

The alt attribute's value is whatever you want displayed in browsers that cannot, for whatever reason, display the image. It can help disabled readers, too.

When working with links of any kind, remember what file structure you have and make links to other sites absolute.

Styling text

HTML supports six levels of headings, paragraphs, line breaks, and lists. Headings and paragraphs will be rendered as per the specifications of the viewer's web browser. Note that these specifications can be overridden by using Cascading Style Sheets (see *CSS*, pages 174–177), and this is the recommended format nowadays.

For headings, paragraphs, and line breaks:

<h1>Heading, size 1 (biggest)**</h1>**
<h2>Heading, size 2**</h2>**
<h3>Heading, size 3**</h3>**
<h4>Heading, size 4**</h4>**
<h5>Heading, size 5**</h5>**
<h6>Heading, size 6 (smallest)**</h6>**
<p>A paragraph of text**</p>**
<p>A paragraph, with a **
**
line break**</p>**

not be able to confidently deliver what is expected of them, the same is true of a web designer with no understanding of HTML. Equally, leaving the clearing up of what are often simple display or functionality issues to a programmer is not a sound use of that person's specialist skills.

Some knowledge of HTML will make you a better web designer and help you make better pages. The same is true of having an awareness of common design pitfalls on the web. The web is not print (see *Converting Print to Web Design*, pages 168–169), and its low resolution means details can be lost and text is harder to read. Basic HTML is not complicated. Essentially, HTML documents are text files containing "markup tags." The tags tell browsers how to display pages. XHTML (see *What is XHTML?*,

pages 172–173) is the new standard. It is similar to HTML, but has stricter rules.

Tags are surrounded by angle brackets, and come in pairs, opening and closing the content. For instance, the following XHTML element displays a paragraph of text in a web browser

Often, the sites that look least professional are those that were designed too rigidly, where the slipping of a few elements has the domino effect of upsetting the overall design. What matters most is having a good grasp of the mechanics of HTML structure.

Besides benefits on the design front it will help you to solve those display or functionality problems without having to use the expensive time of a programmer, leaving him or her free to focus on the more complex coding issues.

To create a bulleted list:
<ul>
<li>item 1**</li>**
<li>item 2**</li>**
</ul>

For a numbered (ordered) list, replace <ul> and </ul> with **<ol>** and **</ol>**.

You can style text with logical and physical styles. Physical styles are perhaps most common, and force browsers to display characters in a certain way, such as ****bold**** and **<i>**italic**</i>**.

Examples of logical styles include:
****emphasis**** and
****strong emphasis****.
How these are displayed depends on browser settings, although most display in italic and bold respectively. Logical styles are more accessible than physical ones because screen readers cater for them.

Working with tables
<table></table> Creates a table. Omitting the end tag usually causes major display problems in web browsers.

Attributes include:

✳ **width** defines the table width—set as a number or percentage.

✳ **cellspacing** sets the space between the table cells.

✳ **cellpadding** sets the padding within each table cell.

✳ **border** sets the size of the border around each cell.

✳ **summary** provides a summary of the contents for speaking browsers.

<tr></tr> Defines a table row.

<td></td> Defines a cell in a row.

This table has one row of two cells:
<table>
<tr> <td></td><td></td> </tr>
</table>

Attributes for the **<td>** tag include:

✳ **valign** top, middle, or bottom, to set the vertical alignment of cell content.

✳ **colspan** numeric, defines the number of columns the cell spans.

✳ **rowspan** as above, but setting the number of rows the cell spans.

This table has two cells in the first row and one in the second, spanning the table width:

<table>
<tr><td></td><td></td></tr>
<tr><td colspan="2"></td></tr>
</table>

EXTENSIBLE HYPERTEXT MARKUP LANGUAGE As more and more diverse devices are used to access the web, XHTML is set to grow in popularity as it allows for greater compatibility across browsers and platforms.

What is XHTML?

Extensible HyperText Markup Language [XHTML] is a reformulation of HTML 4. In the simplest terms, it could be described as the vocabulary (the elements and the tags) of HTML merged with the syntax (the language and the structural rules) of XML.

XML is a language that requires everything to be marked up strictly and correctly. It defines a structure and grammar on which subsets of XML, such as XHTML, are based. This results in documents that are described as "well-formed," meaning that they conform correctly to the rules of XML. XML is used to describe content, not to define how it should be displayed.

There are two main issues that have an impact on the cross-browser, cross-platform consistency of presentation. The first is that different browsers implement the HTML standard in different ways, so certain tags may not be displayed consistently, and some tags aren't supported by some browsers at all.

The second issue results from HTML's flexibility, which means that some designers got into bad habits, such as not quoting attributes and omitting end tags. As well as being a bad habit in general, leading to sloppy approaches to code writing, this can also create inconsistency across browsers, because browsers vary in the way that they render bad markup.

Given the proliferation of devices that are increasingly being used to access web content, such as mobile phones, PDAs, and touch-screens, XHTML represents an attempt to increase the cross-browser, cross-platform compatibility of this content, by using the more disciplined structure and syntax of XML when developing web pages. All this may sound complicated, but in practice, it is quite simple. XHTML markup boils down to a list of rules to follow when coding a web page. These rules are listed in more detail in XHTML markup, right.

XHTML results in web pages that can be read by all XML-enabled devices. While the strictures of XHTML may require some re-thinking of the development process, it offers several advantages:

• It has the advantage of being backward (and forward) compatible.

• It removes the need to code different versions of the same page to cater for different user agents, or browser types.

• When combined with stylesheets, either CSS or XSL, it offers a stable and flexible means of delivering web content.

```
1  DOCTYPE html PUBLIC "-//W3C//DTD XHTML 1.0 Transitional//EN"
        "http://www.w3.org/TR/2000/REC-xhtml1-20000126/DTD/xhtml1-transitional.dtd"

<html><!-- #BeginTemplate "/Templates/wireviewsMain.dwt" --><!-- DW6 -->
2 <head>
<!-- #BeginEditable "doctitle" -->

    <title> 3 reviews - Reviews - Silo - Alloy</title>
    <!-- #EndEditable -->
<style type="text/css" media="screen">
@import url(../wireviews.css);
</style>
 4  <link rel="stylesheet" type="text/css"  5 dia="print" href="../wireviews_print.css">
    <meta name="keywords" content="wire, colin newman, graham lewis, bruce gilbert, robert
gotobed, swim, wmo, he said, omala, immersion, malka spiegel, wir, snub communications, veer
musikal unit, wireviews, music, news, ahead, pink flag, dugga, drill, craig grannell,
reviews">
    <!-- #BeginEditable "metaDescription" -->

<meta name="Description" content="Wireviews - Reviews - Silo - Alloy" />
<!-- #EndEditable -->
    <link rev="made" href="mailto:wireviews@yahoo.com">
    <meta name="revist-after" content="30 days">
    <meta name="author" content="Craig Grannell">
    <meta name="classification" content="music, fanzine">
    <style type="text/css">
<!--
body {color: #000; background-color: "fff}
-->
</style>

  </head>

2 <body>
<div id="wrapper">
    <div class="header"><span class="left"><a href="../index.html"><img
src="../assets/shared/logo.gif" alt="Wireviews home page" width="213" height="23"
border="0"></a></span><span class="right"><span class="label"><a href="../index.html">home</a> | <a
href="../news/index.html">news</a> | <a href="index.html">reviews</a> | <a
href="../artcles/index.html">articles</a> | <a href="../info/index.html">info</a> | <a
href="../wno/index.html">wmo</a> | <a href="../contact/index.html">contact</a></span></div>

<div id="location" class="top"> <a href="../index.html">Wireviews</a> | <!--
#BeginEditable "historyUpper" --><a href="index.html">Reviews</a> | Alloy<!-- #EndEditable
--></div>

       <div id="boxOut">
       <h1><!--"BeginEditable "boxoutTitle" --><span class="boxTitle">ILO</span><br />
       ALLOY <br /> 6
          <span class="label"><Swim Records></span><!-- "EndEditable --></h1>

       <p class="picBoxout"><!-- "BeginEditable "boxoutImage" --><img
src="../assets/cover_art/alloy.jpg" width="140" height=140 title="Cover art" alt="Cover
art" class="image" ?><br />
```

1 A Document Type Definition (DTD) must be included at the top of each XHTML document—see www.w3schools.com/dtd/default.asp

2 <head> and <body>

3 The <title> element

Tags must be correctly nested.

Attributes cannot be shortened. Reference to the XML namespace must be in the <html> element.

4 XHTML tags and attributes must be in lower case.

5 All attribute values, for example the numbers in "height" and "width"

definitions, must have quotation marks around them.

6 All tags must be closed, including those with no content—so <br> becomes <br />. Note the space before the trailing slash—this is included to ensure obsolete browsers display the tag.

CASCADING STYLE SHEETS The use of CSS gives greater design control without affecting the underlying structure of the website.

CSS

CSS (Cascading Style Sheets) is the standard for styling web page elements and is entirely separate from HTML or XHTML, although CSS can be embedded within both types of document. CSS enables you to control all presentational aspects of a web page, from typography to element positioning, all from an external file. By separating such elements from the structural logic of a web page, CSS gives web designers control without sacrificing the integrity of the data—aiding usability and accessibility.

In addition, the defining of typographic design and page layout from within a single, distinct block of code—without resorting to the likes of <font> tags, tables, and spacer GIFs—allows for faster downloads, streamlined site maintenance, greater compatibility, and, when external style sheets are used, instantaneous global control of design attributes across multiple pages from a single external document. CSS can be integrated into your web pages via any of the following means:

- In the header of a given HTML page (called an embedded style sheet).

- Within a given tag (inline style).

- In a external style sheet linked to the HTML page by a reference in the page header.

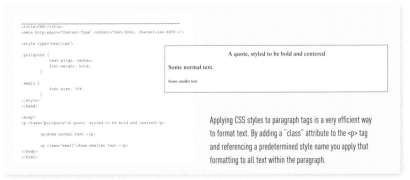

Applying CSS styles to paragraph tags is a very efficient way to format text. By adding a "class" attribute to the <p> tag and referencing a predetermined style name you apply that formatting to all text within the paragraph.

What are styles?

CSS styles are a series of rules that comprise a selector, which is a redefined HTML tag, class name, or ID name, and a declaration, which is made up of property/value pairs, separated by semicolons. Take, for instance, the following CSS rule, which may be found embedded in the head of the HTML document (within a style tag) or found in an external style sheet:

```
p {
color: #000;
size: 12px;
}
```

In this case, "p" is the selector, meaning that the declaration will affect all "p" (paragraph) tags that are found in the HTML document. The declaration has two property/value pairs, which set the color to #000 (hex shorthand for black) and the size to 12 pixels.

It would also be possible to set the style directly within an HTML tag, thus:

```
<p style="color: #000; size: 12px;">
```

Of course, in that scenario, the style would only affect the tag within which it appears, and so the idea of global control over elements is lost (hence the vast majority of CSS being placed in external style sheets). We mentioned classes and IDs. These enable designers to define several styles for the same HTML tag. For instance, we could have the following in our style sheet:

```
.pullquote {
text-align: center;
font-weight: bold;
}
.small {
font-size: 90%;
}
```

Note how the identified element is preceded by a period in the CSS. In HTML we could then have the following:

```
<p class="pullquote">A quote, styled to be bold and
centered</p>
<p>Some normal text.</p>
<p class="small">Some smaller text.</p>
```

Classes give you almost limitless scope for defining styles for your web-page elements and each can be used an unlimited number of times (and also on as many different elements as you wish)—for instance, we could use the above .small style on a heading by typing

```
<h1 class="small">A smaller heading</h1>
```

IDs work in a slightly different way. In CSS, the identified element is preceded by a hash sign (#) rather than a period. The word "id" is used instead of "class," and IDs should only be used once per page. However, they can easily be targeted by JavaScript scripts. Therefore, they are usually used for structural page elements (mastheads, footers, and so on) and dynamic page elements, such as an image that gets swapped. When a page is being viewed with a browser, there may be three style sheets at work:

✳ The author's style sheet, set by the web designer.

✳ The user's style sheet, consisting of personalized browser preferences, such as text size.

✳ The browser default preferences.

Cascading

Cascading is the process by which a style system determines which value for each property to apply to each element. There are four rules that define the process of cascading:

✳ The rule's selector must match the element.

✳ Rules are chosen by weight and origin.

✳ Rules are chosen by the specificity of their selectors.

✳ Declarations are chosen by their order.

Generally speaking, the cascade is toward the element within the web page. Take an external style declaration that reads:

p {color: red; size: 10px}
And an inline style declaration that reads:
<p style="color: green;">

The inline style for color would override the external one, because it's nearer to the element that's being styled. However, because there is no size declaration in the inline style, the size declaration in the external style sheet would still be used. The final result in a CSS-compatible browser would be green text at 10 pixels in size.

CSS POSITIONING (CSS–P) is a flexible layout standard that is the default for web design.

CSS-P

CSS positioning is the most modern and flexible method of working with web-page layout. Unlike the old approach of using tables, CSS enables the precision placement of elements, and each element can act individually, rather than be affected by the page layout as a whole. Therefore, you don't have the problems of merging and splitting table cells, or using invisible GIFs to force page elements into a certain place.

While initially it was most popular with sites that focus on web standards, this technique gained fast popularity. All major sites, such as those of large corporations, like ESPN, the New York Times, and Apple, made the transition to CSS-based layouts years ago, resulting in massive bandwidth savings, greater browser compatibility, and ease of updating. Arguments about these techniques only being supported in "new" browsers are now more superfluous. It is true that advanced CSS positioning is "only" supported by current releases of Opera, Mozilla, Safari, Internet Explorer, and Google Chrome, among others, but that "only" is inclusive of the majority of web users. If you have researched your audience, then you will know which browser they are likely to use, and thus whether they will have viewing problems. As a last resort, advanced features of the design can be "hidden" from obsolete browsers, enabling users to see only the content.

A web page designed using CSS need not feature a table. Working without tables requires a shift in thinking on the part of the designer, in terms of how layouts are planned and implemented. You need to be more organized. Some web design tools aren't yet at the stage where you can easily drag your CSS-styled divisions around a layout. For instance, Adobe Dreamweaver centers around placing unstyled div tags and then using the appropriate dialog boxes to set size, padding, margins, borders, and float properties.

Tables in HTML were intended for the formatting of tabular data, but became the principal means of organizing layout. While apparently suited to layout on the surface, tables are not an ideal for page construction, and CSS-P should be used in preference. As already mentioned, tables bias code towards presentation rather than structure and require nested tables in order to achieve anything other than the most basic of layouts.

To understand CSS-P, you need to recognize the notion of the "normal flow" of an HTML document, where elements are rendered in order (from the top to the bottom of the document) with any CSS styles being applied as the page is rendered. With CSS-P, the element's place within the document can be redefined. There are essentially three different ways an element can be positioned on a page without using tables (see opposite).

Fusce quis justo a mauris lacinia mattis. Aliquam nec eros ac tortor aliquam ultrices. Aliqua pede ante, porta ullamcorper, molestie ac, elementum sed, neque. Aenean eu risus quis metus dapibus tempor. Vivamus est libero, malesuada ac, porta quis, iaculis eget, mauris. Suspendisse potenti. Sed eu elit. Phasellus at lacus eget lorem ullamcorper commodo. Pellentesque habitant morbi tristique senectus et netus et malesuada fames ac turpis egestas. Sed vel lacus non lorem pharetra dapibus. Vestibulum urna turpis, placerat a, lacinia faucibus, feugiat et, diam. Praesent placerat, wisi ut interdum venenatis, risus orci tincidunt justo, sed auctor urna odio in felis. Praesent aliquam, lorem eget condimentum tincidunt, nunc sem aliquam augue, nec blandit sapien enim at eros. Nam pharetra nisl eu enim. Nullam feugiat viverra risus. Nulla dolor. Curabitur viverra. Curabitur commodo dictui metus.

This is an example of absolute positioning - this layer moves with the rest of the text in the document when it is scrolled.

tincidunt justo, sed auctor urna odio in felis. Praesent aliquam, lorem eget condimentur tincidunt, nunc sem aliquam augue, nec blandit sapien enim at eros. Nam pharetra nisi enim. Nullam feugiat viverra risus. Nulla dolor. Curabitur viverra. Curabitur commodo di metus.

This is an example of absolute positioning - this layer moves with the rest of the text in the document when it is scrolled.

Maecenas turpis lectus, ultrices at, egestas at, eleifend sit amet, dolor. Cras cursus, era vitae auctor sollicitudin, mi ligula aliquam nulla, scelerisque viverra ipsum eros ac lacus. ornare turpis eu ligula. Class aptent taciti sociosqu ad litora torquent per conubia nostri inceptos hymenaeos. Vivamus laoreet, orci vel sagittis vulputate, est ante porttitor sapi eget laoreet felis justo sit amet enim. Proin vehicula, neque vel feugiat convallis, felis nui condimentum erat, eu ultrices orci nulla id nisl. Donec eleifend, nulla eget aliquam fringi odio felis hendrerit elit, in tristique diam orci vitae nibh. Aliquam ac neque. Suspendisse lacus. Nam vitae lorem nec.

Absolute positioning

Absolute position lets a developer say where the top left-hand corner of an element should be located, not in relation to the top left corner of the page, but in relation to its parent element.

Pellentesque habitant morbi tristique senectus et netus et malesuada fames ac turpis eg Sed vel lacus non lorem pharetra dapibus. Vestibulum urna turpis, placerat a, lacinia fauc feugiat et, diam. Praesent placerat, wisi ut interdum venenatis, risus orci tincidunt justo, auctor urna odio in felis. Praesent aliquam, lorem eget condimentum tincidunt, nunc sem aliquam augue, nec blandit sapien enim at eros. Nam pharetra nisl eu enim. Nullam feugi viverra risus. Nulla dolor. Curabitur viverra. Curabitur commodo dictum metus.

This is an example of relative positioning - this layer has a value of left: 50 and so is placed 50 pixels from the left of where it appears in the natural flow of the text - it is placed relative to its surroundings

Maecenas turpis lectus, ultrices at, egestas at, eleifend sit amet, dolor. Cras cursus, erat auctor sollicitudin, mi ligula aliquam nulla, scelerisque viverra ipsum eros ac lacus. Nulla o turpis eu ligula. Class aptent taciti sociosqu ad litora torquent per conubia nostra, per inc hymenaeos. Vivamus laoreet, orci vel sagittis vulputate, est ante porttitor sapien, eget la: felis justo sit amet enim. Proin vehicula, neque vel feugiat convallis, felis nunc condimenti erat, eu ultrices orci nulla id nisl. Donec eleifend, nulla eget aliquam fringilla, odio felis hen

Fusce quis justo a mauris lacinia mattis. Aliquam nec eros ac tortor aliquam ultrices. Aliquam pede ante, porta ullamcorper, molestie ac, elementum sed, neque. Aenean eu risus quis metus dapibus tempor. Vivamus est libero, malesuada ac, porta quis, iaculis eget, mauris. Suspendisse potenti. Sed eu elit. Phasellus at lacus eget lorem ullamcorper commodo. Pellentesque habitant morbi tristique senectus et netus et malesuada fames ac turpis egestas. Sed vel lacus non lorem pharetra dapibus. Vestibulum urna turpis, placerat a, lacinia faucibus, feugiat et, diam. Praesent placerat, wisi ut interdum venenatis, risus orci tincidunt justo, sed auctor urna odio in felis. Praesent aliquam, lorem eget condimentum tincidunt, nunc sem aliquam augue, nec blandit sapien enim at eros. Nam pharetra nisl eu enim. Nullam feugiat viverra risus. Nulla dolor. Curabitur viverra. Curabitur commodo dictum metus.

This is an example of fixed positioning - this layer stays in the same place on the screen, regardless of scrolling.

placerat, wisi ut interdum venenatis, risus orci tincidunt justo, sed auctor urna odio in felis. Praesent aliquam, lorem eget condimentum tincidunt, nunc sem aliquam augue, nec blandit sapien enim at eros. Nam pharetra nisl eu enim. Nullam feugiat viverra risus. Nulla dolor. Curabitur viverra. Curabitur commodo dictum metus.

Maecenas turpis lectus, ultrices at, egestas at, eleifend sit amet, dolor. Cras cursus, erat vitae auctor sollicitudin, mi ligula aliquam nulla, scelerisque viverra ipsum eros ac lacus. Nulla ornare turpis eu ligula. Class aptent taciti sociosqu ad litora torquent per mus laoreet, orci vel sagittis vulputate,
This is an example of fixed positioning - this layer stays in the same place on the screen, regardless of scrolling.
to sit amet enim. Proin vehicula, neque erat, eu ultrices orci nulla id nisl. Donec hendrerit elit, in tristique diam orci vitae . Nam vitae lorem nec.

Fixed positioning

Fixed position is a subset of absolute position. When an element is absolutely positioned, it's positioned with respect to the element that contains it. When the page is scrolled, the element also scrolls. Fixed positioning enables you to fix an element, so that regardless of how the page is scrolled, the element stays put. With fixed positioning and the object element in HTML, we can emulate frames-based navigation—at least in theory. A pity, then, that Internet Explorer—the browser used by the vast majority of web users—doesn't support fixed elements.

Relative positioning

Relative positioning is probably a little unfortunately named. Positioning relative to what? A common misconception is that relative positioning is when you specify a position with respect to the parent element, and absolute positioning is when the position is specified with respect to the top left-hand corner of the page. This is not how it works. In essence, relative positioning places an element with respect to where it would statically be positioned. When you relatively position an element, as a developer you are saying to a browser: "take this paragraph, and put it 10 pixels down and 10 pixels to the right of where it would normally be."

TO INTERACT WITH A COMPUTER Tables and layers are useful tools that will be supported for some time yet, despite the development of alternative tools. However, they should be avoided for building sites and only used as a last resort when you cannot easily achieve something with CSS, or you are creating a table of tabular data.

Tables

3

Of the various methods of laying out web pages, from traditional tables through to modern methods, involving complex CSS, each have their advantages and disadvantages—sometimes a combination of methods is required, depending on the project, design, and intended audience. For instance, it is relatively common from a graphic designer's perspective to lay out a page with a very simple HTML table, but use CSS for all internal positioning, although a specialized web designer would avoid tables all together.

HTML TABLES

Despite being designed to contain tabular data, tables have traditionally also often been used to position elements on HTML pages. Although essentially basic grid structures, they can be used to create quite sophisticated layouts that appear consistently in most types of web browser. Working with them can, however, end up being something of a logic puzzle; making sure that content appears where you intend it to requires meticulous planning throughout the design process.

PROS

Ultimately, using tables in this way remains a popular option because pages created in this fashion are so stable across all browsers and because, for those using design tools like Adobe

Dreamweaver, they are easy to create and manipulate in the visual environment.

CONS

On a negative note, there are problems with tables. Complex tabular layouts load slowly due to the way in which a browser has to map them. It's difficult to avoid using "nested" tables (tables within tables) for sophisticated layouts and these place even greater demands on the browser. Such layouts often cause problems when it comes to amending a layout: because cells all rely on each other in order to create the entire table, removing or adding one can wreck an entire layout, causing a designer to curse as they spend time merging and splitting cells until the layout looks fine once again. Even worse, tables cause major accessibility issues, because placing information within them means said information is usually not logically ordered in the HTML document. This is another reason why using CSS for layout is such a good idea.

WORKING WITH LAYERS

One possible alternative to tables is layers, although what's meant by that word depends on who you speak to. Layers were initially introduced as a proprietary Netscape element that has subsequently been deprecated, and is no longer used. If

Heading	Heading
Imsep pretu tempu revol bileg rokam revoc tephe rosve etepe tenov sindu turqu brevt elliu repar tiuve tamia queso utage udulc vires humus fallo 25deu Anetn bisre freun carmi avire ingen umque miher muner veris adest duner veris adest iteru quevi escit billo isput tatqu aliqu diams bipos itopu 50sta Isant oscul bifid mquec cumen berra etmii pyren nsomn anoct reern oncit quqar anofe ventm hipec oramo uetfu orets ritus sacer tusag teliu ipsev 75	Imsep pretu tempu revol bileg rokam revoc tephe rosve etepe tenov sindu turqu brevt elliu repar tiuve tamia queso utage udulc vires humus fallo 25deu Anetn bisre freun carmi avire ingen umque miher muner veris adest duner veris adest iteru quevi escit billo isput tatqu aliqu diams bipos itopu 50sta Isant oscul bifid mquec cumen berra etmii pyren nsomn anoct reern oncit quqar anofe ventm hipec oramo uetfu orets ritus sacer tusag teliu ipsev 75

Heading	Heading
Imsep pretu tempu revol bileg rokam revoc tephe rosve etepe tenov sindu turqu brevt elliu repar tiuve tamia queso utage udulc vires humus fallo 25deu Anetn bisre freun carmi avire ingen umque miher muner veris adest duner veris adest iteru quevi escit billo isput tatqu aliqu diams bipos itopu 50sta Isant oscul bifid mquec cumen berra etmii pyren nsomn anoct reern oncit quqar anofe ventm hipec oramo uetfu orets ritus sacer tusag teliu ipsev 75	Imsep pretu tempu revol bileg rokam revoc tephe rosve etepe tenov sindu turqu brevt elliu repar tiuve tamia queso utage udulc vires humus fallo 25deu Anetn bisre freun carmi avire ingen umque miher muner veris adest duner veris adest iteru quevi escit billo isput tatqu aliqu diams bipos itopu 50sta Isant oscul bifid mquec cumen berra etmii pyren nsomn anoct reern oncit quqar anofe ventm hipec oramo uetfu orets ritus sacer tusag teliu ipsev 75

Should you decide to work with layers, Dreamweaver has the facility to convert layers into tables, or vice versa. This can be useful for creating quick mock-ups; content can be positioned using layers and then the web page can be converted to tables.

Note, however, that overlapped layers cannot be converted. Also, the output from such conversions tends to be substandard, so you should only use these tools for mock-ups and not for live websites.

working in the likes of Dreamweaver, any "layers" that are created are actually absolutely positioned page divisions, internally styled with CSS.

HTML TABLES

Layers provide a certain amount of separation between content and structure that can't be achieved by working with tables. A layer can be drawn out anywhere on a web page and positioned precisely either through inputting coordinates, or by simply dragging it. They offer a designer-friendly working environment that anyone who is used to a DTP application like QuarkXPress or Adobe Indesign can feel instantly at ease with.

STACKING

Layers, as their name suggests, can be stacked (the stacking is measured using a Z-index prop-

erty value). The stacking order can then be altered, or layers can be hidden and revealed, by using JavaScript.

CSS-STYLED PAGE DIVISIONS

The most significant problem with creating layers of this sort in a web-design application is that the result is often unreliable, with little consistency across web browsers and operating systems. Because of this problem, you are often better off ignoring layers completely and creating your own CSS-styled page divisions. This is something that's relatively simple in current versions of Dreamweaver.

Text management on the web is a completely different matter to its print counterpart, and needs careful consideration.

Text management

One of the most limiting factors in web design is the range of fonts that can be safely used on a page, due to few being common across operating system default installs. Although there are various means of using unusual fonts at different sizes, it is important to make specific text management decisions at the start of the web design process.

HTML TEXT

Raw text styled using HTML tags provides the bulk of the content on most of the sites that populate the web today. It's a fairly efficient way of displaying information, since the raw text adds little to the memory size of a document. No plugins are required, so the text can be displayed without the potential for interruptions, and search engine spiders can examine every word that a site visitor is likely to see. However, as we'll see, using HTML to style text is obsolete and has been superseded by CSS.

In order for a page to be displayed showing the same font that it was created with, that font needs to be present on the viewer's system. Therefore most pages are created with text styled using fonts that the designer assumes exist on most computers. Taking into account the various platforms and operating systems that exist, this decision calls for an extremely broad generalization. The result: standard system fonts are used. Essentially, you are restricted to Arial, Arial Black, Comic Sans MS, Courier New, Georgia, Impact, Times New Roman, Trebuchet MS, Verdana, and a few others, and only some of those mentioned are suitable for body copy.

Web best practice involves listing a group of fonts so that, even if the intended font is not present on a user's system, one of the other defaults is. However, you should avoid using an esoteric font as your first choice, because only a tiny minority of your intended audience will see it. A typical HTML font tag looks like this:

`<font face="Arial, Helvetica, sans-serif">Percy Pig </font>`

When the page is displayed in a browser, the words "Percy Pig" should be styled in "Arial." If "Arial" is not present on the system, then "Helvetica" and finally "sans-serif" will be displayed.

The use of font tags has been superseded by CSS. Font tags had to be applied to every element that you wanted to be styled, so updating these styles over an entire website required complex find-and-replace exercises, as opposed to CSS, where you may have to tweak a couple of values in a single, external document. CSS for text formatting has now rendered font tags obsolete.

Arial	AaBbCcDdEeFfGgHhIiJjKkLlMmNnOoPp QqRrSsTtUuVvWwXxYyZz 1234567890
Arial Bold	**AaBbCcDdEeFfGgHhIiJjKkLlMmNnOoPp QqRrSsTtUuVvWwXxYyZz 1234567890**
Verdana	AaBbCcDdEeFfGgHhIiJjKkLlMmNnOoPp QqRrSsTtUuVvWwXxYyZz 1234567890
Impact	**AaBbCcDdEeFfGgHhIiJjKkLlMmNnOoPp QqRrSsTtUuVvWwXxYyZz 1234567890**
Georgia	AaBbCcDdEeFfGgHhIiJjKkLlMmNnOoPp QqRrSsTtUuVvWwXxYyZz 1234567890
Times	**AaBbCcDdEeFfGgHhIiJjKkLlMmNnOoPp QqRrSsTtUuVvWwXxYyZz 1234567890**
Courier	AaBbCcDdEeFfGgHhIiJjKkLlMmNnOoPp QqRrSsTtUuVvWwXxYyZz 1234567890
Trebuchet	AaBbCcDdEeFfGgHhIiJjKkLlMmNnOoPp QqRrSsTtUuVvWwXxYyZz 1234567890

USING CSS FOR TEXT FORMATTING

Every browser has a default style sheet that tells it how to display a web page—certain options can be altered by the user, for example text size and whether or not to show images. The problem with this is that even if a designer specifies the size that he or she wants text to appear in, pure HTML text can only be styled in relative sizes, ranging from 1 to 7, or by using heading tags like <H1>. Allied to this, text sometimes appears differently across Macs and PCs, although such problems are less common today. Typically, differences between the two platforms are now restricted to line-heights and anti-aliasing affecting widths—at least if you use the most suitable methods of defining text size.

Using CSS style sheets (see *CSS*, pages 174–175), however, an exact size measurement can be declared for text. You can use a number of units, although few of them are consistent across browsers and platforms. For instance, points (pt), inches (in), millimeters (mm), and picas (pc) are generally best avoided.

Pixels are commonly used to set the size of website text, mainly because such text tends to look the same across browsers and platforms.

Text management

However, there is one major disadvantage to sizing text in pixels: users of Internet Explorer for Windows cannot adjust this size by going to View > Text Size. Every other browser enables you to amend the size of text defined in pixels, but not IE. Therefore, if using pixels, be careful and ensure everything is readable. Don't fall into the trap of creating pages with small, neat, but ultimately unreadable text.

Ultimately, what's good for a designer is not necessarily best for a user. If you fix the text size of a page, you risk limiting its accessibility—not everyone has the same powers of vision. Instead you may want to think about specifying different style sheets for different kinds of user. With a combination of CSS and JavaScript, it's possible to change every element on a page simply by selecting a choice from a menu. This way you don't automatically end up designing to a common denominator. For more on the accessibility benefits of using CSS, see the W3C page at: www.w3.org/TR/CSS-access.

We've briefly touched on the advantages of CSS over font tags, noting the ability to affect styles on a site-wide basis. However, CSS goes much further than that, and includes a plethora of useful properties for typographers—see box.

There are other properties, too, including (but not limited to) word-spacing, letter-spacing, text-decoration, vertical-align, text-align, text-indent, and line-height. Previously, typographers on the web didn't quite have the same level of freedom as print designers.

BITMAP TEXT IMAGES

Text created as a GIF or JPEG (although the former is the best format for text) is treated the same as any other image on a page. On the plus side the size and typeface will remain faithful to the designer's original styling (it's a fixed pattern of pixels, after all), which can be ideal for title graphics that need to use a font that may not be available on many computer systems.

On the downside, text graphics take up more memory than HTML-based/CSS-styled text, increasing a page's loading time. And if someone views web pages with the images turned off, the text won't appear; so you need to make good use of alt tags. Furthermore, bitmap images cannot be read by a search engine spider, and hinder

Heading 1

Heading 2

Heading 3

Heading 4

Heading 5

Heading 6

Browsers offer ways to increase or decrease text size, a trick that can destroy layouts. Setting sizes in pixels (px) avoids this, but be sure type is readable. H tags demonstrate the range of the old-fashioned relative text scaling controls: less flexible than CSS methods.

search engine optimization. This can be difficult given that if images are used to display text, then that text is often very important. The nuances a spider might look for, such as an H1 or a <b> tag, will never be present.

Also, the visually impaired won't be able to increase the size of graphical text (unless using Opera, which can scale entire web pages), so take care when designing interfaces.

It can be hard to create a web page without using any text that is displayed as an image, especially with regard to titles. Each graphic should have a corresponding alt tag in the HTML code, containing the plain text equivalent of the word or phrase in the graphic. This allows search engines to read the text and makes the page accessible to visually impaired web surfers. One golden rule is never to render body copy as

a graphic: the low resolution of web graphics, would make it invariably hard to read. Furthermore, it cannot be copied, is difficult to update, and even when zoomed, it doesn't get any easier to read.

VECTOR TEXT

Adobe Flash offers an additional range of possibilities for displaying text. Most browsers support the Flash plug-in, but you must check that this applies across your main target audience; some organizations forbid the use of any plug-ins on their browsers, and not all portable devices support Flash, such as Apple's iPhones.

You can use HTML text in Flash, or you can style the text using a font outline embedded in the SWF file (the file created when you export a finished file out of Flash). You can also "break" a word down, so that the text becomes a vector graphic no longer dependent on an embedded font. HTML text will appear the same as it does in an HTML document, but the other two options provide scalable antialiased text.

Generally, the same rules apply to Flash as to images: don't use Flash-based text for the sake of it. It's useful for headings and display copy (and has advantages over images, as files sizes are often smaller). However, don't use it for body copy unless the entire site is to be Flash-based. Doing so may alienate your audience, although Flash at least has fewer problems than bitmap-based text (text can be zoomed, for instance).

ONLINE FONT SERVICES

Services are now available to address the cons of formatting text for the web and using text as graphics. For example, http://webfonts.fonts.com works across any platform and browser with minimal CSS involvement and enables visitors to see your web page as you intend them to.

Working with web color

Even with innovations like sRGB (see page 44), web designers face many problems when using color on the Internet. The difficulty is twofold: first, you cannot plan what setup a user will have when he or she visits a web page, and second, you cannot anticipate how an observer will actually see the color. Arguably, with the former problem, most computer users now possess combinations of hardware and software that enable them to view pages using sophisticated RGB color without experiencing something very differently from another visitor. However, if you take the time to look at how, for instance, most monitors are operated, i.e., with no calibration at all, you'll see that it is crucial to employ some standards. The latter is more often than not completely overlooked by designers, most of whom tend to have very standard color vision, but it is at the core of the accessibility guidelines for web design (www.w3c.org/WAI). Don't forget that color perception is subjective, because it is a biological sensation.

It's useful to summarize the following information in two ways: examining the possible parameters for using color on the web, and then looking at how to implement color text and graphics successfully.

DON'T RELY SOLELY ON COLOR

Ignoring for a moment the issues of seeing the right color from a design point of view, you should bear in mind that many people suffer

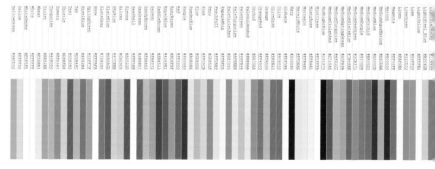

SCREEN DESIGN

from a degree of color blindness, meaning they may not be able to readily differentiate between some combinations at all. In addition, a color page may be viewed on a black-and-white screen—for example, E Ink devices, such as Amazon's Kindle, show pages in black-and-white only. Don't rely solely on color for emphasis. In text, consider using HTML tags or CSS to add weight to a word. Also, navigation systems where choices are based on color are very rarely the best ones. Make sure that foreground and background colors provide enough contrast to be clearly visible. Both of these points are outlined in the W3C web content accessibility guidelines, and a full, authoritative account of how to use color on the web can be found at: www.w3c.org/Conferences/WWW4/Papers/53/gq-alloc.html.

Below: The W3C HTML and CSS standards list only 16 valid color names, which are aqua, black, blue, fuchsia, gray, green, lime, maroon, navy, olive, purple, red, silver, teal, white, and yellow, although most browsers recognise a wider range of color names as this chart from w3schools.com shows. It is always best to specify web colors by their Hexadecimal values

Web design color considerations

Take into consideration the slightly different way color behaves on screens. Because what's seen is created by light shining out at the viewer rather than light bouncing off the surface of paper, white and pale colors can be relatively dazzling.

The question of how many colors to use on a page is hard to answer. It seems obvious to avoid using too many colors, but how many is too many, and is this really a hard-and-fast rule?

If a number of different shades of one or two colors are used, the effect can be very subtle and sophisticated. On the other hand, using fewer but clearly different colors can look a mess if not handled carefully. It is all really a matter of good design sense, just as it would be in print. Experiment with the way colors work together on screen and note how bright and dark tones and hues behave. Watch out for dazzling combinations that make text hard to read, and always ensure there's enough contrast between text and background—it's harder to read screen-based text than printed material. Be aware of the effect of clashing complementary colors, and remember that bright, saturated colors on screen can appear a lot stronger than they do in print. If you remember to analyze how things look as you work, you should avoid color disasters.

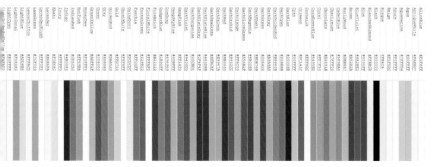

Managing images on the web

The way that you work with your images is critical and always rests on keeping a high-quality source image independently of the resized, converted, and compressed versions that might be created from it.

LOW-QUALITY WEB IMAGES

Many images used in web work are low-resolution, 72dpi (dots per inch) scans. Without the original, imagine the difficulties that would occur if a printed version of the image were required (as they often are, usually for marketing purposes). A 72dpi scan leaves no room for maneuver: try to scale it up and you'll lose image quality; attempt to improve image quality and you'll soon find you're working with a very limited number of pixels in the overall image, which means that any adjustments risk looking obvious. Because there aren't sufficient pixels to allow for a smooth transition over an area, you'll find yourself working in a very intolerant environment.

COMPRESSED IMAGES

Many images, such as pictures from a digital camera, are initially generated as JPEGs, a "lossy" file format designed to provide efficient image compression (see Compression formats for the web, right). Digital cameras, unless set otherwise, tend not to compress images particularly heavily, so quality isn't usually an issue with original shots. However, there may be a temptation to save on storage space by compressing the originals further, or by optimizing the original rather than saving a new copy. Try to resist this temptation, and keep your camera set at as high a quality as possible, while still allowing for a good number of pictures on the storage card.

Once you have your images ready, it's worth spending time planning a file management strategy before moving everything to your computer. If you always archive original images and work with copies, returning to the original whenever a new, edited version is needed, then you'll always have access to the best-quality images for any purpose.

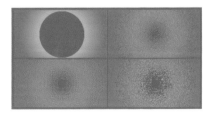

Photoshop's GIF transparency dither options, shown clockwise from top left: No dither,

Diffusion dither, Noise dither, and Pattern dither.

Compression formats for the web

File compression may be either "lossless" or "lossy." In lossless compression, all of the original data contained in a file will be restored when it is decompressed into another format. GIF images are an example of a lossless compression format. Lossy compression, by contrast, relies on permanently removing information. In JPEG images, for example, increasing amounts of image data are removed as the degree of compression increases, or as files are opened and resaved. Obviously, lossy compression can create files of a smaller size (in general, though there are exceptions) than lossless compression, but with the trade-off of worse image quality.

Interlacing

If an image is interlaced, a low-resolution version will appear in a browser almost immediately following the user's download request. The image will then continue to be redrawn until it reaches its maximum resolution.

Transparency

A color in an image's palette can be selected to display transparently in the GIF and PNG formats. This technique is useful for blending an image with a background color. Note that this isn't the same as alpha transparency: only a single color is removed. If you blend red to transparent, and then place the GIF on a web page with a blue background, you'll see the original blend is replaced with an abrupt color change. You can get around this to some extent using Photoshop's transparency dithering controls, but the results are seldom brilliant.

GIF

The Graphics Interchange Format is best used for drawn graphics with flat colors rather than photographic images, as it is limited to a maximum of 256 separate colors. GIF files can be incredibly compact, and are well suited to bitmap images of text and simple logo graphics. GIF is a good cross-platform format, making it ideal for use on the Internet, and comes in two varieties: GIF 87a and GIF 89a. The latter type supports animation and interlacing.

JPEG

This lossy format is ideal for any images with continuous tones, such as photographic images, because it supports 24-bit (millions of colors) images without the need for large file sizes. JPEG does not support transparency or interlacing. The more recent JPEG2000 format does support an alpha channel.

PNG

A relatively new file type, the Portable Network Graphics format was designed specifically for the web. It supports lossless 24-bit image compression with 8-bit transparency, although the latter feature is not supported by all browsers. While a good web format, PNG files are larger than JPEGs and GIFs.

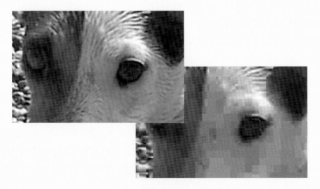

A bitmap image can be compressed to dramatically small file sizes when saved in the JPEG format. However, this involves losing quality in order to save space; the higher the JPEG compression, the lower the image quality will be. Many programs offer ways to compare different compression settings side by side to help you find the right balance of size and quality.

COLOR/IMAGE

4

COLOR MATTERS

THE APPROPRIATE AND EMOTIVE use of color is integral to the competence of the digital graphic designer. In our consumer-led, information-rich, entertainment-orientated society, the designer must understand thoroughly both the nature of color and the way in which it works in order to use it effectively.

There are several reasons why the nature and the workings of color are important. First, when designing on screen with color (and when screen color is actually used in web and multimedia projects), that color is transmitted directly from a white light source. However, when color is reproduced through the use of printing inks, the colors are not transmitted but reflected. Crucially, the range of colors that can be printed with inks is smaller than and different from the range that can be created from white light on a computer monitor. So the final digital file, particularly one used for print, must contain reliable information about color output.

WHERE DOES COLOR COME FROM?

All color comes from pure, white light. Light passed through a glass prism splits into the colors of the spectrum; the colors seen from the prism are transmitted directly onto the retina. Similarly, colors seen on a computer monitor are also transmitted directly onto the retina. Since all the data that constructs computer imagery is digital, monitors need a method whereby colors of the spectrum can be quickly simulated. The method used displays only the three primary colors that make up white light, in a grid of pixels. By using up to 256 different intensity levels of each primary color to display each pixel, you get a total of 6.7 million colors (256 x 256 x 256). The three primary colors used are red, green, and blue—RGB. If we only viewed on screen, our understanding of primary colors could stop there. However, most designers also produce design for print, so they have to simulate color through printing inks. Ink colors are perceived by the viewer through the reflection of light from the printed surface. The RGB primaries apply exclusively to transmitted light, and for reflected light we need a second set of three colors. These are cyan, magenta, and yellow—CMY.

Opposite: This powerful poster by Nicklaus Troxler shows how vibrant colors contribute to the verve of the subject matter and help to delineate the composition.
DESIGN BY NICKLAUS TROXLER

25 Jahre Kleintheater Luzern

ADDITIVE AND SUBTRACTIVE COLOR It is important for the digital graphic designer to understand the different ways colors are created.

Color theory

TRANSMITTED OR ADDITIVE COLOR

When one primary transmitted color is combined with another, more light is perceived than with one color alone. For this reason, red, green, and blue are referred to as the additive primary colors. All three colors add up to white. Thus, combining red light with green light, for instance, produces a color that starts to approach white light (in fact, yellow). Similarly, a combination of red and blue produces magenta, and a combination of blue and green produces cyan. It will be seen that each primary additive (or transmitted) color appears the way it does because each represents white light minus two primaries. Thus, for example, red is white light minus green and blue.

REFLECTED OR SUBTRACTIVE COLOR

In our material world, everything we see has a particular color because most matter absorbs white light (which we get, with varying degrees of purity, from sunlight and artificial light) to a greater or lesser extent. Black objects absorb all the white light that shines on them, whereas white objects reflect all the white light that hits them. What is generally understood to be an object's color is, in reality, only the reflection of certain amounts of the three primary colors. It is a combination of these that is perceived and

Below: The human eye is able to see a greater range of color than either CMYK printing or RGB monitors are able to reproduce. Generally, more vibrant colors are available on screen than can be printed.

A = CMYK process
B = RGB monitor
C = The visible spectrum

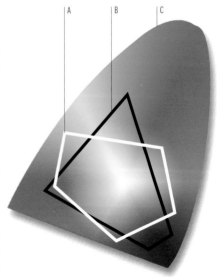

COLOR/IMAGE

Additive color

This diagram represents Red, Green, and Blue light falling onto a white surface. Yellow is formed when Red and Green overlap because there is additional light in that area. When all three colors overlap, we see white since all the components of white light are now present.

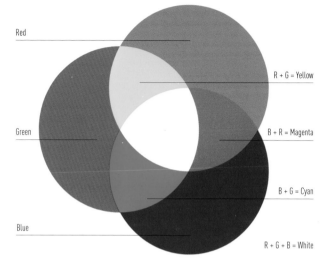

Red

R + G = Yellow

Green

B + R = Magenta

B + G = Cyan

Blue

R + G + B = White

Subtractive color

Here, three primary subtractive colored inks have been printed onto paper. Each of these colors has one of the additive primaries subtracted so, where two overlap, two primary colors are subtracted leaving only one of the primaries visible. Once all three subtractive colors overlap then all three components of white light are absorbed; no light escapes and black is perceived. In practice a small amount of light does get reflected and a true black is not achievable using only Cyan, Magenta, and Yellow. To correct this printers use a fourth ink, Black, to create deep shadow areas necessary for good color-image reproduction.

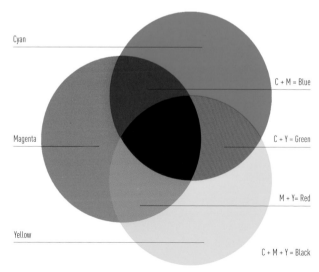

Cyan

C + M = Blue

Magenta

C + Y = Green

M + Y = Red

Yellow

C + M + Y = Black

Color theory

interpreted as a particular color. For example, if an object appears red, it means that the material of which it is made is absorbing all the green and blue light, leaving only the red part of the spectrum to be reflected. Paints, inks and all other kinds of coloring pigment behave in the same way, by subtracting (absorbing) a certain amount of light and reflecting the rest.

Since pigments subtract color from white light, it should be easy to see why red, green, and blue inks cannot be combined to mix colors for printing on white paper (which reflects the red, green, and blue that compose white light). Remembering that each primary additive color is white light minus two other primaries, it should be clear that mixing any two primaries as pigments (making them part of the reflective surface rather than transmitted light) will result in color being absorbed.

If the goal is to mix a wide range of printing colors from a small number of basic hues (say three), colors that absorb only one primary color must be identified. You will recall that the secondary colors—cyan, magenta, and yellow—are each achieved by absorbing (subtracting) just one primary color from white light. Similarly, mixing two secondary colors will absorb (subtract) two transmitted colors and leave the third. Thus, mixing cyan pigment with yellow pigment would produce green; mixing cyan with magenta would produce blue; and mixing magenta and yellow would produce red. All printing devices can therefore use cyan, magenta, and yellow as printing primary colors.

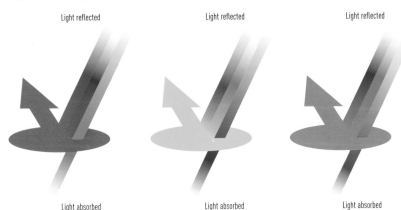

Light reflected   Light reflected   Light reflected

Light absorbed   Light absorbed   Light absorbed

COLOR/IMAGE

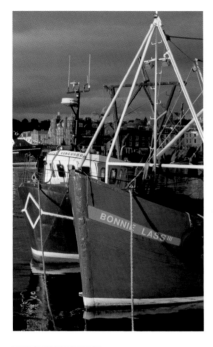

RGB

Red

Green

Blue

Photoshop's Channels palette shows how an image is composed in RGB or CMYK mode. On the right are the four channels of CMYK, which appear very much like the proofs taken from each lithographic printing plate. The channels displaying RGB (left) are instantly recognizable by the areas of black in each channel, which represent the absence of light.

CMYK

Cyan

Magenta

Yellow

Black

Note that the top images in these palettes are not channels themselves but provide a view of the combined channels.

SINCE THE COMPUTER MONITOR generates white light, it is able to display virtually all the colors that the eye is capable of seeing. However, it is a fact of physics that (mirrors excepted) all objects absorb some light, even if only a very small amount. Thus the entire spectrum can never be reflected.

Color gamut

The white of a computer screen is always much brighter than the whitest of white printing papers. This is because paper does not reflect all the white light that falls on it. The rich and vibrant pigments used in paints and inks cannot match the brilliance of the computer screen.

It is also impractical to use thousands of different colored inks to reproduce colored images. In printing, therefore, the three basic colors of cyan (C), magenta (M), and yellow (Y) are "mixed" to simulate real-world color as closely as possible. Black (K) ink is also added to boost shadow areas and make them crisper. Mixing is achieved by printing formations of tiny dots, each of a separate color, that merge when read. This method of reproduction is known as four-color process (CMYK, or just "process"). The use of only cyan, magenta, yellow, and black thus produces a restricted range of colors known as process colors.

PANTONE MATCHING SYSTEM

If a job only requires one or two colors, it would be unnecessary to run a four-color press. A special color of ink would be much more useful than a mix of cyan, magenta, yellow, and black. Many printers once held stocks of inks from a number of different ink manufacturers but, for practical reasons, the range of colors was somewhat limited. The PANTONE Matching System was devised to meet

the needs of designers who want to specify a special color. It is essentially a set of basic ingredients (standardized pigments) and a recipe book in the form of a color sampler containing hundreds of colors that can be created by mixing the specified amounts of the standardized pigments. By following these color recipes, printers across the world can accurately mix and match any PANTONE color from their basic stock and use it on their presses. The resulting colors are solid ink colors, known as spot colors or specials, and they are quite unlike the colors simulated by halftone dots in the four-color printing process. Thanks to the stronger and wider range of pigments used, many PANTONE color mixes can be more vivid and vibrant than those achievable using only CMYK.

To give the digital graphic designer the widest range of color choice, for print, almost all graphics arts software shows the full range of PANTONE colors as well as providing cyan, magenta, yellow, and black (CMYK) controls for mixing process colors. The designer has the option of choosing either a PANTONE color to be printed as a spot color, or one to be simulated by cyan, magenta, yellow and black. Simulation can be successful but in many cases a good match cannot be achieved because the PANTONE color is beyond the range achievable by the four-color process (out of gamut).

Above: Some of the brighter and subtler shades of color will be lost when an image goes to CMYK printing. In these illustrations Photoshop's gamut warning is shown in green, revealing the shades that will be lost from the original RGB image when it is printed in CMYK.

Right: When a PANTONE color is mixed according to the recipes shown on the swatch, it is inks that are being mixed to produce a single colored ink. This is radically different from the simulation of a color by the use of small dots of CMYK, which creates the illusion of color change.

PANTONE® Color Form
PANTONE® Color
PANTO
PANTONE® Color Formula Guide

PANTONE 483 C	8 parts PANTONE 8 parts PANTON 4 parts PANTON		PANTONE 3935 C	16 parts PA 1/8 part PA 160 parts PA	PANTONE 3242 C	PANTONE 2635 C	1 part PANTONE Violet 15 parts PANTONE Trans. White	6.2 93.8
PANTONE 484 C	8 parts PAN 8 parts PA 1 part PA		PANTONE 3945 C	16 parts 1/8 part 30 part	PANTONE 3252 C	PANTONE 2645 C	2 parts PANTONE Violet 14 parts PANTONE Trans. White	12.5 87.5
PANTONE 485 C	8 part 8 par		PANTONE 3955 C	16 1/8 7	PANT 3262	PANTONE 2655 C	4 parts PANTONE Violet 12 parts PANTONE Trans. White	25.0 75.0
PANTONE 486 C			PANTONE 3965 C		PA 32	PANTONE 2665 C	8 parts PANTONE Violet 8 parts PANTONE Trans. White	50.0 50.0

COLOR ATTRIBUTES Whether color is transmitted directly onto the retina or reflected from printed pigments, it has various attributes which can be measured and specified to define it. There are many different ways of describing color, some useful for technical purposes, others more intuitive as a way of thinking about the appearance of color and the relationship between different colors and shades.

Describing color

One of the most useful ways to describe color is in terms of hue, saturation, and brightness (referred to as either HSB or HSL, "lightness" replacing brightness). These terms underpin dialogues between users throughout the graphic arts industry.

HUE

Hue is essentially interchangeable with the word "color" as we normally use it. The colors of the spectrum are often displayed in a circle or "color wheel," and we can use basic names to identify each main color: red, orange, yellow, green, blue, cyan, magenta, violet . . . When we refer to a color as being "orange," we are identifying its hue. Whether it is vibrant, dull, pale, or dark, we still recognize it as orange.

SATURATION

Saturation refers to the vibrancy and purity of a color. The colors we see are made up from the three primary colors. A total absence of light—no red, green, or blue—of course is black. If there are equal, full strengths of red, green, and blue, white is perceived (white light, as you will recall from prism experiments at school, contains all the colors). As gray lies between black and white, it must be made up of equal amounts of less-than-total red, green, and blue. It is the fact

that the amounts are equal that makes gray "desaturated"—neutral.

If we now, for example, gradually increase the red element, while decreasing the blue and green, the gray will turn redder and eventually become a totally saturated red. The more balanced its red, green, and blue components, the less saturated a color appears.

BRIGHTNESS

Brightness (sometimes referred to as lightness or tone) refers to how much light is present. Saturation or desaturation of a color depends on the ratios of red to green to blue, not necessarily the overall quantity of light. If a large amount of light is used to create a color, irrespective of the ratios of red, green, and blue, the color will be bright (or light). If little light is used overall, then the color is perceived as being dark.

COLOR MANAGEMENT

In the digital realm, we can describe color in terms of hue, saturation, and brightness by setting each on a scale, typically from 0 to 100 (a familiar scale to humans) or 0 to 255 (familiar to computers). But what exactly does this scale refer to? We could fire the electron guns in a CRT monitor in the proportions directly dictated by our HSB values, but the progression through the scale might be quite uneven, and the result would be different on each monitor.

Decades before the advent of desktop computers, it was realized that the industry needed a way to describe how color appeared to the human eye and brain in such a way that a numeric color specification would refer precisely to a certain perceived color. The solution was the Munsell system, which formed the basis of new "color models" devised by the CIE, an international commission.

In the 1990s, the ICC (International Color Consortium)—founded by Apple, Adobe, and other digital companies—devised an industry standard for swapping color definitions accurately between digital devices. The particular way a device chooses to define colors, within the range of colors it can actually handle, is known as its "color space." To be ICC-compatible, each device must come with a "color profile" that relates its color space to a CIE color space. Armed with a CMS (color management system) and a profile for each device involved in production (including software programs), a computer can ensure color images are transferred accurately from one device to the next, all the way from taking a digital photo, for example, to seeing it printed on a magazine page.

At least, that's the theory! In practice, few people know how to set up color management effectively. Apple naturally added an ICC CMS to its own Mac operating system, under the name ColorSync, and most Mac products are ICC-compatible. Windows now also has a CMS built in, but Microsoft does not encourage anyone to use it. Instead, it recommends that every device should use the "sRGB" color space, a general purpose model. That would work fine, except that sRGB is not a very good color space, and converting color imagery (such as professional digital photos and scans) into it risks compromising quality.

Ideally, the color profile of any hardware device shouldn't just be the preset or "canned" one supplied by its manufacturer; you should test or "calibrate" the device at regular intervals and recreate a profile according to its exact color performance. This requires extra hardware and software. Calibrators for monitors are quite affordable, though, and professional designers should seriously consider investing in one. If the screen you are looking at is not representing color accurately, there is little hope that the system as a whole will deliver the results you expect.

The Saturation level of the top picture is high and that of the bottom picture is very low.

The Brightness level of the top picture is low and that of the bottom picture is very high.

IMAGE CREATION

4

IMAGES created on the computer can range from a simple icon printed in one color to a multi-layered photographic montage using all the colors of the spectrum.

Different types of image include diagrams, charts, graphs, maps, technical illustrations, logos, icons, symbols, photographs, collages, montages, and photomontages, any of which might be incorporated into a design to inform or entertain, or both.

Images are designed in different styles, both for aesthetic reasons as well to meet production limitations. They may be in black and white, grayscale, or full color, and may be produced as monotones or duotones. They may be square, rectangular, or geometrically shaped, or appear unbounded on the page or surface.

What images are, what they do, and how they are created are of considerable importance to the graphic designer. Image-making requires care, a rich visual language, a sense of purpose, and sensitivity to the way in which the outcome can affect the viewer.

Many graphic designers concerned with image-making are, or become, photographers and illustrators, with much of what they create being integral to their own designs. The graphic designer's motivation often springs from a client-generated brief, the parameters of which will often dictate the use of type and image.

WHERE TO OBTAIN IMAGES

Rich sources of copyright-free art are available on CD and the Internet, which, together with images generated by the designer, can provide a springboard for inventive, image-based design solutions. Collections of imagery can inspire the designer into developing, simplifying, or synthesizing them to support a project. This can often be detected in icon or logo design, where several visual references may have been modified and fused into a single graphic symbol. Much of the time, however, the graphic designer is the creative

Opposite: Mood and atmosphere can be generated from creative image manipulation in a bitmap editing application. Qualities of layering, transparency, and depth are obtained by the inventive use of various Photoshop functions.

DESIGNED FOR MACUSER MAGAZINE BY TOM HINGSTON STUDIO, UK

manager of visual components and uses images created by illustrators and photographers. A balance has to be maintained between giving the illustrator or photographer creative freedom and ensuring that the commissioned work complements the project. Building a good working relationship and establishing a rapport with other artists is essential to professional working practice and to getting the right results.

The advent of digital control over images has almost immeasurably expanded the creative scope of illustrators and photographers. With accessible, powerful software for creating and manipulating images at their fingertips, digital graphic designers can produce a wide range of graphic effects to incorporate into existing or newly created images. Respect for the integrity of other image-making professionals is, of course, extremely important. It is not ethical either to alter another professional's work or to manipulate it gratuitously. However, by agreement or in collaboration, it is possible to modify the original dimensions, mood, and meaning of an image.

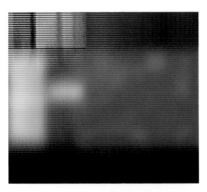 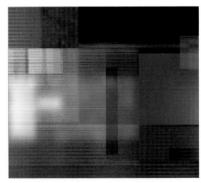

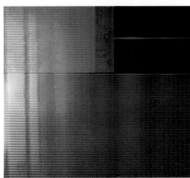 

THE DEVELOPMENT OF SOFTWARE for easy and creative image-making continues in leaps and bounds. Just when the designer exhausts all the tools of one program, an updated version hits the market, adding a plethora of new features.

Imaging software

As programs become feature-rich, they attempt to be all things to all people, and in doing so may mask the fact that the behavior of some aspects of image creation is not entirely compatible with others. It is easy to be overwhelmed by the multitude of features available, so it helps to have an appreciation of some of the underlying principles.

There are essentially two different types of image-making program: bitmap, also known as "painting" or "photo editing" software, and

Below opposite: Libraries of images on CD or DVD are widely available, as well as web-based "royalty-free" picture collections. Images are offered at varying resolutions to meet different requirements, and often the price will vary according to file size. Low-resolution images (72-96dpi) are suitable for screen-based work; high resolution (around 300dpi at A4 size) is required for commercial print quality; and extra-large images will be needed for full-bleed spreads or where part of the picture is to be blown up.

Right: Bitmap images (above right) may be available in full color or as "grayscales" printed in a single color. Images with no gradations between black and white are called line art, sometimes also referred to as "bitmap" images (right), although the correct term in this case would be "1-bit." "Bitmap" is also used to refer to one-color digital images.

drawing, also referred to as "vector." The two ways of storing graphics are completely different, but they can be used within the same program and combined within the same artwork or layout.

BITMAP EDITING PROGRAMS

The industry-standard bitmap program, used by digital graphic designers, photographers, web designers, and the printing industry, is Adobe Photoshop. There are various other bitmap programs used by artists and illustrators, such as Corel Paint Shop Pro and Corel PhotoPAINT, as well as specialist tools such as Corel Painter which, unlike other "painting" programs, really does simulate paint—along with pencils, pastels, and many other real world art media.

Bitmap programs are used for creating single images, not multi-page documents. Their pri-

mary function is to adjust the color values of the pixels that—in a grid of anything up to several million locations—make up every digital image, such as a photo from a digital camera. From a distance, of course, you don't notice the individual square pixels within an image, only the overall effect. Equally, you don't have to be aware that the software is modifying pixels; it appears to make subtle changes across all or part of a picture. Many different "filters" can be used to adjust color balance, increase the impression of sharpness, change the balance of light and shadow, and so on. Alternatively, you can "paint" with the mouse directly on to the part of the image you want to change, or more literally paint blobs and lines of color onto a blank "canvas." Photoshop and some other bitmap editors now also provide vector drawing

Imaging software

tools, and can store type as scalable vectors, "rasterizing" it to a bitmap when you finish off your artwork.

BITMAP ADVANTAGES

Bitmap software is the best way to manipulate photographic and other "continuous tone" images, such as paintings or scanned artwork. In the real world, hues and shades merge imperceptibly with each other in every direction. This "continuous tone" effect would be impossible to reproduce using discrete shapes, as in vector drawing. Instead, the digital camera or scanner divides what it sees into a fixed grid of squares and measures the color in each. When these colors are displayed on the monitor as pixels, they recreate the visual impression of the scene with its continuously varying tone. Software tools can alter pixel values in a gradual way, maintaining realism.

The amount of detail that can been seen in a scanned image (the same applies to any digital image) depends entirely on how many times per inch the scanner is made to record the color values. This figure is the resolution. High resolution is obtained when pixel information is recorded at, say, 300 points across every inch (300ppi); a low-resolution scan might record 72 points per inch (72ppi).

BITMAP DISADVANTAGES

Bitmap images have two disadvantages. First, in terms of digital storage, they are very space-

Above: The essence of a bitmap image is that shapes and images are made up entirely from the uniform arrangement of varying colored pixels. There is no underlying structure to describe this shape.

hungry. The color values of every pixel in the image—typically several million—must be identified and recorded. This large amount of information can be reduced to some degree by using "data compression" techniques such as LZW or JPEG, but only up to a point. Second, because a bitmap image has no structure other than a sequence of pixels arranged in a grid, when you enlarge it the pixels just get bigger. The viewer will soon lose the illusion of a smooth image and become aware of the individual colored squares. Unless the image can be recreated from scratch at a higher resolution (for example by re-scanning an analogue photo), you can never scale up a bitmap beyond a certain point without its visual quality suffering badly.

Left: These images have been scanned at 300ppi, 150ppi, 72ppi, and 36ppi. The lower the scan resolution the less information captured and therefore the coarser the image. In order to display these images the same size, on screen or in print, we have had to enlarge the low-resolution images.

Above: Bitmap applications provide photo-realism and are useful for applying graphics such as logos or advertising into real-life situations. Here a corporate identity has been digitally applied to a photo of a vehicle so the look can be tested before implementing the design.

Above: Duotones are usually grayscale images overprinted black onto a copy of the image, which has been printed in spot color to provide depth and interest. Generally the angle of screen for the black is set at zero and the angle of screen for the spot color

is set at 450, which allows the color to be more visible. Digitization of the image allows for considerable control of the tonal range across the black and spot-color versions of the image.

PHOTO / ED SEABOURNE

Imaging software

VECTOR-BASED PROGRAMS

Vector-based programs describe the shape of an object as a series of strategically placed points connected by lines controlled by mathematical formulae—rather like a "join the-dots" picture with the added benefit that the connections between points can be precisely described as straight or curved lines. The line is called a path or a vector. Paths can have thickness (stroke) and color, and the shapes or objects they create can also be filled with a color, gradient, texture, and so forth. Each object can be moved around a page independently, which allows them to be arranged and rearranged, overlaying or underlying each other as appropriate. By altering the position of the points and the ways in which the paths connect them, the vectors and the resulting shapes they make can be re-formulated.

Vectors are an ideal way of describing the outline shape of letterforms, and in fact font files are essentially a collection of outline vectors. Vector images allow for good-quality scaling both on screen and when output from a printer's RIP (see page 92). When a vector image is re-sized, the mathematical formulae ensure that all the points and paths are repositioned so as to maintain their original relationships. Since coloring is simply the filling-in of a defined shape, the scaled shape is automatically refilled. Objects described by outline information are memory-efficient, since a relatively compact set of numbers can describe quite complex shapes and color fills. Vectors, however, cannot produce photo-realistic images, since realism needs a constantly shifting description of tone and color that can be satisfactorily carried out only by the subtle changes in pixel color achievable by bit-map techniques.

This page: Even apparently rough-edged images benefit from being created by vectors. This logo for Chronicle Books has been enlarged greatly from the same small-scale Adobe Illustrator file seen below, but still keeps a clean, sharp edge. This would have been impossible from a small-scale bitmap file.

COLOR/IMAGE

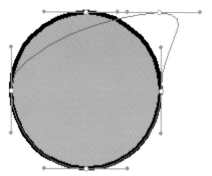

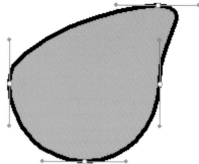

Above: The fundamentals of vector shapes are points joined by straight or curved lines controlled by either moving these points or adjusting the curves between them by means of curve levers. All drawing applications use this method of creating simple or complex paths and shapes. It is well worth taking the trouble to master how to use the Path or Pen tools as they are absolutely essential to digital image creation.

Below: Pamela Geismar of San Francisco's Chronicle Books was able to color up the humorous illustrations of Thorina Rose, taking advantage of Illustrator 9's transparent colors, for the book Office Kama Sutra. It was essential to be able to lay transparent colors in Multiply mode to allow the gray tones to show through.

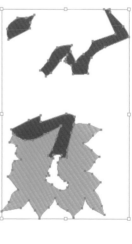

Imaging software

VECTORS AND BITMAPS TOGETHER

Most major graphic arts programs can handle both vectors and bitmaps, although they represent different imaging technologies. However, one or other technology generally dominates each program. For example, all page-layout and drawing programs are essentially vector-based, but they also have the ability to import bitmap pictures. The bitmap is usually contained within a placement holder, such as a "picture box," that may or may not have a visible frame. Vectored objects such as typographic elements, graphic shapes, rules, drawn logos, and technical illustrations may lie over or under imported images.

Unless it is appreciated that an image composed of a grid of pixels is fundamentally different from a vector image, whose component parts are described as outlines and filled shapes, much confusion may occur. The designer may be left wondering why certain tools and functions do not work for both kinds of image.

Page-layout programs such as QuarkXPress and Adobe InDesign now have features that allow for quite a large amount of control over the imported bitmapped images beyond simply changing shape and size or applying tints, and can integrate vector and bitmap elements quite effectively, though less so than Photoshop. InDesign is the more advanced in this area. Adobe Illustrator, FreeHand, and CorelDRAW, all drawing programs, have the capability of modifying imported bitmapped images using various effect filters, and are also able to convert (rasterize) vector objects into bitmaps. Once rasterization has taken place, the vector information is lost and the result is merely a collection of pixels.

Below: Here, a bitmap image is converted into a vector file by placing points and vectors to create outlines around significant bitmap areas of tone and/or color. The resultant outlines can then be filled with color using a drawing application like Illustrator.

COLOR/IMAGE

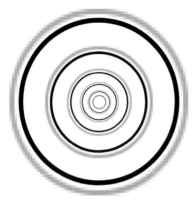

Left: A series of circles of increasing size produced from a single bitmap file, compared to those produced from a single vector file. It is not difficult to see which is which.

Above: A cube drawn in a vector application (left) has been "rasterized" when opened in Photoshop (right). The process converts the vector drawing to a bitmapped (pixel-based) image.

Right: A vector (left) and bitmap (right) version of an image. In order to maintain a similar quality of reproduction when enlarged to 200% the bitmap image must be re-scanned at a much higher resolution than before, resulting in a much larger file size. By comparison, the same vector file may be used at any size. Bitmap images create smooth transitions throughout all the subtle tonal changes; vector images show defined, hard-edged shapes.

By contrast, Photoshop, a bitmap program, has very capable vector-based tools. One use of these is to enable the user to make accurate and smooth selections with the aid of paths. Additionally, text can be created using the outline (vector) information from the font files and still remain editable. In the end, however, vectors and editable text will need to be converted to bitmaps before they can be fully integrated into an image.

Working in the opposite direction, Illustrator, FreeHand and CorelDRAW can process bitmap images and produce outlines (vectors) where colors and tone change. This can be done through the Live Trace feature in Illustrator, or the auto-trace facility in FreeHand.

SCANNING AND RESOLUTION To work successfully with bitmap pictures, the impact of several different but interrelated technologies must be considered. In planning graphic reproduction the intended result needs to be established before the appropriate preparatory steps can be decided upon. In other words it is usually advisable to start from the output end and work backwards to the beginning.

Scanning

SCANNING FOR PRINT

The Print section in Part 2 of this book explains how a printing plate must be made for each color in order to transfer the color-filtered components of the image onto paper. In four- or six-color process, the colored areas of an original image are analyzed for how much of each printing ink is required to simulate the color at any given point. Then the location of each required ink color is transferred to the appropriate plate as tiny, close-printing dots in a conversion procedure called halftoning. The dots in a full-color halftone vary in size according to how much of their ink color is required at a given spot, but even the biggest of dots is so small that it merges almost

There is much confusion about the terminology regarding resolution. Dpi, ppi, lpi—what's the difference? It is quite common for lay persons and professionals alike to use dpi (dots per inch) to describe any type of resolution. Strictly speaking we use the term samples per inch (spi) when referring to scanned bitmaps—but now mostly ppi is used. Pixels per inch (ppi) refer to monitor displays and dots per inch (dpi) refer to particles of ink, toner, or light that are used by printing devices to create images. Halftone dots, created from the smaller printer dots (dpi), are arranged in lines to form a mesh, or screen, and so halftone screens are expressed in lines per inch (lpi).

Above: When an area is enlarged on screen for a zoomed-in view, the application's software creates squares of identically colored pixels to give the illusion of enlargement. Pixels are still displayed at the rate of 72ppi but the illusion is that they have "grown." A similar effect is seen when an image scanned at a low resolution is printed and there are not enough pixels per inch for every halftone dot required. So a few neighboring halftone dots will use the same information and therefore appear identically, both vertically and horizontally. This results in little, visibly definable squares and the picture appearing pixellated.

COLOR/IMAGE

Right: One of the most important concepts to grasp when working with Photoshop is that when the application shows 100% in the bottom left of the picture window, it does not mean the picture is being viewed at actual size. It means that the screen is displaying each scanned pixel with one monitor pixel (pixel for pixel). It can be seen that if an image is scanned at 72ppi (the same resolution as a Mac monitor, which is fixed) then it will appear the correct size. If an image is scanned at, say, 300ppi, then the monitor will require 4.16 inches to show 300 pixels, resulting in a bigger-looking picture. It is not possible to mix pixel resolutions in the one image so when images of variable resolutions are copied and pasted, they will appear to shrink or expand in order to fit the pixel grid of the host image.

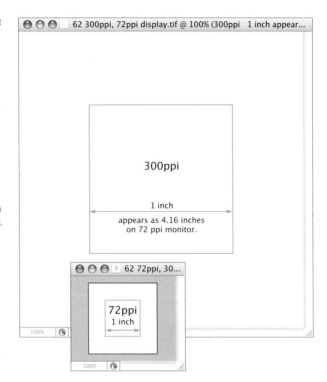

62 300ppi, 72ppi display.tif @ 100% (300ppi 1 inch appear...

300ppi

1 inch

appears as 4.16 inches on 72 ppi monitor.

62 72ppi, 30...

72ppi
1 inch

imperceptibly with the surrounding dots to create the illusion of a visually smooth change of color, tone, and intensity.

Imagesetters (output devices used to generate reproduction-quality copy for printing) have a device resolution of up to 3000 dots per inch (dpi). For most printing work, halftone dots are required at a rate or output resolution of 150 halftone dots per inch. Dividing the imagesetter resolution by the output resolution, we find that a 3000-dpi imagesetter has 20 dots with which to construct the largest halftone dot required.

Since these rates per inch are linear, the largest (100 per cent) halftone dot would be 400 dots in area (20 dots square) and a 10 per cent dot would be around 40 dots in area. That is more than enough to ensure fine reproduction.

The designer's file must obviously contain all the image detail to produce all the tiny halftone dots that represent how much ink falls where. In fully digital printing and direct-to-plate (DTP) imagesetting, the dots transferred to the plate come directly from the designer's file. More conventionally, there is an intermediate stage in

Scanning

which the imagesetter produces prepared photographic negative film, through which the plate's light-sensitive, emulsion-covered surface is then exposed to light. In this case, it is the film that comes directly from the designer's file.

In order to produce output at 150dpi (output resolution), the imagesetter must receive information at a minimum of 150 pixels per inch, or ppi (input resolution). If a picture file has been scanned at a lower resolution, there will be insufficient information to satisfy the imagesetter. In the absence of such information, it will make identically sized halftone dots until new

information reaches it. For instance, if a file can only provide 50ppi (one-third of the necessary linear resolution), an imagesetter set to output at 150dpi must create three identical dots in a row both across and down. This results in a group of 9 identical dots which, when printed, will look like a little square to the naked eye. Worse, the whole image will be made up of these little squares. The way to avoid this is to scan at a high enough resolution to provide at least 150 unique pieces of information for the 150 demands made by the imagesetter.

That is the theory—but there is one small, added complication. Halftone dots are arranged at angles to each other, with a unique angle for each process color. The objective is to ensure that any pattern in the dots does not distract the human eye, so that the image appears smoother and more realistic. Since images are scanned horizontally and vertically rather than at an angle, and since imagesetters lay down the dots from left to right, the requirement to work at an angle

Below: The ideal resolution for print work is 300ppi (left). If the resolution is too low or the image is enlarged too much—thereby reducing the effective resolution—then unwanted pixellation occurs (center). If no halftone dots need to be created, as in line-art images, one may scan at the maximum resolution of the output device, which could be as much as 3,000dpi. However a scan at 600ppi will normally be sufficient to obtain a visually sharp edge (right).

 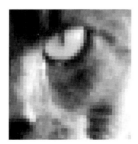 

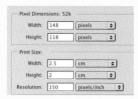

Left and center: Image size and resolution are interlinked. When an image is scanned it may be expressed in two ways. First, by how many pixels it measures horizontally and vertically. This need not dictate how big it will print, just how many bits of information record the picture. Secondly, we are able to give the picture a physical size so that when sent to a printer there is some reference as to how big the picture should be reproduced. Top and center are two versions of a picture that has been scanned once—its pixel size is 148pixels x 118pixels. The top picture is described physically 2.5cm x 2cm at a resolution of 150ppi, whereas the lower picture is described 5cm x 4cm at a resolution of 75ppi. This is very similar to looking at a mosaic on a wall close to or from a distance—the number of squares that make up the picture do not change, it is the viewing distance that makes the picture appear bigger or smaller and coarser or smoother respectively.

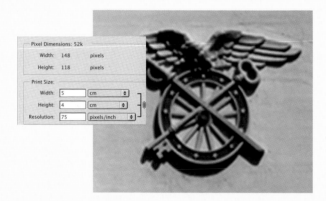

By contrast the picture on the bottom has been given the same physical dimensions as the one in the center but has been scanned at a far higher resolution (300ppi) so that the pixel size is 591pixels x 472pixels.

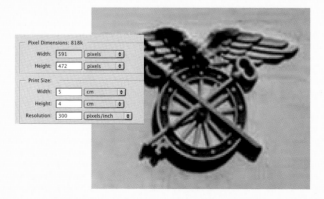

Scanning

increases the demand for accurate information across the inch. For this reason, it is recommend that images should be scanned at between one-and-a-half times and twice the intended output resolution. Most designers tend to err on the side of caution and stick to scanning at double the halftone rate. So, for most general commercial offset litho printing, pictures are scanned at 300ppi. There will be no quality problems if a picture is scanned at higher resolution, but equally there will be no quality improvement. However, there will be an enormous increase in file size and processing time, which will slow all processes down.

If an image is to be printed in solid process color, requiring no halftone dots, it is known as line art. Theoretically, for the best results you could scan that image at 3000ppi to match every imagesetter dot. However this is impractical for file size reasons. For crisp results, line work should be scanned at about 600-1200ppi. Any extra quality obtained from scanning at much above this level of resolution is imperceptible.

The resolution of an image must be correct for the size at which it will be printed. It is no good scanning a picture at 300ppi and then enlarging it dramatically in a page-layout program. Your original picture file will still contain the same information, but it will now be stretched two or three times beyond its original dimensions. This has the effect of substantially lowering the resolution relative to its new size. A small amount of scaling up or down may not result in print quality problems, but it is always best to scan a picture at the correct resolution for the intended output size. Fortunately, most scanning software allows the user to set a resolution and a scaling ratio. The scanner then ensures that the picture is scanned so that the resolution is correct at the new image size.

When buying a scanner, it is important to ascertain the highest resolution actually achievable. Some manufacturers claim a very high output, but this is sometimes achieved by interpolation—the software recalculates its best actual result to add more pixels per inch. Although interpolation will smooth out an image, it will capture no more detail, so always judge by "optical" not "interpolated" resolution. Interpolation also takes place when an image or parts of it are rotated or transformed in some way. Sometimes, owing to looming deadlines or unavailability of the original image, a designer will need to increase a picture's resolution directly in the file. Photoshop can interpolate and increase the number of pixels in an image; if this proves necessary, the bicubic method should always be used for the best results.

FOR SCREEN PRODUCTS

Resolution issues for image use in web pages or multimedia production are much more straightforward than for print, since the designer knows that the audience will be viewing images on a monitor not dissimilar to the one on which the design was created—so the size you see is the

size you'll get. At 96ppi, roughly the resolution of the average modern PC monitor, images contain just 9,216 pixels per square inch, about a tenth the size of a 300ppi file. Apart from bringing file size (with compression) down within a practical range for Internet transmission, this also means the designer's software will work faster than when editing high-resolution print files.

Banding, like posterizing, is normally caused by too much post-scan adjustment of image levels or curves settings.

Preview and adjust levels or curves in the scanner software before making the final scan.

In-scanner adjustments

Compare the difference between applying curves and levels adjustment at the point of scanning with applying it to a plain scan later in Photoshop. The histogram for the pre-adjusted scan is complete, but the plain scan that has been Photoshop-adjusted to achieve the same result clearly suffers from a loss of color information.

The spiked histogram below clearly shows the amount of color information that is lost if adjusting curves and levels is done in Photoshop rather than during the scan.

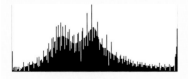

Transparency scanning

In order to scan a transparency, an average flatbed desktop scanner uses a transparency adaptor containing a second light source. The adaptor is mounted above the scanner bed and passes over the transparency, shining light through it on to the sensor arm keeping step below.

Scans of 35mm slides made in this way are rarely impressive because desktop scanners are not designed to scan such small items, which are also hard to press flat against the glass, so results can be a little out of focus.

The solution is to use a dedicated slide scanner. These have lenses and very high-resolution sensors, and can deliver images suitable for use at 8 x 5 inches and even letter sizes at good print resolutions. These devices are fairly specialist, however, and if not restricted to the 35mm format, tend to be very expensive.

WORKING WITH BITMAP IMAGES IN PAINTING PROGRAMS Working on a bitmap image is much more flexible than working with the object-oriented, structured nature of vector shapes. Tools, generically termed "painting tools," can be drawn across a field of tiny pixels to alter them in various ways.

Image manipulation tools

Whether you have selected the eraser, pencil tool, or one of various brush styles, the tool is referred to as a brush. Its "diameter"—the size of the area it affects—is measured in pixels, from 1 up to almost any size. Painting tools can also be assigned an opacity level to determine the extent to which the color applied with the "brush" overwrites existing pixels. The color is chosen by setting the program's current foreground color, although some brushes may use the background color as well to create variation, or may have a preset color scheme.

Left: The three fundamental painting tools of Photoshop - Brush, Pencil, and Airbrush. Most significant is the default antialiasing of the Brush and Airbrush compared to the Pencil. Antialiasing is a technique used by software to place intermediate pixels of lighter tone between one color and another to create an impression of smoothness. Antialiasing replicates the way the eye sees and helps create photo-realistic imagery.

Brushes can either be set up as "pens," consisting of an ellipse (a scalable vector shape) which can be angled for calligraphic effects, or based on a small bitmap image that is repeated along the stroke you paint.

A graphics tablet is a plastic-coated board, ranging in size from around A6 to A2 (though with a smaller "active area"), accompanied by a stylus that is held like a pen. As you touch the stylus to the surface and move it around, its position is transmitted to the computer. This, and various other parameters, such as pressure (how hard you press down) and tilt (the angle at which you hold the stylus), can be assigned to control aspects of the brush as you "paint," allowing more subtle effects to be created.

CLONING
A special form of brush is the clone tool, sometimes called a rubber stamp. With this, you select a point within an image as the "source." When you start to paint, pixels from around this point are applied, so that you are effectively copying one part of the image over another. Because the effect is seamless, this can be used to cover unwanted elements in a photo, or remove scratches and blemishes from scans, leaving the manipulation unnoticeable.

Above and below: Transformations in Photoshop include scaling, rotating, distorting, and perspective.

The History palette shows each move taken and allows the user to go back several stages if desired.

Above: Probably the most useful painting tool in all of Photoshop's armory, the Rubber Stamp tool (Cloning tool) allows one part of an image to be painted across to another part. Combining subtlety of brush size and strength of opacity it is possible to eradicate unwanted material and replace it with other image-forming pixels. In the window to the right can be seen a circle, indicating the size of the active Rubber Stamp brush.

Image manipulation tools

SELECTING

A number of selection tools, including rectangular and elliptical marquees, lasso, and magic wand, can be used to isolate the area of the image you want to change. The edge of the area defined can be "feathered" so that changes fade off gradually rather than leaving a hard outline. You can then apply an adjustment or effect to this entire area, or use it as a mask: brushes will have no effect outside the selected area.

TRANSFORMATIONS

Photoshop menus allow for either the whole image or a selected area to be rotated, mirrored, distorted, or inverted (colors reversed). More complex transformations are also possible.

GLOBAL COLOR ADJUSTMENT

Global color adjustment allows the designer to modify either the entire image or a selected area for color balance, brightness and contrast, saturation levels, color replacement, and general fine-tuning. The effect can be adjusted in a dialog box, and calculations are carried out and implemented by the software according to the type of adjustment selected.

Below: Replace Color in Photoshop allows a certain color range within an image to be adjusted (by manipulating its hue, saturation, and lightness) without affecting other tones. The Fuzziness control dictates the extent of the area changed.

COLOR/IMAGE

LAYERS

Layers exist to help create montage work as well as to allow changes and additions to a picture to be made without irreversibly altering it at each stage. Adding a layer is a little like putting a sheet of clear film over your image and painting onto it. The original image can be seen through the layer, and parts of the film can be cut out and discarded. Areas of a layer can be "masked" to allow the underlying image to show through, but are not actually deleted.

ALPHA CHANNELS AND MASKS

A color file image has a "channel" dedicated to each primary color (RGB or CMYK). Extra channels—alpha channels—can be used to store masks as grayscale images. A mask can represent a selection: where there is white in the channel, those areas are selected, while areas that are black in the channel are unselected, and gray areas partially selected (so that any adjustment or effect applied will take partial effect, as if its opacity had been lowered). So you can use alpha channels to save selections made with the selection tools. An alpha channel saved within the final image file can be accessed by page-layout programs to create "soft cutouts," where an irregularly shaped image is placed over other graphics or text and blends in seamlessly at the edges.

COLOR ATTRIBUTES AND BLENDING MODES

In applying color using brushes or global fills, it is possible to paint with attributes of color rather than with the color itself. For instance, if a vibrant red is selected from the palette and a brush set to the blending mode Luminosity, the underlying pixels will not change to red when painting starts but will simply be brightened or darkened to match the luminosity of the red. If a color is applied with the Color blending mode, the underlying pixels

will change hue but the image's light and shade qualities will remain unchanged. There are many different blending modes to choose from, each affecting the underlying pixels uniquely.

SPECIAL EFFECT FILTERS

Filters apply effects to images or selected areas, enabling many interesting and novel results to be achieved quickly. Photoshop and other image editors are supplied with a wide range of useful standard filters, many of them highly controllable using several parameters set numerically or by dragging sliders in a dialog box. A real-time preview is usually provided so that you can adjust the effect by eye before applying it to the image, which may take longer. Hundreds of other filters are available from third-party manufacturers.

Left and above: The beauty of masks is that they can be saved and called up at any time to select a particular area of an image. Furthermore, a mask can be added to and subtracted from, using any of the usual painting tools, brush sizes, and/or opacities. The mask can optionally be shown as a red tint, allowing it to be edited with the image visible for reference.

WORKING WITH DRAWING (VECTOR) PROGRAMS The vectors used in drawing programs are called Bézier curves. All drawing programs handle Bézier curves in a similar fashion: a pen tool allows the user to set a series of points on the page, and these will automatically be joined by lines.

Vector drawing tools

The shape of these lines is dictated by the way in which the pen is manipulated by dragging and clicking the mouse. Each point, or "node," when selected, will display one or two non-printing "handles." A given point may be selected later and the handles manipulated to modify the curves. The points themselves can also be repositioned entirely at will.

Drawing programs give the digital graphic designer many powerful tools with which to create complex shapes, to apply special effects, and to speed up otherwise laborious tasks. Not all programs offer identical tools, although most of them do share a core set of features. The menus and terminology employed may also differ, as may the graphical presentation of tools.

For example, both Adobe Illustrator and FreeHand can convert type into points and vectors; the operation is called Create Outlines in Illustrator, but Convert to Paths in FreeHand.

Finished drawings should be saved in the "native" format of your drawing program to ensure all features can be read back in. For transfer to other programs, such as a DTP package, all type should be converted to outlines and the drawing saved as EPS (encapsulated PostScript). Illustrator's native format is an adaptation of this standard format, and files from earlier versions of Illustrator can thus be read by many other programs. The advanced features recently introduced into drawing packages, however, cannot be saved as regular PostScript. It may be possible to export as an EPS with certain effects converted to simpler vector forms (with the same final appearance, though no longer editable) and others rasterized to bitmap images incorporated within the file. Output errors are not uncommon, and in some cases the best option is to rasterize the whole drawing to a 300dpi bitmap image at the required size.

Opposite and below: Illustrator Lawrence Zeegen uses FreeHand to assemble and manipulate a combination of bitmap and drawn images. When displayed in "artwork" form it is easy to see the entire structure and layout of object-oriented components.

DESIGN BY LAWRENCE ZEEGEN, UK

Some of the features offered by drawing programs

✳ Typographic functions are comparable with those found in leading page-layout programs, so that all character and paragraph formatting and spacing can be applied, together with layout functions such as multiple columns and text flow.

✳ Text can be converted to paths so that letterforms can be used in the same way as any other hand-drawn object.

✳ Shapes may be stroked (given a colored outline), filled, cut, rotated, skewed, distorted, duplicated, mirrored, scaled, and added to. They may also be grouped, fused, cropped or used to crop others, used as a mask, used to contain a picture, and used to make patterns.

✳ User-defined color palettes can be made up from RGB, CMYK, and HSB models as well as from color libraries such as PANTONE.

✳ Many guides, grids, and views are available to support image construction. Views such as "artwork" mode show only points and paths, without color or fills, to help to clarify highly complex pictures and speed up screen rendering.

✳ Layers can be used to build up images in coherent groupings. These layers may be locked against accidental deletion and may also be hidden while other layers are being worked on.

✳ Numerous filters are available to create special alterations and effects with shapes or groups of shapes.

✳ Shapes or groups of shapes can be rasterized, which enables them to be used with an imported bitmap image.

✳ A range of bitmap-only filters may be applied to any imported bitmap or rasterized image.

✳ Multiple blends may be used between two shapes to act as a morphing technique.

✳ Spacing and alignment tools allow for swift arrangement of disparate elements.

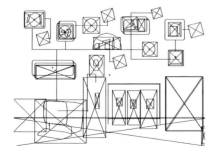

REFERENCE

5

Professional practice

A design studio manager, or anyone else occupying a similar position, is in the middle of a complicated series of relationships. For everything to go well, these relationships need to be successfully managed. Not all of the relationships described here will apply in all situations. If you are working for yourself, for instance, and are not using suppliers, then you will have no one to worry about apart from the client. In some situations the client may be internal, which changes the relationship slightly. At times it may seem that you need the combined skills of an air-traffic controller, a diplomat, and a traveling salesman to keep everyone happy and to keep everything moving forward.

BE HONEST

You need to be prepared to adopt different approaches to suit each type of working relationship. You may also need to be economical with the truth on occasions: the delivery date you agree with your client, the one you specify to the printers, and the one you give your staff and freelancers may, for example, all need to be slightly different. However, don't let these sleights of hand get out of control. Acting a part and concealing the truth are hard to keep up. As far as possible, be yourself and stick to the facts. In particular, it's always in your best interests to

be clear about costs. Lack of clarity about money is the one thing that can be guaranteed to discourage people from working with you again.

BE CONSISTENT

Few things are more demotivating than a perception among staff of favoritism by a manager. This can be a particular problem when working with in-house staff, where inconsistencies of treatment will rapidly be noticed. Moreover, when you say you're going to do something, make sure that you do it; you can then reasonably expect the same from everyone else.

BE ASSERTIVE

It is important to be clear about what you want out of a relationship or situation from the outset; demands that are made later may be harder to achieve. Make sure you keep your side of any arrangement by, for example, making sure suppliers and freelancers get paid on time. If the relationship starts to deteriorate, step in quickly and sort it out—don't wait for a crisis.

BE ORGANIZED

Ensure you keep your records for a particular job, such as costs, budgets, and schedules, on hand and up-to-date. If you aren't on the ball, don't be surprised if no one else is either. If problems emerge, be prepared to come up with solutions, or to approve those suggested by others. Above all, make sure that everyone knows where their responsibilities start and end and to whom they report. Remember that "responsibility" means just that—you're not just lumbering people with work, but also making them responsible, within certain limits, for how it's done. Don't interfere in this, or get snarled up sorting out minor problems, more than you have to. Being organized and delegating effectively also involves not needing to know every minor detail of every job.

BE POSITIVE

Your ultimate objective is to produce a top-quality job, on time and on budget. Remember not to let human relationships, unexpected problems, or interesting diversions distract your attention from this goal. It is possible (although not necessarily easy) to achieve this while at the same time keeping everyone else involved feeling they were well treated and well rewarded. Aggressive, manipula-tive, or melodramatic behavior may, at the time, seem the only way to get the job done, but ultimately it can lead to disappointment. The next time that you need the same people to work with you, it's unlikely that they'll want to reciprocate.

IF YOU ARE THE FREELANCER...

Much of what is written elsewhere about business relationships from the point of view of a studio manager is also relevant to a freelancer. Some additional points to bear in mind include:

* For all relationships, consider the "do as you would be done by" principle. If you treat people in an unprofessional way, is it reasonable to expect them to behave any better to you?

* Keep your quotes clear. Price any possible extras and warn your client in advance before invoking them

* Agree on your responsibilities and make sure you have the right information (style sheets, etc.) to do the job

* Keep your invoices clear. Establish who they should be sent to and specify the job name and number. Be aware that many firms only do check runs once a month. Be polite to the client's accounts department

* Be clear whether you are assigning copyright of the work you create

Below: The studio manager is the central focus of the various relationships involved in a working design studio. You'll need to be calm, honest, and assertive at all times to keep everything under control and running smoothly.

PROFESSIONAL PRACTICE

225

Professional practice

USING FREELANCERS

One of the great advantages of using freelancers or independent contractors is that they generally work elsewhere, so you will not be responsible for any telephone bills, travel, depreciation, or other costs except by prior arrangement. Sometimes, however, you may find that it's convenient to have freelancers working in your office, in which case you'll generally provide equipment and materials. In either case, your arrangement with the freelancer needs to be defined by some kind of contract. This should reflect your company's needs and must also comply with state common law of contracts.

CONTRACTUAL ISSUES

Get standard terms agreed upon with a lawyer and use them as the small print in all agreements. Include a conspicuous statement near the signature line drawing attention to the small print. Remember that most problems arise from matters not being clear at the outset. Agree upon the details, confirm them in writing, and make sure you both adhere to them. Points to be covered in a design contract are:

ASSIGNMENT OF COPYRIGHT

Be clear who owns the completed work. The act of paying for the job does not necessarily mean that the copyright automatically passes to you: legally it should be specifically assigned.

The freelancer needs to assure you that, in producing the work, he or she has not infringed on anyone else's intellectual rights, trademarks, and the like, and to indemnify you against his or her actions.

QUALITY AND DELIVERY

Specify what's required, by when, and in what format. Specify that freelancers use their "best endeavors" to eliminate errors (this demands more thoroughness than "reasonable endeavors") and that late or sub-standard work may result in deductions from the fee.

PAYMENT TERMS

The simplest terms are when everything owed is paid when the freelancer has finished the work. For long jobs, staged payments might be appropriate. If so, you'll have to be clear about what triggers them. Phrases like "when the job is 50 percent complete" can be hard to define. Payments should be tied to events or "milestones" about which you can both agree.

REJECTION FEES

Sometimes freelancers might demand payment for design work that has been completed, but rejected as being unsuitable (as you might do to your clients). How reasonable this is largely depends on which side of the transaction you're on. If your policy is not to pay them, make this clear from the outset. If you can be convinced otherwise, agree upon the details before work starts.

WORKING WITH CLIENTS

Most of the information on this page concerns client relationships: but it also describes your suppliers' and employees' dealings with you. An advantage of being in the middle is that you can empathize and learn from both sides. Imagine a cartographer being late with a map, and offering a pathetic excuse. Imagine your client thanking you for an excellent job. How would you feel in each case? If this were you, talking to your client or your supplier, would their reactions be different?

SETTING THE RIGHT TONE

First impressions, good or bad, are hard to dispel. It's better to be too formal than too friendly. The time for jokes and flippant emails may come, but the first contact is not the place to start. Empathy is the key to good client relationships. Try to treat your clients in the way that you would want to be treated in their place. Key watchpoints are:

Below: Cover all relevant angles in your contract as clearly as you can, but try not to make it seem alarming. The aim is to ensure that your clients understand issues such as the ramifications of mid-project changes or delays. Get the balance right and your professional relationship will be off to a very good start.

- Listen to your client
- Try to understand his or her needs
- Do what you say you're going to do
- Ensure good communication with your client
- Avoid regarding the meeting of your client's requirements as a problem

CONTRACTS

The job will need to be confirmed in writing. If this is clear, logical, and accurate, you will be seen to be so, too. Key points to specify include:

- The precise work you will be doing, covered by the fee—such as resizing images or generating layouts, for example
- The work that you will not be doing—such as scanning or retouching images
- The work that you might be doing, and that might be charged as extra—such as picture research or photography
- Decisions still to be made—such as the extent
- The schedule and the format in which the material will be supplied

If you have a dispute, the contract will be evidence of what was agreed. But don't overanticipate problems or your client might suspect all your jobs end in disaster.

Extra cost. If new photography is needed for the design stage, we will charge $350 for each 8-hour day of art direction and attendance at the photo shoot. Client will be consulted before any additional costs are incurred.

3. Payment schedule

Each poster/leaflet will be invoiced upon its completion. Payment is to be made 15 days from receipt of each of the individual invoices.

4. Rejection/cancellation of project

The client shall not unreasonably withhold acceptance of—or payment for—the project. If, prior to completion of the project, the client observes any nonconformance with the design plan, we must be notified promptly.

Recording time and money spent on a job will ensure more accurate planning and budgeting in the future.

Records and timesheets

The production of anything, from a 6-inch nail to a 900-page book, requires the expenditure of resources. In crude terms, profit is the difference between what you receive in payment and what you pay out in costs. A printer can estimate exactly how much paper is needed to produce a given book, and how long it will take. For a designer, however, your major expenditure is time—by you, by your staff, and by your freelancers. At the start of a job you need to consider how many hours will be spent on it and continue monitoring throughout the job. This process ends at the job's conclusion, when you use this information to assess how profitable it has been.

If the job is quoted on a flat rate, the client won't care how many hours are spent on it. If you've outsourced everything to suppliers on a similar basis, then you probably won't care either. In both cases, if everything's done right and on time, then how long it has taken is someone else's problem. There are, however, some common circumstances where the picture changes. If any of the following apply to your organization or to any of the jobs you do, timesheets become useful:

- If you charge your clients by the hour
- If you produce regular titles
- If you employ staff

Asking employees to record what they do on timesheets is, on the face of it, reasonable and logical. Badly handled, however, it can lead them to draw sinister conclusions. What, someone might ask, is their real purpose? Who will see them? How will this affect me? Be prepared to sell the idea by outlining the potential benefits. Projects monitored in this way will be more efficient and profitable. The information gathered will enable appropriate resources to be allocated from the outset in the future. Involve staff in the costing process at the beginning of jobs and compare projection with reality at key stages during it. Above all, make it clear that the records are being used, in a constructive way, to everyone's benefit.

Right: This shows part of the weekly timesheet for Jane Smith, who's been doing a variety of tasks on several jobs in a busy production department. This chart enables time to be analyzed by the task and by the project. Such information is invaluable for internal or external charging and accounts; when planning future projects; and when considering outsourcing all or part of a similar job in the future.

Jane Smith	Week	Task
03/445	proofing	
03/445	photo res.	
03/460	proofing	
03/461	meeting	
03/461	chasing copy	

Job number

If you produce regular titles, you should know pretty much exactly how long each stage will take. Saying "the whole thing takes about three weeks" may be fine for most cases, but if someone is ill, or leaves, or if part of the work needs to be outsourced, you'll need to know more precisely what is involved. Sometimes, timesheets are required by a higher level of management, perhaps for some boardroom argument about outsourcing. If so, be honest with your staff. It's also worth considering the use of timesheet and project-management software.

Timesheet software can be especially helpful for freelancers, where the marking of time spent is critical. The software can prompt you to record hours, warn you in advance of meetings, and even sound a buzzer every hour to remind you of the passage of time.

It is assumed that anything you are charged for, such as printing costs, will be properly recorded. Time, often the most expensive item, has been discussed already. What's left is the swamp of "overheads," or "consumables," into which unattributed costs can be tossed, eventually to reappear spread equally across all jobs in your accounts regardless of where they were actually expended. Allocating individual items of expenditure is sometimes not worth the effort—for example toner and paper. Such incidentals, however, can mount up. These might include:

- Color-printer consumables (such as ink and coated paper)
- On-line data transmission
- Couriers and mail
- Travel and entertainment

Even if you don't charge the client for these "consumables," it is often worth allocating the costs against the job. Your accounts department may demand it and it will also be useful evidence when quoting on reprints or similar future jobs.

Any records you maintain during a project should be filed away at the end of it. This should contain the hard-copy correspondence, quotes, samples, job-costing sheets and—certainly until the job is paid for—proofs; and a copy of the finished job. This should complement any computer folder you have for digital files. Being able to lay your hands on this information in the future can save considerable time and money.

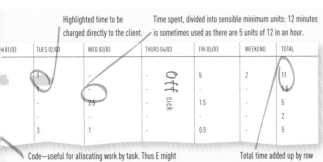

Highlighted time to be charged directly to the client.

Time spent, divided into sensible minimum units: 12 minutes is sometimes used as there are 5 units of 12 in an hour.

MON 01/03	TUES 02/03	WED 03/03	THURS 04/03	FRI 05/03	WEEKEND	TOTAL
1	-		- Off	5	2	11
1	-	-	sick	-	-	1.5
-	2.5		-	1.5	-	5
-	-		-	-	-	2
3	1		-	0.5	-	5

Code—useful for allocating work by task. Thus E might be editorial work: E1 is for proofing, E2 writing, and so on. A is admin, D is design, S is sales related, and so on.

Total time added up by row (task) and by column (day).

Timesheet checklist

✓ Be consistent—ensure everyone complies

✓ Don't let their completion and analysis become time-consuming jobs in themselves

✓ Consider the results—and discuss these with staff

✓ Remember that you are analyzing the task—not necessarily the person doing it

✓ The figures are only the means to an end

Creating a workflow model

Like the journey of a train along a track, the progress of a design project through various "stations" en route may be predicted in advance and then measured as it occurs. In fact, many design projects involve not one train but several: one carrying editorial, another graphics, another design, proofs, print, and so on, each moving at its own speed along its own piece of track and having its own obstacles with which to contend. Each train must connect with others at crucial junctures. A workflow model is a timetable of these journeys, a visible representation of the structure and schedule of the job's production.

One complicating factor is that while some stages of production can overlap without disrupting the progress of the job, others cannot. For example, while certain chapters in a book may still be written after other chapters have been laid out on the page, the layout process cannot begin until the design has been finalized and the first batch of text has been approved.

WORKFLOW PRINCIPLES

Workflows may be computerized or handwritten, but should always be clear. Most follow the principle of allocating periods of time for the completion of various tasks, against which progress may be logged. Details will vary, but what must be clear to everyone is that the schedule is being monitored and updated in a practical, consistent, and useful way. It's pointless allocating a task to someone to be completed by

JOB	ALLOCATED	DELIVERY	OUTPUT	COPY	GRAPHICS	LAYOUT
445/ XYZ PLC LOGO	27/7 LUCY	28/8 LONDON	PRINT 10K	27/7 EDITS REQD.	2 CHARTS & 4 PIX—ALL SUPPLIED	BASED ON 02/016 BUT NOW 8x5IN

a certain date and then failing to react if the task remains unfinished.

Above all, a workflow model must be simple to operate and to interpret. If it's going to be updated by several people, make sure they understand its importance and how it works. It's dangerous to devise a model so complex that no one else will know what it means—what will happen if the model's originator is absent from work?

SIMPLE WORKFLOW

The workflow shown below is for a relatively simple job, such as a brochure, and might be part of a larger chart that covers many projects, most of which do not merit a chart of their own. It offers a summary of what has happened and what has yet to happen, under the control—in the case of this job—of Lucy B. Such charts may also be useful as historical records if completed projects or periods need to be reviewed.

Workflow junctures

Any workflow model must identify the "fixed points" of a job's timetable, the nonachievement of which can delay the entire project. Each job will be different, but such fixed points might include:

* Allocating tasks
* Finalizing the design
* Finalizing the flat plan
* Passing all the printer's proofs
* Printing slots
* Delivery date

This simple workflow chart lists the key deliverables of the job, giving a completion date and relevant extra details below each heading.

PROOF	CLIENT PROOF 1	CLIENT PROOF 2	NOTES	DELIVERY
6 AUG. B.Q.	SENT 9/8– TEXT CORR'S & 1 NEW PIC	SENT 11/8 OK 14/8	2 COPIES OF EACH PROOF– SEE JOB BAG	TO PRINT 18/8 L.B.

PRINTER LIAISON Changes in technology have revolutionized the relationship between designer and printer.

Working with printers

You should always plan exactly what you need to know before contacting a printer and asking for a quote. This ensures that you will always get the correct information, and that you will have the same information from each printer, allowing you to easily compare them. If you're seeking competitive quotes, send each printer exactly the same specifications, always check the payment terms for any contract, and make sure all the areas are covered: schedules, courier costs (for proofs), delivery costs, etc.

If the job has possible variations (such as different page extents, paper stock weights, or color-falls), ensure that you express these clearly and ask that they be provided separately from the main price. Optional extras (such as extra proofs, extra deliveries, or bound-in inserts) should have their scale of prices agreed upon at the outset, as should the basis upon which corrections will be charged.

Satisfy yourself that the printer has a fully functioning prepress workflow system that will cope with your PDFs in the form in which you supply them and minimize interventions. That way you're more likely to end up with the result you want and confirm the order in writing, specifying all details of the job.

Ensure that you are given a prepress contact. Get him or her to send you details of exactly how the material should be supplied. If this is as PDFs, there should be a standard set of instructions and a job options file for your Acrobat Distiller settings folder. Do a test file, send it to the repro house or printer, and then get them to send you a proof from their RIP. Reconfirm the schedule to this person and discuss any likely or potential problems.

Agree upon who will be taking delivery of the printed job, you or your client. If you are receiving the job on their behalf, then ensure in advance that you have enough room to stock it.

USING A PRINT BROKER

This can be worth it, particularly if you're unsure whether your suppliers are offering the best deal (especially if the printer is in a distant country where you have no knowledge of local rates or competition) or if you're moving into, say, web offset for the first time. A possible drawback is that you may have to have all contact with the printer via the broker.

VISITING THE PRINTER

Unless the job is very complex or if you're very worried about color fidelity, it's now less crucial to pass proofs on press. If time is tight, it can be a useful way of delivering the last files, seeing the last proofs, watching the first pages, and meeting the people you've been phoning and emailing.

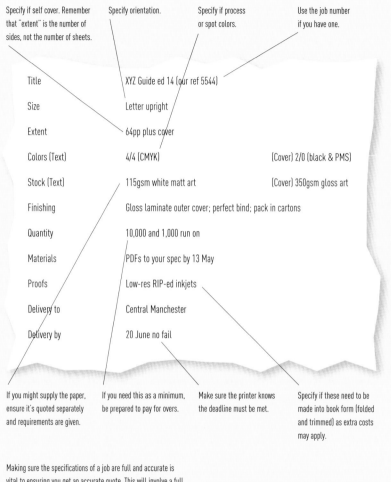

Specify if self cover. Remember that "extent" is the number of sides, not the number of sheets.

Specify orientation.

Specify if process or spot colors.

Use the job number if you have one.

Title	XYZ Guide ed 14 (our ref 5544)	
Size	Letter upright	
Extent	64pp plus cover	
Colors (Text)	4/4 (CMYK)	(Cover) 2/0 (black & PMS)
Stock (Text)	115gsm white matt art	(Cover) 350gsm gloss art
Finishing	Gloss laminate outer cover; perfect bind; pack in cartons	
Quantity	10,000 and 1,000 run on	
Materials	PDFs to your spec by 13 May	
Proofs	Low-res RIP-ed inkjets	
Delivery to	Central Manchester	
Delivery by	20 June no fail	

If you might supply the paper, ensure it's quoted separately and requirements are given.

If you need this as a minimum, be prepared to pay for overs.

Make sure the printer knows the deadline must be met.

Specify if these need to be made into book form (folded and trimmed) as extra costs may apply.

Making sure the specifications of a job are full and accurate is vital to ensuring you get an accurate quote. This will involve a full understanding of the different aspects of the production process, so ask for information from reliable sources rather than making guesses.

THE PRINCIPLES OF COPYRIGHT can be a minefield. In theory, you cannot reproduce anyone else's work without their permission, but in practice there are exceptions.

Copyright

Copyright is the exclusive right to control the reproduction of a literary or artistic work. As a designer or publications specialist, copyright will affect you in two main ways: establishing rights over your own work; and avoiding infringing the rights of others. The basic principle of copyright is straightforward. However, there are many variations and nuances upon that principle that can and do render the field a very complex one—as reflected by the number of thriving legal practices specializing in copyright.

Copyright happens automatically. It doesn't have to be claimed or registered. However, in the United States, an author has to register copyright in order to assert his or her rights. Under US law, it lasts until 70 years after the author's or artist's death. You can only copyright something that exists as a product or entity (in our context, something that has been put down on paper or on a computer). You cannot copyright ideas, as such.

If writing or designing is the normal part of your job as an employee—if you are the layout person on a magazine, for instance—then copyright will usually devolve automatically to your employer. If, however, you are working as a freelancer, or independently, and you have been commissioned to write or draw a piece of work, the commissioning employer should specify whether or not they want the rights to the work. They may insist upon it; this is not unusual, nor is it generally unreasonable. But before you sign a contract and start work, think about what the loss of copyright will mean for you and try to establish exactly what you will be "signing away." Will you be able to use your work, or part of it, elsewhere? Will they? And will you mind if they do? If you have any doubts, ask, and get the answers down in writing.

Bear in mind that copyright is both conditional and transferable. Authors may arrange with publishers for the copyright on, say, a book to rest with the publisher for five years and then revert to the author. A photographer may insist that a picture agency may sell a certain picture in some countries, but retain the copyright for him/herself in others. There are endless permutations, and thus copious grounds for potential dispute.

As far as written material is concerned, the precise conditions governing the use of other people's work make for a difficult and often contentious area. Strictly speaking, you should ask permission to quote anything copyright; in practice, nobody minds very much provided you use the material "within reason" and quote the source. As a rough guide, it's usually acceptable to quote a passage of up to 100 words in length

The iconic Ché Guevara photograph

For 35 years, this instantly recognizable photo has adorned many a student's bedroom wall. Photographer Alberto Diaz Gutierrez, who goes by the name Alberto Korda, never asked for payment and never objected to its reproduction; in short, he did not assert his copyright over the image. Not, that is, until August 2000 when a London advertising agency, Lowe Lintas, used the photo to promote Smirnoff vodka. Korda, incensed at what he viewed as a slur on non-drinker Ché Guevara's "immortal memory," successfully sued the agency, along with the company that supplied the image, Rex Features. In an out-of-court settlement, he received an undisclosed sum (which he donated to children's medical care in Cuba) and, perhaps more important, official recognition of his copyright.

Copyright

without direct permission provided the source is accredited in full. For example:

"You can't just rip off images from magazines, download any old image from the Internet, or re-use that agency photo 600 times over in your work." (Computer Arts, May 1999, page 22).

SPECIFIC PROBLEMS FOR DESIGNERS

For most designers the more pressing question is, "What use can I make of someone else's work in my own?" The short answer is: you may use whatever the person concerned—or their publisher—has given you permission to use; without that permission you may use very little indeed.

The issue regularly arises in relation to images (including logos and clip art) and especially since access via the Internet has made acquiring these so easy. It can be tempting, and simple enough, to download an image and incorporate it into your own work. Don't do it unless you know that you have the right to use the material. The fact that you are physically able to copy material does not imply that you have the right to do so, and near-invisible watermarks can identify images even after editing.

Always ask for permission, no matter how common the image. Most publishers will grant this, sometimes for a fee, sometimes free. Allow enough time for them to contact the author or artist and for the reply to come back. Above all, don't rely on a verbal agreement: get it in writing.

Ask, too, how they would like the source to be acknowledged. The copyright owner might make it a condition of the permission that they are credited.

Copyright is a large subject, fraught with contentious issues, most of which are outside the scope of this book. If you have any concerns either about material you want to use or about your own rights over work you have done, seek advice. There are some good reference books on the subject, and more information is available on Internet sites such as the Library of Congress site: http://www.copyright.gov.

COPYRIGHT AND SOFTWARE

All of the software that you are likely to have on your computer will be subject to the law of copyright. You are breaking the law if you make copies (beyond whatever backup copies the software manufacturer allows you to make), and if you distribute these, or allow them to be distributed, to other people.

Some software manufacturers even forbid you to give your own copy away; they insist that what they have sold is a license for you (the registered user) and only you, to use a particular copy of their application.

You are also not even allowed to rent it to a third party. Technically, they would say, you should return the software if you no longer want it, although in practice we have never heard of anyone being asked to do so.

Copyright applies to shareware too. If you read the fine print then you will often discover that, even when the author of the software

Some common myths

"I got it from a website, so it's all right to use it."

Not true. Think of the Internet as a library, where websites are the books that someone has written, published, and placed there. The fact that the "pages" are electronic and therefore physically easier to copy makes no difference. Remember the absence of a notice does not mean copyright does not apply.

"There is no copyright symbol, so it isn't protected."

Not true. An author does not have to formally claim or register his or her copyright for copyright protection to exist (but he or she will have to in order to assert it).

"I know it's someone else's work but I have altered it and combined it with my own, so that's all right."

Absolutely not true. This is plagiarism, pretending that you are the author of somebody else's work.

"I have scanned a direct copy of a newspaper article: anyone can see its source, so that's legitimate."

Not true. Newspapers—and online newspapers—are quite explicit about their copyright restrictions, which protect both staff writers and freelancers. Each time you want to use material from a newspaper, you must ask for permission first.

"I have acknowledged the source of the material, so copyright has not been breached."

Not true. You should acknowledge the source, but that does not absolve you from obtaining prior permission.

"I bought the original painting so the copyright is mine now and I can reproduce it as I like."

Not true. The copyright on works of art remains with the artist, whose permission must be sought and who is entitled to receive payments if the artwork is reproduced.

allows you to distribute copies, they generally do so only as long as you include specific files that contain their copyright details.

In the United States, fonts cannot be protected by copyright. However, this is not the case in some other countries, such as the United Kingdom. Fonts being protected by copyright almost inevitably leads to problems when transferring documents to freelancers and sending completed work off to print.

Purchasing image rights

"Rights-protected," or "rights-managed" images are priced according to the use to which you intend to put them, and the number of copies and territories the book will be sold in, in the case of publishers. Although traditional photo libraries are comparatively expensive, they have the advantage of giving you exclusive or near-exclusive use of the image for a set period. Rights-protected images may be used only in the size (usually as a proportion of page size) and for the purpose specified in the deal.

Royalty-free images, by contrast, may usually, but not always, be used as many times and for as long as you like for a set fee. You may also manipulate the image and use it at different resolutions and on different media. Their major disadvantage is that other people will have bought the same image and so you may find it appearing on a competitor's material. Don't be confused by the term "copyright free " as there is no such thing as a copyright-free image. If you come across this term, it more than likely means "royalty free."

American paper sizes

Eight Crown
1461mm x 1060mm
57.5in x 41.75in
4140pt x 3006pt

Antiquarian
1346mm x 533mm
53in x 21in
3816pt x 1512pt

Quad Demy
1118mm x 826mm
53in x 32.5in
3168pt x 2340pt

Double Princess
1118mm x 711mm
53in x 28in
3168pt x 2016pt

Architectural-E
1219mm x 914mm
48in x 36in
3456pt x 2592pt

ANSI-E
1118mm x 864mm
44in x 34in
3168pt x 2448pt

Architectural-F
1067mm x 762mm
42in x 30in
3023pt x 2160pt

Quad Crown
1016mm x 762mm
40in x 30in
2880pt x 2160pt

ANSI-F
1016mm x 711mm
40in x 28in
2880pt x 2016pt

Double Elephant
1016mm x 686mm
40in x 27in
2880pt x 1944pt

Architectural-D
914mm x 610mm
36in x 24in
2592pt x 1728pt

Double Demy
890mm x 572mm
35in x 22.5in
2520pt x 1620pt

ANSI-D
864mm x 559mm
34in x 22in
2448pt x 1584pt

Imperial
762mm x 559mm
30in x 22in
2160pt x 1584pt

Princess
711mm x 546mm
28in x 21.5in
2016pt x 1548pt

Architectural-C
610mm x 457mm
24in x 18in
1728pt x 1296pt

Demy
584mm x 470mm
23in x 18.5in
1656pt x 1332pt

ANSI-C (Broadsheet)
559mm x 432mm
22in x 17in
1584pt x 1224pt

Super-B
483mm x 330mm
19in x 13in
1367 x 935pt

Brief
470mm x 333mm
18.5in x 13.13in
1332pt x 945pt

Architectural-B
457mm x 305mm
18in x 12in
1296pt x 864pt

ANSI-B (Ledger; Tabloid)
432mm x 279mm
17in x 11in
1224pt x 792pt

Legal (Legal-2)
356mm x 216mm
14in x 8.5in
1008pt x 612pt

Legal-1
330mm x 216mm
13in x 8.5in
935pt x 612pt

Folio (F4)
330mm x 210mm
13in x 8.25in
935pt x 595pt

Foolscap E
330mm x 203mm
13in x 8in
935pt x 575pt

Architectural-A
305mm x 229mm
12in x 9in
864pt x 648pt

ANSI-A (Letter)
279mm x 216mm
11in x 8.5in
792pt x 612pt

US Government
279mm x 203mm
11in x 8in
792pt x 575pt

Quarto
275mm x 215mm
10.75in x 8.5in
774pt x 612pt

Executive
267mm x 184mm
10.5in x 7.25in
756pt x 522pt

Index Card 10 x 8
254mm x 203mm
10in x 8in
720pt x 576pt

Crown Quarto
241mm x 184mm
9.5in x 7.25in
684pt x 522pt

Royal Octavo
241mm x 152mm
9.5in x 6in
684pt x 43pt

Statement
216mm x 140mm
8.5in x 5.5in
612pt x 396pt

Demy Octavo
213mm x 137mm
8.38in x 5.38in
603pt x 387pt

Foolscap Quarto
206mm x 165mm
8.13in x 6.5in
585pt x 468pt

Index Card 8 x 5
203mm x 127mm
8in x 5in
576pt x 360pt

Crown Octavo
181mm x 121mm
7.13in x 4.75in
513pt x 342pt

Photo 7 x 5
178mm x 127mm
7in x 5in
504pt x 360pt

Photo 6 x 4
152mm x 102mm
6in x 4in
431pt x 289pt

Post Card
148mm x 100mm
5.82in x 3.94in
419pt x 284pt

Photo 5 x 4
127mm x 102mm
5in x 4in
360pt x 288pt

Photo 5 x 3
127mm x 76mm
5in x 3in
360pt x 215pt

Business Card
89mm x 51mm
3.5in x 2in
252pt x 144pt

ISO paper sizes

The following table shows the width and height of all ISO A and B paper formats, as well as the ISO C envelope formats:

A Series Formats

4A0	1682mm x 2378mm	66.22in x 93.62in	4768pt x 6741pt
2A0	1189mm x 1682mm	46.81in x 66.22in	3370pt x 4768pt
A0	841mm x 1189mm	33in x 46.81in	2384pt x 3370pt
A1	594mm x 841mm	23.39in x 33in	1684pt x 2384pt
A2	420mm x 594mm	16.54in x 23.39in	1191pt x 1684pt
A3	297mm x 420mm	11.69in x 16.54in	842pt x 1191pt
A4	210mm x 297mm	8.27in x 11.69in	595pt x 842pt
A5	148mm x 210mm	5.83in x 8.27in	420pt x 595pt
A6	105mm x 148mm	4.13in x 5.83in	298pt x 420pt
A7	74mm x 105mm	2.91in x 4.13in	210pt x 298pt
A8	52mm x 74mm	2.05in x 2.91in	147pt x 210pt
A9	37mm x 52mm	1.46in x 2.05in	105pt x 147pt
A10	26mm x 37mm	1.02in x 1.46in	74pt x 105pt

B Series Formats

B0	1000mm x 1414mm	39.37in x 55.67in	2835pt x 4008pt
B1	707mm x 1000mm	27.84in x 39.37in	2004pt x 2835pt
B2	500mm x 707mm	19.69in x 27.84in	1417pt x 2004pt
B3	353mm x 500mm	13.9in x 19.69in	1001pt x 1417pt
B4	250mm x 353mm	9.84in x 13.9in	709pt x 1001pt
B5	176mm x 250mm	6.93in x 9.84in	499pt x 709pt
B6	125mm x 176mm	4.92in x 6.93in	354pt x 499pt
B7	88mm x 125mm	3.47in x 4.92in	249pt x 354pt
B8	62mm x 88mm	2.44in x 3.47in	176pt x 249pt
B9	44mm x 62mm	1.73in x 2.44in	125pt x 176pt
B10	31mm x 44mm	1.22in x 1.73in	88pt x 125pt

C Series Formats

C0	917mm x 1297mm	36.1in x 51.06in	2599pt x 3677pt
C1	648mm x 917mm	25.51in x 36.1in	1837pt x 2599pt
C2	458mm x 648mm	18.03in x 25.51in	1298pt x 1837pt
C3	324mm x 458mm	12.76in x 18.03in	918pt x 1298pt
C4	229mm x 324mm	9.02in x 12.76in	649pt x 918pt
C5	162mm x 229mm	6.38in x 9.02in	459pt x 649pt
C6	114mm x 162mm	4.49in x 6.38in	323pt x 459pt
C7	81mm x 114mm	3.19in x 4.49in	230pt x 323pt
C8	57mm x 81mm	2.44in x 3.19in	162pt x 230pt
C9	40mm x 57mm	1.58in x 2.44in	113pt x 162pt
C10	28mm x 40mm	1.1in x 1.58in	79pt x 113pt

The ISO paper sizes are based on the metric system. The ratio (height divided by the width) of all formats is the square root of two (1.4142). This ratio does not permit both the height and width of the pages to be nicely rounded metric lengths. Therefore, the area of the pages has been defined to have round metric values. As paper is usually specified in g/m2, this simplifies calculation of the mass of a document if the format and number of pages are known.

ISO 216 defines the A series of paper sizes based on the following simple principles:

The height divided by the width of all formats is the root of two (1.4142)

Format A0 has an area of one square meter

Format A1 is A0 cut into two equal pieces. In other words, the height of A1 is the width of A0 and the width of A1 is half the height of A0

All smaller A series formats are defined in the same way. If you cut format An parallel to its shorter side into two equal pieces of paper, these will have format A(n+1)

The standardized height and width of the paper formats is a rounded number of millimeters. For applications where the ISO

A series does not provide an adequate format, the B series has been introduced to cover a wider range of paper sizes. The C series has been defined for envelopes

The width and height of a Bn format are the geometric mean between those of the An and the next larger A(n-1) format. For instance, B1 is the geometric mean between A1 and A0; that means the same magnification factor that scales A1 to B1 will also scale B1 to A0

Similarly, the formats of the C series are the geometric mean between the A and B series formats with the same number. For example, an A4 size letter fits nicely into a C4 envelope, which in turn fits as nicely into a B4 envelope. If you fold this letter once to A5 format, then it will fit nicely into a C5 envelope

B and C formats naturally are also square-root-of-two formats

Accents and diacriticals

Macintosh: These are accessed by simultaneously pressing both the Option/Alt key ⌥ and the character (as listed below) or the Shift ⇧ Option and character keys all together.

Windows: Characters are accessed by pressing the Alt key, then typing the appropriate number as listed below. For example, Alt + 0199 produces Ç (the character appears after the Alt key is released). Some applications, such as Microsoft Word, have their own shortcuts for generating special characters.

Character	Sym	Mac	Win
Acute	´	⌥E	0180
Acute, cap A	Á	⌥Y	0193
Acute, cap E	É	see note	0201
Acute, cap I	Í	⇧⌥S	0205
Acute, cap O	Ó	⇧⌥H	0211
Acute, cap U	Ú	⇧⌥;	0218
Acute, cap Y	Ý		0221
Acute, l/c a	á	see note	0225
Acute, l/c e	é	see note	0233
Acute, l/c i	í	see note	0237
Acute, l/c o	ó	see note	0243
Acute, l/c u	ú	see note	0250
Acute, l/c y	ý		0253
Broken bar	¦		0166
Bullet	•	⌥8	0149
Caron, cap S	Š		0138
Caron, cap Z	Ž		0142
Caron, l/c s	š		0154
Caron, l/c z	ž		0158
Cedilla	¸		0184
Cedilla, cap	Ç	⇧⌥C	0199
Cedilla, l/c	ç	⌥C	0231
Cent	¢	⌥4	0162
Circumflex	^	⇧⌥N	0136
Circumflex, cap A	Â	⇧⌥M	0194
Circumflex, cap E	Ê	see note	0202
Circumflex, cap I	Î	⇧⌥D	0206
Circumflex, cap O	Ô	⇧⌥J	0212
Circumflex, cap U	Û	see note	0219
Circumflex, l/c a	â	see note	0226
Circumflex, l/c e	ê	see note	0234
Circumflex, l/c i	î	see note	0238
Circumflex, l/c o	ô	see note	0244
Circumflex, l/c u	û	see note	0251
Copyright	©	⌥G	0169
Dagger	†	⌥T	0134
Danish cap O	Ø	⇧⌥O	0216
Danish l/c o	ø	⌥O	0248
Decimal	·	⇧⌥9	0183
Degree	°	⇧⌥8	0176
Diaeresis, cap A	Ä	see note	0196
Diaeresis, cap E	Ë	see note	0203
Diaeresis, cap I	Ï	⇧⌥F	0207
Diaeresis, cap O	Ö	see note	0214
Diaeresis, cap U	Ü	see note	0220
Diaeresis, cap Y	Ÿ	see note	0159
Diaeresis, l/c a	ä	see note	0228
Diaeresis, l/c e	ë	see note	0235
Diaeresis, l/c i	ï	see note	0239
Diaeresis, l/c o	ö	see note	0246
Diaeresis, l/c u	ü	see note	0252
Diaeresis, l/c y	ÿ	see note	0255
Diaeresis/umlaut	¨	b U	0168
Diphthong, cap AE	Æ	⇧⌥'	0198
Diphthong, cap OE	Œ	⇧⌥Q	0140
Diphthong, l/c ae	æ	⌥'	0230
Diphthong, l/c oe	œ	⌥Q	0156
Divide	÷	⌥/	0247
Double dagger	‡	⇧⌥7	0135
Ellipsis	…	⌥;	0133
Em dash	—	⇧⌥-	0151
En dash	–	⌥-	0150
Eszett	ß	⌥S	0223
Euro currency*	m	⌥2	0128
Florin	ƒ	⌥F	0131
Grave, cap A	À	see note	0192
Grave, cap E	È	see note	0200
Grave, cap I	Ì	see note	0204
Grave, cap O	Ò	⇧⌥l	0210
Grave, cap U	Ù	see note	0217
Grave, l/c a	à	see note	0224
Grave, l/c e	è	see note	0232
Grave, l/c i	ì	see note	0236
Grave, l/c o	ò	see note	0242
Grave, l/c u	ù	see note	0249
Guillemet, close double	»	⇧⌥\	0187
Guillemet, close single	›	⇧⌥4	0155
Guillemet, open double	«	⌥\	0171
Guillemet, open single	‹	⇧⌥3	0139
Icelandic eth, cap	Ð		0208
Icelandic eth, l/c	ð		0240
Icelandic thorn, cap	Þ		0222
Icelandic thorn, l/c	þ		0254
International currency*	¤	⇧⌥2	0164
Logical not	¬	⌥L	0172
Macron	¯	⌥,	0175
Multiply	×		0215
Mu/micro	µ	⌥M	0181
One half fraction	½		0189
One quarter fraction	¼		0188
Ordfeminine	ª	⌥9	0170
Ordmasculine	º	⌥0	0186
Paragraph	¶	⌥7	0182
Per mille/thousand	‰	⇧⌥E	0137
Plus or minus	±	⇧⌥=	0177
Quote, close single	'	⇧⌥]	0146
Quote, double baseline	„	⇧⌥W	0132
Quote, close double	"	⇧⌥[	0148
Quote, open double	"	⌥[	0147
Quote, open single	'	⌥]	0145
Quote, single baseline	‚	⇧⌥0	0130
Section	§	⌥6	0167
Spanish exclamation	¡	⌥1	0161
Spanish query	¿	⇧⌥/	0191
Sterling	£	⌥3	0163
Superscript 1	¹		0185
Superscript 2	²		0178
Superscript 3	³		0179
Swedish cap A	Å	⇧⌥A	0197
Swedish l/c a	å	⌥A	0229
Three quarters fraction	¾		0190
Tilde, cap A	Ã	see note	0195
Tilde, cap N	Ñ	see note	0209
Tilde, cap O	Õ	see note	0213
Tilde, l/c a	ã	see note	0227

Tilde, l/c n	ñ	see note	0241
Tilde, l/c o	õ	see note	0245
Tilde, small	˜	⊕⍂N	0152
Trademark*	™	⍂2	0153
Trademark, registered	®	⍂R	0174
Yen	¥	⍂Y	0165

Note

Some accented characters are only accessible on Macintosh computers by two keyboard operations in succession (rather than simultaneously). For example, an a acute is generated by first pressing ⍂ + E together, then a (or ⊕ + A for a cap A acute). These are as follows (but note that some accented capitals have their own keys, listed above, which should be used in preference):

Acute: ⍂ + e then character
Á É Í Ó Ú á é í ó ú

Grave: ⍂ + ` then character
À È Ì Ò Ù à è ì ò ù

Diaeresis: ⍂ + u then character
Ä Ë Ï Ö Ü Ÿ ä ë ï ö ü ÿ

Tilde: ⍂ + n then character
Ã Ñ Õ ã ñ õ

Circumflex: ⍂ + i then character
Â Ê Î Ô Û â ê î ô û

Some accents are only accessible on Macintosh computers via the Character Palette or InDesign's "Glyphs" palette.

The following are only accessible by keyboard shortcut on Macintosh computers; in Windows they are available from Character Map.

Apple (Mac only)		⊕⍂K
Approximately equal	≈	⍂x
Breve	˘	⊕⍂.
Carib diacritic	ˇ	⊕⍂T
Delta	Δ	⍂J
Dot accent	˙	⍂H
Dotless i	ı	⊕⍂B
Fraction bar	⁄	⊕⍂1
Greater than or equal	≥	⍂.
Hungarian umlaut	˝	⊕⍂G
Infinity	∞	⍂5
Integral	∫	⍂B
Less than or equal	≤	⍂,
Ligature, fi	fi	⊕⍂5
Ligature, fl	fl	⊕⍂6
Lozenge	◊	⊕⍂V
Not equal to	≠	⍂=
Ogonek diacritic	˛	⊕⍂X
Omega	W	⍂Z
Partial differential	∂	⍂D
Pi	ϖ	b P
Pound sign**	#	⍂3
Product	∏	⊕⍂P
Radical	√	⍂V
Ring	°	⍂K
Summation	Σ	⍂W

* In some Macintosh fonts where b 2 generates the Euro currency symbol, the ™ symbol is generated by typing cb 2

** Depends on language; the pound sign can be generated by c 3 on some keyboards, on others b 3 generates the sterling (£) symbol.

US envelope sizes

Number	Height	Width
6 1/4	3 1/2in	6in
6 1/2	3 1/2in	6 1/4in
6 3/4	3 5/8in	6 1/2in
7	3 3/4in	6 3/4in
7 3/4	3 7/8in	7 1/2in
*Monarch	3 7/8in	7 1/2in
Data Card	3 5/8in	7 3/4in
Check Size	3 5/8in	8 5/8in
9	3 7/8in	8 7/8in
10	4 1/8in	9 1/2in
11	4 1/2in	10 3/8in
12	4 3/4in	11in
14	5in	11 1/2in

*Pt. Flp.

ISO envelope sizes

For postal purposes, ISO 269 and DIN 678 define the following envelope formats:

Format	Size [mm]	Content Format
C6	114 x 162	A4 folded twice = A6
DL	110 x 220	A4 folded twice = 1/3 A4
C6/C5	114 x 229	A4 folded twice = 1/3 A4
C5	162 x 229	A4 folded once = A5
C4	229 x 324	A4
C3	324 x 458	A3
B6	125 x 176	C6 envelope
B5	176 x 250	C5 envelope
B4	250 x 353	C4 envelope
E4	280 x 400	B4

The DL format is the most widely used business letter format. Its size falls somewhat out of the system and equipment manufacturers have complained that it is slightly too small for reliable automatic enveloping. Therefore, DIN 678 introduced the C6/C5 format as an alternative for the DL envelope.

Glossary

animation The process of creating a moving image by rapidly switching from one still image to the next. Traditionally achieved by drawing or painting each frame, now possible with a variety of software (qv) running on personal computers.

antialiasing The strategic insertion of pixels (qv) of various shades into a bitmapped graphic (qv) to smooth out "jagged" transitions between contrasting tones, for example along a diagonal line.

ADSL Acronym for "asynchronous digital subscriber line," a form of broadband (qv) Internet connection created by boosting the capacity of existing copper telephone wires. Typically the speed achieved for uploading (sending files out from the user's computer) will be half that for downloading (receiving files, including webpages being viewed by the user), hence "asynchronous." The more general term "DSL" is more commonly used in North America.

Apple Macintosh The brand name of Apple Computer's range of PCs (qv). The Macintosh (or "Mac") was the first personal computer to make use of the graphical user interface that had been pioneered by Xerox at the Palo Alto Research Center. The use of this interface provided the platform for the software (qv) applications that gave rise to desktop publishing, revolutionizing graphic design.

authoring tool Software (qv) for creating interactive presentations or websites. Such programs typically include text, drawing, painting, animation (qv), and audio features. These are combined with a scripting language that is used to determine how each element of the page or screen behaves—for example, it may be used to ensure that a movie is played when a certain button (qv) is pressed.

bandwidth The measure of the speed at which information is passed between two points (for example, between two modems (qv) or from memory to disk). The broader the bandwidth, the faster the data flow. Bandwidth is usually measured in cycles per second (hertz) or bits per second (bps).

Bézier tools Vector-based (qv) drawing tools, employed by most graphics programs. A pen tool allows the user to place a series of points on the page; the points are then automatically joined by a line. Two "handles" on each point control the curve of the line.

bit A contraction of "binary digit," the smallest unit of information that a computer can use. A bit may have one of two values: on or off, 1 or 0. Eight bits form a byte.

bitmap An image composed of dots, such as a digital photo. A bitmap is a table of values corresponding to the pixels (qv) that make up the image. "Bitmap fonts," for example, contain such an image of each character, with each pixel represented by one bit, which can be either black or white. Color images typically use at least 24 bits (three bytes) for each pixel, allowing millions of colors to be represented. The finite number of pixels in a bitmap limits the maximum size at which it can be reproduced at acceptable visual quality, unlike vector (qv) graphics.

bleed The margin outside the trimmed area of a sheet, which allows for tints, images, and other matter to print beyond the edge of the page. For printing without bleed, the designer must leave a blank margin around the page.

body text The matter that forms the main text of a printed book, excluding captions (qv), headings (qv), page numbers and so on.

brand guardian A person who is employed, usually by the client of a design or advertising agency, to ensure that the corporate brand identity of the client company is consistently presented.

broadband Used to describe any telecommunications link with a high bandwidth (qv), enabling a fast rate of data flow; specifically, a digital Internet connection made via ADSL (qv) or cable modem (qv).

browser An application that enables the user to view (or "browse") web (qv) pages across the Internet (qv). The most widely used browsers are Netscape Navigator and Microsoft Internet Explorer. Version numbers are particularly important in the use of browsers, as they indicate the level of HTML (qv) that can be supported.

button An interface control, usually in a dialog box, that is clicked by the user to designate, confirm, or cancel an action. Default buttons are usually emphasized by a heavy border and can be activated using the Return or Enter keys.

cable Shorthand for a broadband (qv) Internet connection made using digital land lines installed by a cable telecoms company. In domestic installations this is typically sold as a package with digital cable TV, but provides a separate connection point for a personal computer.

cable modem A book-sized box that connects a computer to a cable (qv) service. Also known as a "digital modem," although not strictly a modem (qv) at all.

CAD Acronym for "computer-aided design." May refer to any design carried out using a computer, but usually to three-dimensional design, such as product design or architecture. Software (qv) may control the entire process from concept to finished product, sometimes termed CAD-CAM (computer-aided manufacturing).

caption Strictly speaking, a caption is a headline printed above an illustration, identifying the contents of the image. However, the word is now used to describe any descriptive text that accompanies illustrative matter, usually set below or beside it at a small size. Not to be confused with "credit," the small print beside a picture that identifies the illustrator, photographer, or copyright holder.

CD-ROM Acronym for "compact disk, read-only memory." A CD-based method for the storage and distribution of digital data. Based on audio CD technology, CD-ROMs can store up to 650 megabytes of data, and are available in record-once (CD-R) or rewritable (CD-RW) formats for computer use.

character A letter of the alphabet, numeral or typographic symbol. The table of contents of a font is its character set.

CMYK In four-color process (qv) printing, an abbreviation for cyan, magenta, yellow, and black (black being denoted by "K" for "key plate").

ColorSync Apple's color management (qv) system.

color management The process of controlling the representation and conversion of color information. The designer's computer should have a color management system (CMS) such as ColorSync (qv) which is used by software to help ensure colors appear consistently on all devices, including the monitor.

compression The technique of rearranging data so that it either occupies less space on disk, or transfers more quickly between

devices or along communication lines. Different kinds of compression are used for different kinds of data: applications, for example, must not lose any data when compressed, whereas images, sound, and movies can tolerate a large amount of data loss.

contrast The degree of difference between tones in an image (or computer monitor) from the lightest to the darkest. "High contrast" describes an image with light highlights and dark shadows, whereas a "low contrast" image is one with even tones and few dark areas or light highlights.

corporate identity A design or set of designs for use on corporate stationery, livery, etc.

CSS Abbreviation for "cascading style sheets." These extend the capabilities of HTML (qv), allowing the web (qv) designer to exercise detailed control over layout and typography, applying preset formats (qv) to paragraphs, page elements, or entire pages. Several style sheets can be applied to a single page, thus "cascadin." Correct use of CSS helps create pages that display as intended in all browsers.

default settings The settings of a hardware device or software (qv) program that are determined at the time of manufacture. These settings remain in effect until the user changes them; such settings will be stored in a "preferences" file. Default settings are otherwise known as "factory" settings.

digital press A printing press that outputs pages directly from digital files, typically using some form of inkjet technology.

Director Adobe's multimedia authoring software (qv).

display type Text set in large-size fonts (qv) for headings (qv), or any

matter that is intended to stand out. Fonts too ornate for general text, or specially designed for larger sizes, are referred to as display faces.

download The transfer of data from a remote computer—such as an Internet (qv) server—to a PC (qv).

dpi Abbreviation for "dots per inch." A unit of measurement used to represent the resolution (qv) of devices such as printers and image setters. The closer the dots (i.e., the higher the value), the better the quality. Typical values include 300dpi for a laser printer, and 2450dpi+ for an imagesetter. Dots per inch is sometimes erroneously used as a value when discussing monitors or images; the correct unit in these cases is ppi (pixels (qv) per inch).

Dreamweaver Leading web design software (qv) from Adobe.

DSL See ADSL.

DVD Abbreviation for "digital versatile (or video) disk." A storage disk similar to a CD-ROM (qv), but distinguished by its greater capacity (up to 17.08 gigabytes).

embedded fonts Fonts (qv) that are fixed within files, meaning that the original font folder does not need to be provided in order for the file to be printed or set.

embossing Relief printing or stamping in which dies are used to impress a design into the surface or paper, leather, or cloth so that the letters or images are raised above the surface of the paper.

EPS Abbreviation for "encapsulated PostScript." A graphics file format used primarily for storing object-oriented or vector (qv) graphics.

Glossary

An EPS file consists of two parts: PostScript (qv) code, which tells the printer how to print the image; and an on screen preview, usually in JPEG (qv), TIFF (qv), or PICT format.

film The material that provides the template for printing plates. A cellulose acetate-based material, coated with light-sensitive emulsion so that images and text can be recorded photographically.

finishing As the name implies, the final part of the print production process. It encompasses various processes, including collating, trimming, folding, binding, embossing (qv), laminating (qv), varnishing (qv), and so on.

Fireworks A web-specific graphics production tool by Adobe.

Flash Adobe software (qv) for producing vector (qv) graphics and animations for web (qv)presentations. Flash generates small files that are quick to download (qv) and, being vector-based, the graphics may be scaled to any dimension without an increase in file size.

font A complete set of type characters of the same size, style and design.

format In printing, the size or orientation of a book or page.

four-color process Any printing process that reproduces full-color images which have been separated into three basic "process" colors—cyan, magenta, and yellow—with a fourth color, black, added for greater contrast. See also CMYK.

frame (1) A decorative border or rule surrounding a page item.

frame (2) In page-layout software (qv), a container for text or image.

frame (3) On the Web (qv), a means of splitting a page into several areas which can be updated separately.

FreeHand Vector-based (qv) drawing software by Adobe.

Freeway A website layout program produced by SoftPress.

GIF Acronym for "graphic interchange format." A bitmapped (qv) graphics file format that compresses (qv) data without losing any, as opposed to JPEG (qv), which discards data selectively.

glyph A letter, number, or symbol in a particular typeface, referring to its visual appearance rather than its symbolic function. Any number of alternative glyphs may represent the same character (qv).

gobo A metal or glass disk with designs printed onto or cut into it, for use with a projector or spotlight.

graphic A general term that is used to describe any illustration or drawn design. May also be used for a type design based on drawn letters.

grid A template (qv)—usually showing such things as column widths, picture areas, and trim sizes—used to design publications with multiple pages, to ensure that the basic design remains consistent.

hairline rule The thinnest line it is possible to print, with a width of 0.25pt.

halftone The technique of reproducing a continuous tone image, such as a photo, on a printing press by breaking it up into a pattern of equally spaced dots of varying sizes.

heading A title that appears at the top of a chapter, or at the beginning of a subdivision within the text.

hierarchy of information The technique of arranging information in a graded order, which establishes priorities and helps users to find what they want.

hinting In typography, information contained within outline fonts (qv) that modifies character shapes to enhance them when they are displayed or printed at low resolutions (qv).

HSB Abbreviation for "hue, saturation, and brightness."

HTML Abbreviation for "hypertext mark-up language." A text-based page-description language used to format documents on the web (qv) and viewed on web browsers.

hue Pure spectral color that distinguishes a color from other colors. For example, red is a different hue from blue. Light red and dark red may contain varying amounts of white and black, but they are the same hue.

hyperlink A contraction of "hypertext link," a link to other documents that is embedded within the original document. It may be underlined or highlighted in a different color. Clicking on a hyperlink will take the user to another document or website.

ICC The International Color Consortium, which oversees the most widely used standards for color management (qv) systems.

Illustrator Vector-based (qv) drawing software by Adobe.

image map An image, usually on a webpage, that contains embedded links to other documents or websites. These links are activated when the appropriate area of the image is clicked on. Most image maps are

5

now "client-side," stored within the page's HTML (qv) code rather than accessed from a server.

imposition The arrangement of pages in the sequence and position in which they will appear on the printed sheet, with appropriate margins for folding and trimming, before platemaking and printing.

InDesign Leading desktop publishing software (qv) from Adobe.

ink A fluid comprising solvents and oils in which is suspended a finely ground pigment of dyes, minerals, or synthetic dyes, which provide color. There are many different types of ink for the various printing processes.

inkjet printer A printing device that creates an image by spraying tiny jets of ink on to the paper surface at high speed.

Internet The entire collection of connected worldwide networks which serves as the medium of transmission for websites (qv), e-mail, instant messaging ("chat") and various other digital services.

Internet Explorer Web-browsing software (qv) from Microsoft.

intranet A network of computers similar to the Internet (qv), to which the public does not have access. Mainly used by large corporations or governmental institutions.

ISDN Abbreviation for "integrated services digital network." An obsolescent telecommunications technology that transmits data digitally via telephone lines.

ISP Abbreviation for "Internet (qv) service provider." Any organization that provides access to the Internet. Most ISPs also provide other services, such as email addresses.

JavaScript Netscape's Java-like scripting language, which provides a simplified method of adding dynamic effects to web (qv) pages.

JPEG Abbreviation for "Joint Photographic Experts Group." This International Standards Organization group defines compression standards for bitmapped (qv) color images, and has given its name to a popular compressed (qv) file format. JPEG files are "lossy" (lose data during compression), but work in such a way as to minimize the visible effect on graduated tone images. Pronounced "jay-peg."

kerning The adjustment of space between adjacent type characters to optimize their appearance. Not to be confused with tracking (qv), which involves the adjustment of spacing over a number of adjacent characters.

lamination The application of transparent or colored, shiny, plastic films to printed matter to protect or enhance it.

layers In some applications, a level to which the user can consign an element of the design being worked on. Individual layers can be active (meaning that they can be worked on) or non-active.

layout The placement of various elements—text, headings (qv), images—on a printed page.

leading The spacing between lines of type.

Mac OS The operating system used on Apple's "Macintosh" computers.

master page In some applications, a template (qv) that includes attributes that will be common to all pages, such as the number of text columns, page numbers, and so on.

Media Player A widely used audio and video player application. Supplied with Microsoft Windows (qv) and also available for Mac (qv).

modem Contraction of "modulator–demodulator." A device that converts digital data to analogue, and back, for transfer from one computer to another via standard telephone lines.

mounting The process of sticking artwork on to a thick piece of board, usually for display or presentation.

MP3 Abbreviation for "MPEG audio layer 3." A popular compressed (qv) audio file format.

offset lithography A common bulk printing method involving the use of photographic plates.

OpenType A relatively new digital font format that can contain either PostScript (qv) or TrueType (qv) data and allows large numbers of characters to be stored in one file.

PageMaker The original page make-up software, launched by Adobe. Now defunct.

PANTONE The proprietary trademark for PANTONE's system of color standards, control and quality requirements, in which each color bears a description of its formulation (in percentages) for subsequent printing.

PC Abbreviation for "personal computer." The term is generally used to denote any computer that is IBM-compatible and runs the Windows (qv) operating system (as opposed to the Mac OS (qv), for example).

PDF Abbreviation for "portable document format." A multi-purpose format from Adobe that allows complex, multi-featured documents to be created, retaining all text,

Glossary

layout, and picture formatting, then to be viewed and printed on any computer with PDF "reader" software (such as the free Adobe Reader) or, if correctly formatted, used for final output on a printing press.

Photoshop Powerful, industry-standard image manipulation software from Adobe.

pictogram A simplified graphic symbol representing an object or concept.

pixel Contraction of "picture element." The smallest component of a digitally generated image, such as a single dot of light on a computer monitor. In its most simple form, one pixel corresponds to a single bit (qv): 0 = off, or white; 1 = on, or black. In color and grayscale images (or monitors), one pixel may correspond to several bits: an 8-bit pixel, for example, can be displayed in any of 256 colors (the total number of different configurations that can be achieved by eight 0s and 1s).

plug-in Software (qv), usually developed by a third party, that extends the capabilities of a program. Plug-ins are common in image-editing and page-layout software for such things as special effects filters. They are also common in web (qv) browsers for playing such things as movies and audio files.

PNG Abbreviation for "portable network graphics." A rarely used file format for images on the web that provides 10 to 30 per cent "lossless" compression (qv).

point The basic unit of Anglo-American type measurement. There are 72 points to an inch.

PostScript Adobe's proprietary page description language for image output to laser printers and high-resolution (qv) imagesetters.

pre-press Any or all of the reproduction processes that occur between design and printing, especially color separation.

proof A prototype of a job (usually a printed document) produced to check quality and accuracy. An accurate on-screen preview of a job is known as a soft proof.

QuarkXPress Industry standard page-layout program.

QuickTime Apple Computer's audio and video delivery technology, compatible with both Windows (qv) and the Mac OS (qv).

raster Deriving from the Latin rastrum (rake), a "raster image" is any image created as rows of pixels, dots, or lines in a "raking" sequence, i.e. from top to bottom of a page, monitor, etc. On a monitor, the screen image is made up from a pattern of several hundred parallel lines created by an electron beam that "rakes" the screen from top to bottom. The speed at which the image or frame is created is the "refresh" rate, quoted in hertz (Hz), equal to the number of times per second. Converting a vector (qv) image to a bitmap (qv) for output on screen or printer is "rasterization."

Real Media A set of audio and video file formats and players from Real Networks, often used on the web.

resolution The quantity of data points, such as pixels, with which an image, sound, or other phenomenon is stored digitally. Higher resolution means better definition, clarity, and fidelity, at the cost of larger files.

RGB Abbreviation for "red, green, blue." The primary colors of the "additive" color model, used in color monitors and for web (qv) and multimedia graphics.

RIP Acronym for "raster image processor." Used by a printer to convert and rasterize (qv) page-layout data, typically in a PostScript (qv) or PDF (qv) file, for printed output, as a proof or on press.

rollover The rapid substitution of one or more images when a mouse pointer is rolled over the original image. Often used for navigation buttons on web (qv) pages.

rule A printed line.

Safari Web browser (qv) software from Apple, standard on Macs (qv).

sans serif The generic name for type designs that lack the small extensions (serifs, qv) at the ends of the main strokes of the letters. Sometimes called "lineal type."

saturation The variation in color of the same tonal brightness from none (grey) through pastel shades (low saturation) to pure color with no grey (high or "full" saturation).

scamp A preliminary drawing showing a proposed design.

scanner An electronic device that uses a sequentially moving light beam and sensor to digitize artwork from paper or photographic film. Most scanners are flatbed, with a glass surface on which the original document is placed.

serif The short counterstroke or finishing stroke at the end of the main stroke of a type character.

ShockWave A Adobe technology used for delivering Director (qv) presentations to browsers (qv) via the web (qv).

silkscreen printing ("screen printing") A method of printing in which ink (qv) is forced through a stencil fixed to a screen made of silk. Modern printers more commonly use a screen made of synthetic material .

software The generic term for any kind of computer program, as opposed to the physical hardware.

spot colors A printing color that has been specifically mixed for the job, as opposed to using the four-color process (qv) colors.

streaming A method of playing audio or video files as they are received (for example via the web), minimizing initial waiting times.

tags Formatting commands in HTML (qv) and related mark-up languages. A tag is switched on by placing a command inside angle brackets ‹command› and turned off by the same command preceded with a forward slash ‹/command›.

template A document created with pre-positioned areas, used as a basis for repeatedly creating other documents in the same style.

TIFF Acronym for "tagged image file format." A graphics file format used to store bitmapped (qv) images with no loss of data and optionally with extra features such as layers (qv). Widely used in graphic design and pre-press (qv).

touch screen A computer screen that responds to touch, avoiding the need for a mouse or keyboard. Often used for public access displays.

tracking The adjustment of spacing between characters in a selected piece of text. See also kerning.

traffic In an advertising context, elements of client business that an agency is handling.

trapping Settings in DTP programs that determine the interaction of overlapping colors. Also refers to printing problems when one solid color completely overprints another. Trapping preferences are complex and best left to the service bureau or printer.

TrueType Apple Computer's digital font (qv) technology, developed as an alternative to PostScript (qv) and now used by both PCs (qv) and Macs (qv). A single TrueType file is used for both printing and screen rendering, while PostScript fonts require two separate files.

typography The art of type (qv) design and its arrangement on a designed page.

Unicode A system used to identify which glyphs (qv) in a font represent which characters (qv).

URL Abbreviation for "uniform resource locator." The unique address of any page on the Web (qv), usually composed of three parts: protocol (such as "http"), domain name, and directory name.

varnish A liquid that dries to form a hard, usually shiny surface. Varnish can be applied on press to printed matter, especially covers.

vector A straight line segment of a given length and orientation. "Vector graphics"—which can involve more complex forms than straight lines, such as Bézier (qv) curves—are stored as numeric descriptions that can be scaled to reproduce the same visual result at any physical size, rather than broken up into discrete pixels as in the case of bitmapped (qv) images.

Windows The PC (qv) operating system devised by Microsoft, which uses a graphical user interface (GUI) similar to the Mac OS (qv).

web Also known as "world wide web" (www). An amorphous entity comprising pages created in HTML (qv) and delivered via Internet (qv) servers to users' web browsers (qv).

XHTML A combination of HTML (qv) and XML (qv) used to create Internet content for multiple devices.

XML An acronym for "extensible markup language," which is broader than HTML (qv).

Index

Index

Index

Index